Scarcity and Choice in History

For
W.H.H.C. 1873–1964
and
A.E.B. 1882–1952

Scarcity and Choice in History

W. H. B. Court F.B.A.
Professor of Economic History
in the University of Birmingham

EDWARD ARNOLD

© Edward Arnold (Publishers) Ltd 1970

First published 1970
by Edward Arnold (Publishers) Ltd
at 41 Maddox Street, London, W.1.

SBN 7131 5484 5

PRINTED IN GREAT BRITAIN
BY W & J MACKAY & CO LTD, CHATHAM

Contents

Chapter

1	Growing Up in an Age of Anxiety	1
2	The Years 1914–18 in British Economic and Social History	61
3	Two Economic Historians: Richard Henry Tawney Sir John Clapham	127
4	What is Economic History?	151
5	The Communist Doctrines of Empire	180
6	Problems of the British Coal Industry between the Wars	195
7	A Warwickshire Colliery in the Eighteenth Century	225
8	Industrial Organization and Economic Progress in the Eighteenth-Century Midlands	235
	Index of Subjects	250
	Index of Persons	254

Acknowledgements

The author and publisher wish to thank the following for permission to reprint articles by the author: Routledge and Kegan Paul Ltd. and the University of Toronto Press for 'What is Economic History?' from *Approaches to History* edited by H. P. R. Finberg, 1962; the Clarendon Press for 'The Communist Doctrines of Empire' from *Survey of British Commonwealth Affairs*, vol. 2, edited by Sir Keith Hancock, 1940; A. Oosthoek's Uitgevers N.V. for 'Problems of the British Coal Industry between the Wars' from *Economic History Review*, vol. XV, 1945, and for 'A Warwickshire Colliery in the Eighteenth Century' from *Economic History Review*, vol. VII, 1937; the Royal Historical Society for 'Industrial Organization and Economic Progress in the Eighteenth-Century Midlands' from *Transactions*, vol. XXVIII, 1946; and Verlag J. C. B. Mohr, Tübingen for 'Sir John Clapham' from *Architects and Craftsmen in History, Festschrift für Abbott Payson Usher*, 1956. In addition the author and publisher wish gratefully to acknowledge permission given by Cambridge University Press to print extracts from *The Study of Economic History—An Inaugural Lecture* by J. H. Clapham, 1929, and from *Economic History of Modern Britain* by J. H. Clapham.

Preface

The papers which follow have been written at various times and on different occasions. Some have been printed elsewhere. It is hoped that readers may find it convenient to have these brought together. The larger part of the book has not been published before.

The special interest of economic history lies in the economic problem in history, born of the perpetual conflict between the extent of men's resources and the urgency of human need and desire. The concern of the economic historian lies in what economic decisions have been taken, by whom and under what circumstances, how far they were rational, to the extent that the means employed reached or missed the desired aim, what alternatives were possible, and what the consequences of action were. We men take economic decisions because we must. Whether as communities or individuals, we cannot but choose between the alternative uses of resources which are always relatively scarce. What we call economic history is the path through time of our decisions, often obscure or impossible to trace, sometimes issuing in terrible events.

History as men write it does not exist independently of the observer, a person brought up and living in a particular place at a particular time. This relativity of the observer affects our general notions of cause and effect. We all have such notions. The only question is whether we are aware of what they are and where they come from. It also affects the values which we bring to history and those which we are capable of understanding. A scale of economic preferences in itself assumes a sense of time, a measurement of quantities and a set of values if a choice is to be made. Where and how did the owners of the scale acquire their values? How and where did the historian collect his, since they affect both his selection and his handling of historical problems? We can only be candid and study ends as well as means, the historians' values as well as those of other people. In an age of changing tradition, with all practical and philosophical problems on the move, this brings an element of self-analysis into the writing of history, if only for the sake of its impersonality and its usefulness.

The essay here called 'What is Economic History?' first appeared in *Approaches to History*, edited by H. P. R. Finberg (1962). The paper on 'Communist Doctrines of Empire' was written as an appendix to Sir Keith Hancock's *Survey of British Commonwealth Affairs*, vol. 2 (1940). 'Problems of the British Coal Industry between the Wars' was an article in the *Economic History Review*, vol. XV, nos. 1 and 2 (1945) and was reprinted in slightly altered form in *Coal*, in the *History of the Second World War, United Kingdom Civil Series* (H.M.S.O., 1951). 'Industrial Organization and Industrial Progress in the Eighteenth-Century Midlands' was first read as a paper to the Royal Historical Society and printed in their *Transactions*, 4th series, vol. XXVIII, 1946. 'A Warwickshire Colliery in the Eighteenth Century' appeared in the *Economic History Review*, vol. VII, no. 2 (1937). Of the more personal papers, that on Sir John Clapham was contributed to *Architects and Craftsmen in History, Festschrift für Abbott Payson Usher* (Tübingen, 1956). My thanks are due to those who have allowed these papers to be printed here.

Of the other papers, that on Richard Tawney was read to the Maitland Society at Downing College, Cambridge and the Economics Society of the University of Hull. The themes of 'The Years 1914–18 in British Economic and Social History', extracted from a longer study, were the subject of lectures in 1968 to members of the universities of Western Ontario and Toronto in Canada, Wisconsin and Northwestern universities in the United States. I owed the opportunity for this visit to the Nuffield Foundation of London, the William Waldorf Astor Foundation of New York, the Hoover Institution, California and the Institute for Advanced Study at Princeton.

In these days, when students are unpopular, even inside universities, it should perhaps be admitted that some students helped, although without knowing it, to find a title for the book while others, by their patient listening, might even be said to have written parts of it. The final typing was carried out by Miss Theresa A. Gossage, formerly of the Faculty of Commerce and Social Science at the University of Birmingham. For a lot of tedious work on the indexing, I have to thank my sister, Mrs. E. C. Hayes and Mrs. Arlene Lenaghan.

1 Growing Up in an Age of Anxiety

(The paper which follows had an accidental origin. In 1964 I was in hospital for some time with a pulmonary embolism and lung tuberculosis. It was a part of the convalescence, agreed with my physician, that I should 'not allow my mind to rot'. This was advice one was very willing to take. But conditions were difficult. I could write, but I was not allowed to pick up heavy books or to move more than a small distance each day. History writing was out of the question. Fortunately, while in hospital I had read, but cannot remember where, a review article. According to this, some Continental philosophers had found it worth their while to write as part of their work what was described as an 'intellectual autobiography'. The purpose of this was to explain to their readers how they came to hold the philosophical views which they did. How they performed this self-imposed task I did not know, for I had no example to go upon. But it occurred to me that, while writing history had become for me impossible, I might do worse than try to explain to myself how I became the sort of historian that I am. What seemed puzzling was how I had come to write history which in some ways was traditional while in other directions it diverged sharply from tradition. Perhaps the secret is that, beyond the deep personal level at which our first knowledge of human nature comes to us, our views of history are very much a matter of the social values we were brought up with or have since acquired. It seems doubtful, to say the least, whether an historian's outlook can be inferred entirely from the books he has read or the learned men he has met. How society looked to him from the start, how it has come to appear, is the elusive source of many of his beliefs. Self-analysis leads one quite a long way back, although probably not so far as the psycho-analyst, concerned with the origins of personal psychology, would like. The limited intention of the essay, which was not intended to be either psycho-analysis or general reminiscence, dictated its form. It deals perhaps not so much with events as with what was assumed to be the case. For I was brought up in a world of tremendous assumptions and of conflicts between them which were no less extreme.

The early part of the paper was written in illness and convalescence. The rest was added, at different times, when it appeared that what I had written interested other people. The Audenesque title now given to it is not intended to be mysterious. It refers to the fact that I was nine years of age when the first war broke out in Europe, thirty-four at the beginning of the second war. The years between 1914 and 1939, for anyone who lived then and in Europe, may not unfairly be described as an age of anxiety.)

I

Time and place are usually conceded to have a good deal to do with our being the persons that we are. Even if, as one must accept, there is much in every man and woman which does not depend in any obvious way upon the society they were born into and have grown up in, the circumstances of birth must decide far more than we can ever be aware of. What circumstances do decide, and how they do so, must remain a matter of dispute. I have spent the best years of my life trying to introduce into the writing of modern English history the adjustments, the major changes of method and outlook, which are necessary to account for the development of a powerful industrial society out of a traditional one and for its far-reaching consequences. But my early surroundings were most unindustrial.

The time of my birth was the 12th October 1904 and the place Cirencester in Gloucestershire. A small town in the Cotswold hills, it was extremely countrified. My father used to say that when he went there, a few years before I was born, there were as many hounds and sheep in its streets as people.

The rural England I was thus born into was in many ways half feudal and medieval, despite all the changes wrought by the modern centuries. Local society, nicely graduated according to Edwardian ideas of what was good and proper, was dominated by two great institutions. These stood one at each end of the street where my father lived. Cirencester House, which had been a great country mansion since the early eighteenth century, lay on the western edge of the town. From the market-place rose the tower of the parish church, a monument of old wool-stapling days. Lord Bathurst, seldom seen but well known locally, and the vicar of the church, whoever he might be at the time, represented the ruling powers in the town of the old county families and the established church.

The street in which I and my elder sister and younger brother lived, until our father left the town and removed to Berkshire in 1920, ran almost direct from the walls of Cirencester House to the church. It passed on its way one or two establishments more interesting to a child than the usually empty gates of the house or the soaring stillness of the church which awoke only for services. Shops and dwelling-houses apart, there was a butcher's slaughter-yard, the doings in which were a great source of fascination and anger to us as children. An old lady, whose sweetness of personality still somehow lingers in my memory, lived over it. She could neither read nor write and occasionally brought letters across the street for my father to read for her. Next to our house stood an ironmonger's shop and a smithy where horses were shod. Horses left overnight could be heard by us kicking and rustling in the stables. Other stables, kept by the same man, were full of breeding canaries, finches and bantam fowl. There was a public house at either end of the street, one superior, the other inferior. Both were, of course, out of bounds for us. But children are great seekers out of life. If we did not speak to the publican, it was because we preferred a conversation with his tame magpie. From an upper window of the other, the superior public house, an old gentleman with whom we made friends and who was kept by illness in his room could sometimes be persuaded to toss us a bag of sweets.

True poverty did not live in our street. It dwelt round the corner in a near-by yard. There, according to our childish eyes, both the people and the houses looked different.

We children were great reporters of the talk of the street at home and we took part in its doings whenever we could, even when this was, strictly speaking, not allowed. There was a controversy which seemed to go on for ever between the youth of the neighbourhood and a street newspaper-seller known as Dobbin. The profound topic was whether snakes possessed legs. Youth adopted at the top of its voice the orthodox belief. Dobbin delighted his hearers by his growing incoherence in defence of the opposite proposition. This saga was known to us in its minutest particulars. We even contributed one or two episodes by teasing Dobbin. At times we angered my father by holding the heads of his customers' horses in front of the shop in return for pennies. There were horses everywhere in the town and tall gangling hounds, for this was foxhunting country.

Our style of life was so quiet that at all times of the year we children were well aware whether the grass in Earl Bathurst's park grew green, whether it flowered, seeded or faded. We had also full leisure to note how other boys and girls touched by disease withered like the grass and died. This was a world of childish doings and imaginings in which the first cowslip or the early cuckoo seemed and to us was more important than the life of a man.

Meanwhile the society of our parents was changing and transforming itself. When I was not yet two, in the early months of 1906, an important general election took place. This returned the liberal Campbell-Bannerman-Asquith administration that governed the country till 1915. It introduced a season of lively political passion. In that age before radio and television it fell to my father as the chief newsagent in the town to read out the telegraphed results of the election as they came through to a dense crowd waiting in the street outside his shop. They greeted him with friendly irony as 'the returning officer'. Keenly political himself, on the conservative side, he never forgot the excitement in the town.

Eight years later came the European war. Even the quiet currents of life in a Cotswold town began to run a little faster and with some complications in the autumn of 1914. Our rambling house on the street, while it remained a home for us, became a billet for soldiers. I see the flash of the Sam Browne belt of the billeting officer still, as he took the turn on the stairs. The man within the belt died on the Somme, I believe. South Wales miners dressed in the uniform of South Wales Borderers, men from the Orkneys and Glasgow recruited into the Cameron Highlanders, old Indian Army 'sweats' full of beer and odd stories came into the house and went away again. They left for lands which we children gazed at uncomprehendingly on the map. Sooner or later the big front door of the house closed on their heavy boots and packs, their rifles, their anxieties and their jollity. Through them and even more perhaps through the set face and the strange silence of people whom we knew in the town, the war sank into our youthful imaginations. We felt vaguely the presence of a tragedy which we did not and could not understand.

The war in Europe was without a doubt the dominant public event in the lives of all those born before 1914. For the men and women of my parents' generation, who were in middle age when the war began, it was a change from one era in their life to another, from old certainties to new insecurity. But for a boy in his early teens the war was little more than a background to life, forgotten for weeks and months at a time despite my assiduous reading of newspapers and the stories which we children read and wrote about the war. School, our hobbies and amusements occupied us almost wholly. It was only later that I began to realize something of the incomprehensible vastness of the experience through which our elders had passed. After the war my father, whose business included bookbinding, showed me one day in great secrecy a document which had been left with him to be bound. It was a record, kept by a British officer who was present, of the famous conversations in the railway carriage at Compiègne, between Marshal Foch and the delegates of the German Army, which led to the armistice of 1918. I suppose that this was the first historical document I ever saw and I was horrified by it. A schoolboy, knowing nothing of the implacable emotions of men at war, I was startled and shocked by what seemed to me the deliberate inhumanity of the proceedings.

Echoes of these tremendous events pursued us as we grew up. When I went up to Cambridge in 1923 one of my first acts was to go to a public lecture by the economist Maynard Keynes. He was speaking on the Versailles Treaty and the problem of the payment of reparations by Germany then still much talked about. The lecture was a brilliant performance, but it was scarcely calculated to encourage admiration for the wisdom of our elders. The truth was that the war had shattered the simple loyalties which fed the emotional life of an older generation. We undergraduates found that we thought about the war and its consequences differently from our parents. For us it was a war that should never have taken place.

If I found myself at Cambridge in the mid-twenties discussing politics and contemporary history, this was owing mainly to my father and his personal influence upon me. In the society of a small country town such as Cirencester he was something of an exception. Among the professional people and the small traders who were his daily companions and acquaintances he stood for London-owned business—he was the manager of W. H. Smith and Son's bookshop—and he was not a Cirencester-bred man. This was a point of some importance. He was too intellectual and independent to be very representative of anyone except himself. But from one point of view he was representative, for he brought into Cirencester the special and unmistakable air of the textile democracy of Stroud and the Stroud Valley where he had been brought up. If I attempt some sort of profile of him and of his parents, it must be because for years he was, as a father tends to be to a son, the pattern I was most anxious to imitate and also the model I most wished to avoid.

His own father came from Somerset and was the son of a man, said to be of French Huguenot descent, who carried the mail in Devon in saddle-bags on horseback at a time when the railway had not got further west than Exeter. This man later drove the coach between Porlock and Minehead. In the coachman's large family only one boy was trained for a skilled job. The boy was my grandfather, who became an apprenticed currier and leather-worker. He left Somerset for Gloucestershire and married a girl, young but already a widow. She worked as a cutter in a cloth mill at Stroud in the Cotswolds. The pair left Gloucestershire and went to London. There, in the trade boom of the early seventies, my grandfather found employment in the tanneries of Bermondsey south of the Thames. In this way my father came to be London born. But not London bred, for when the boom broke my grandfather went in search of work elsewhere, settling down again at last in Stroud. Here he and his wife were out-workers for one of the mills, that is they made up clothes to order in their own house, including the sailor suits which were fashionable for small boys early in the century. I recollect the room in which they worked, where we played with the bobbins from the sewing-machines. I asked my father many years later how much money they made. He said three or four pounds in a good week. This was when trade was lively. When the mill ceased to give out work in bad times and the boys had left home the want of income could be extreme. My aunt, the single girl in a family of boys, remained at home. She traces to such a desperate period of lack of employment mental moods and impressions unerased after seventy years.

Poverty was the common lot of wage earners in Victorian times. What was rare about my grandfather's household in Stroud was its combination of material bareness with intellectual liveliness. This bright spark of thinking and feeling it owed chiefly to my grandmother. She was a mill girl born to the mill, for her mother worked in it before her. Slightly built with finely drawn features, she had a sense of humour which never deserted her, perhaps because she used it as often against herself as other people. Like many mill girls she was not particularly interested in or good at housework. She must have liked the company and the talk of the mill. She enjoyed most of all listening to the conversation of her sons, a cut and thrust about politics, books, and everything under the sun. When the argument rose high she knew how to stop a quarrel, for her personality was as strong as theirs.

Much has been written of the political and economic interests of the working classes of Victorian England and their pursuit of what they regarded as their proper share in the making of the law and in the distribution of the national income. English history in that century turned largely upon it. Less has been said of the search of some men and women in those classes for a civilization which they had never known or which had been denied to them. In the attempt to make the education of the mind and the emotions their own and to enter into possession of themselves, such people were in a small minority. People interested in these things were a minority in every class. The working classes did not differ in this respect from the classes above them. Scientific or religious or artistic interests were rare throughout English society. But the interests of a minority of the working class had a significance extending well beyond themselves. They were the true justification of the wide economic and political claims which were being made for the class to which these people belonged. For throughout the century in advancing those claims the majority of the nation found themselves faced by the fixed belief of the upper classes that in the social structure of Victorian England not only did wealth rule poverty and education ignorance but men who were superior by nature governed those who by nature were inferior. The governed were held to be for ever incapable of understanding the civilization they had been born into. This doctrine they denied. They asserted against it, not a counter-belief in the superiority of their own class, but the proposition that in all classes it was one and the same human nature one was dealing with, whether poor or rich, educated or uneducated. In their own way and subject to the limits of their experience they were believers in the unity of mankind. The roots of this faith lay deep in Victorian religion and intellectual life. It was these roots which they explored, in their own way and following in the first instance the only guides they had, the experience and the thinking of the educated classes above them.

The intellectual interests of my Stroud grandmother seem to have come from her father. He was in the family memory a shadowy figure who appeared in Gloucestershire in the early years of the nineteenth century. According to my father he was supposed to have had something to do with the Chartist agitation in the north of England. He certainly bore a Lancashire name, refused to discuss his past with his wife, and left letters from the north unanswered. By trade he was a bookbinder and he kept, as bookbinders did in those days, a set of his own tools.

From him and from other ancestors unknown to me his daughter derived a temperament in which religion, intellectual and musical interests were about equally blended. Perhaps the religion came from her mother, a mill girl who was a strong church-goer all her life. Church-going was conventional in Victorian times and there were social gains to be made by it. But one gets an impression, in these two women, of a personal faith which could only find its satisfaction in this way. It certainly survived the conditions of a hard life. Music was a natural delight to her, for she was the fortunate possessor of a fine soprano voice which she took care to cultivate. Her intellectual curiosity she satisfied wherever she could read, sometimes at home, sometimes under the street lamps coming home from the mill. She was not committed to solemnity. She admired George Eliot, both as a novelist and as a woman. But she was a student also of the romances of Rose Braddon and the mysteries of Eugene Sue.

Her mental vitality came out in far bolder form in her children, particularly in my father and his younger brother Arthur. As men they pursued very similar careers. Both left school early, in my father's case at thirteen. Both had minds which would have made their way in any profession, if Victorian England had thought it worth while to recruit the professions from working-class homes. From delivering newspapers and railway bookstall clerking they graduated to bookselling, in an age when bookselling and newsvending were becoming large-scale business. They were hard readers in a curious variety of fields. My uncle's idea of light reading was Henry Hart Milman's *History of Latin Christianity*.

My father's range was even wider. He respected science, as every educated late Victorian did. It was from him that I acquired a taste for natural history—he and his brothers, in their poor bedroom, were great collectors of all sorts of natural objects—and some inkling of the importance of the work of Charles Darwin and Alfred Russell Wallace. But he took seriously also the conflict between science and religion and studied it in his own scholarly way. One grew used to finding books on the historical geography of Palestine and the folklore of the Old Testament scattered about the house and to hearing of J. G. Frazer and other anthropologists. He had a way of taking up current economic controversy in the same spirit and insisted on mastering the arguments on both sides. When the gold standard was under fire in the nineties he became a student of bimetallism. But perhaps the best example of his methods was the effect upon him when he was over thirty of the publication of A. E. Zimmern's *Greek Commonwealth* in 1911. It says something for the idealistic ardour of politics in those days that my father, who had inherited from his parents keen political interests on the conservative side, forthwith began to teach himself Greek in order to learn more about these people who ran a democracy and an empire before the Romans were heard of. He collected the English historians of Greece and, since with him everything became linked with his religion, he took to following the lessons in church until his last years in a Greek New Testament. In much the same spirit, when he was nearly ninety he heard me talk about a book on Chinese history which I had been reading. I got the impression that with a little encouragement he would have begun the study of Chinese in order to get the Chinese point of view.

My father's father belonged to the generation of working man who got the vote in 1867. These men believed, or the best of them did so, that they had been called upon to govern themselves. It is arguable that this was no more than an illusion, even that they had been deceived. What is indisputable is the vigour of their political convictions and behaviour. For my grandfather a general election was hardly complete which left his shirt whole. A Disraelian Tory living in a Liberal stronghold at Stroud, he rejoiced to burn blue lights on the top of his garden wall when he knew that a Liberal procession was coming that way. This could usually be trusted to create an interesting situation. His political conduct contrasted strongly with his normal demeanour, which was gentle and unassuming. A mild man, he possessed an unexpected streak of physical and moral courage which was of help to his neighbours on more than one occasion. His political interests descended to his sons. This man was known only to have given one order to them. It was that they should never go into domestic service. They never did.

On re-reading what I have written I notice that while I have tried to describe my father I have said nothing about my mother. She never shared my father's intellectual life, but the eyes with which I look at the world must be partly hers. She was the daughter of a railway signalman at Ashchurch in Gloucestershire and remained in her interests always very much the country woman, with a preference for her garden and simple family jokes over other things. Her father carried an Italian surname Bassano, which is my third name. This must have sounded odd in an English country district. He spoke sometimes of a tradition in his family that they had come to England from Italy in the sixteenth century and were related to the Bassani, Venetian painters, some of whose pictures hang at Hampton Court. I never had time to examine this attractive and unusual story. Family legends have a way of being both right and wrong at the same time. The name Bassano appears in the Patent Rolls, I am told, as early as 1617, but who the man then mentioned was, whether he or his ancestors came from Bassano on the Brenta, the home town of the painters, and whether he was an ancestor of the Gloucestershire railwayman, I do not know. Scraps of evidence suggest some connection between my grandfather's family and the silk industry, which brought a number of Italians to England, notably to Derby, where my grandfather was born.

Despite my father's enthusiasms, historical and political interests with me were late in growing. My first school in Cirencester was rough. My brother and I attended because it was near to our house and because it was a church school. Powell's School by name, it had been founded in past times by a charitable woman for the children of poor weavers. None of us were the sons of weavers, but many were poor. Some must have been very poor indeed. I still remember the rags and the smell of the class on hot summer days, which made me feel sick. Discipline was extremely strict. Fist fights and teasing the weak-minded boys were the chief recreations. Fortunately children easily develop interests more harmless than these, even when they are not encouraged to do so. The streets of a Gloucestershire country town in those days were quiet and free from traffic. We played marbles in the gutters on the way to and from school. I was often intensely miserable at this school and often intensely happy. I still remember the names and faces of a few of my schoolmates and like to suppose that they may even remember me.

My world changed for me in my eleventh year. I won a free place, as it was called, at the boy's grammar school in the town. In the same year my eyes were tested and I was given glasses to wear. With great delight I found that I could now tell the time by the church clock. The ability to see birds and flowers probably seemed as important at the time as going to a new school. I attended this school, my brother, too, until we left Cirencester five years later. I cannot believe that it was a very good school, although as a teaching institution it was competent to the level then thought proper for the boys of a country town. Old diaries suggest that I was seldom at the top of the form, but content to drift along somewhere near it. They also make it clear that I was far more interested in the plants and animals of Gloucestershire than I was in my schoolwork. Natural history was a passion with me, as it is with many children. Most of my spare time which was not spent in collecting, observing, sketching and noting, was passed in reading about my favourite subject. In this way I came into touch with what had been one of the most powerful intellectual interests of Victorian England. I read Darwin and Huxley long before I opened Gibbon or Adam Smith and my first serious ambition was to become a zoologist. For some years I was possessed by the ardent faith that life is lived best in the Bird Room of the British Museum (Natural Science).

This taste for natural history was stimulated not only by living in a country district but also by a big house and a remarkable man. The house was Chesterton House, on the outskirts of Cirencester, and the man was Sir Charles Brooke, who died in 1917 but had ruled the state of Sarawak in the island of Borneo ever since mid-Victorian times. 'Rajah Brooke', as he was called in the town, stayed at Chesterton House whenever he was in England. He had built on the edge of the town a museum and aviaries, where those who wished might see for themselves the birds and animals and products of his East Indian kingdom. This domain of the white Rajah was a very strange place and for children it was utterly absorbing. Like many another schoolboy, I became, under its powerful influence and that of the books I read, a kind of camp follower of Victorian science in the days of Alfred Russell Wallace and Joseph Dalton Hooker, when all the animals and plants of the world were being catalogued and the question of the origin of species became an urgent scientific problem. Not that all our thoughts rose to this philosophic level. I seem to remember leaving a sweet in the hand of a stuffed orang-utan, to see whether it would still be there in a fortnight's time.

Biological ambitions were encouraged by a young aircraftsman who visited our house at Cirencester in the later years of the war. He came not to talk to me but to pay attentions to my sister. Talk he did, however, fluently and well. Walter Batt was a demonstrator in the laboratories at King's College, London, in peacetime. He was the first man with some scientific training I ever met. It was from listening to him that I first came to learn something of the scope of the Darwinian theory of evolution by natural selection and from my father's reserved attitude towards it something of the crisis which this had produced in Victorian religious faith and morals. These scientific conversations, if they can be called such, must have been one of the influences which in my early teens carried me away, although unconsciously rather than consciously, from the beliefs taught in the great church at the end of the street. I became interested in animal habit, in the conflict of instincts, and in the idea which I had read in Lloyd Morgan, that this conflict was the beginning of reason.

My biological ambitions, probably always misplaced, had to be given up when the family moved from Cirencester to Newbury in Berkshire in 1920. Neither in my old nor my new school was biology taught and my interest in physics, chemistry and mathematics were limited. My urgent intellectual and emotional needs at this stage of life attracted me strongly towards the idea of a university, but if I wished to attend a university I must win an open scholarship or exhibition to do so. My parents' income was far from adequate to maintain me there unaided. Other possibilities besides a scientific career had to be looked at and other interests besides zoology came to the fore. They had certainly begun to do for some time past.

This boyish passion for science had one curious result. My first piece of published work was not the scientific monograph I had once hoped it might be, but it had something to do with the history of science. It was the life of Mark Catesby, a naturalist and traveller who collected plants and animals in Florida and the Carolinas early in the eighteenth century. This I wrote for the first edition of the *Dictionary of American Biography* when I was a research student at Harvard. I chose his name from among a number which were offered by Samuel Eliot Morison to his historical research seminar, because it reminded me of old interests.

By that time, in the mind of a graduate student working in the America of Calvin Coolidge and Herbert Hoover, natural history was quite crowded out by the new interests of history and politics. The change had begun in my last years at school, with the need to alter the direction of my thinking if I ever wished to go to college. It was also owing to the influence of a remarkable schoolteacher. Someone was needed to counter with me the influence of the biologists and to point out that there were questions of human society just as difficult as any which Charles Darwin had faced and equally deserving of study. This counter influence came through the headmaster of Newbury Grammar School, Edward Sharwood Smith.

A tall man, with intelligent eyes and large mobile mouth, he was, although I did not know it, approaching his final years as a teacher and retired a few years later. But he exercised in a short space of time a shaping influence on my life, as on many other boys who were his pupils. He was a born teacher, whose personal career had been altered, strange as that may seem, by the Education Act of 1902. Brought up in the public-school tradition, he believed that the time had come to devise good secondary schools for the broad social classes which had been left out of, not to say excluded from, the public schools in the nineteenth century. With characteristic enthusiasm and energy he accepted the headmastership of an old and neglected grammar school in a sleepy country town in order to make the experiment.

He was a classics man himself and taught classics. There were some extremely serious limitations to his point of view. He knew nothing of natural science and not a great deal about the medieval and modern history of Europe. What he really taught was a conception of human nature, partly Hellenic, partly Christian in origin, reconciled according to a highly personal formula. This hardly did justice to the reality of the conflict between Greek and Christian ideals. But he insisted that we should study the classical model of man in the original sources and languages, with full regard for historical conditions. We did not know where his views came from. We only knew his superb teaching powers. He made Greeks and Romans live, showed us how views of the human person and society in which nineteenth-century England still believed first came into the world and urged us to examine them for ourselves instead of taking them on trust. To my surprise I found myself reading Greek and Latin history. To rouse indifferent boys to this degree of interest was an astonishing achievement, and his hearers, sometimes entranced, sometimes scornful, never forgot it.

Some things he could not do. He taught the classical wisdom—know yourself—and it would be a fair criticism of him to say that he expected us to accept in the main the classical answers. Outside our schoolroom conceptions of human nature which had lasted for two thousand years were being criticized and taken to pieces much as in the seventeenth and eighteenth centuries the classical idea of the physical world had been pulled apart and replaced by the experimental scientists. The works of Freud and Marx were waiting for us to make it clear just how hard it is for men to understand either themselves or others. These were our problems, not his. He could hardly be expected to solve them. At least when we left his hands we knew something of the weapons with which intellectual battles were fought. It was customary to react violently against his influence if and when one went to college. I was no exception. But the fact remained that it was he and no one else who shook us awake. He had a knack of turning boys intellectually into men. What we did afterwards was our concern, not his. This was very much in keeping with the character of the man. He once defined a school as 'a community of individuals, who respect one another's individuality'.

He was a great informal as well as formal teacher. He did much for me, for example, simply by lending me a translation of Goethe's autobiography to read. Perhaps I was less under his influence, although no less under his spell, than some of my schoolmates. I did not specialize in classics and was a poor classics scholar. But I received valuable encouragement from him to read history, when biology looked impossible. On ways and means he was enigmatic. It was like him to warn me against textbooks. 'Read the big books. Read Maine's *Ancient Law*.' Fortunately there was someone in the school who knew something about history textbooks, although less than Sharwood Smith about the big books. With some help from the history master, who, however, was inclined to sleep in the cricket pavilion while we worked at our books under the trees in the sports field, and even more from a good school library, I went up to Downing College, Cambridge, in October 1923 as an unselfconfident undergraduate. I had won a small open scholarship to read history.

Reading history at Cambridge meant entering the History School and coming under the influence of its dominant personalities. The teaching on the English history side I found rather boring, although I admired the subtle and resourceful teaching of constitutional history. European history, both modern and medieval, I found more interesting. In one's third year it became necessary to study a special period. British economic history, taught by the late Sir John Clapham, had interested me in the first year, but I felt no inclination at that time to go on with it. Harold Temperley was trying to make Cambridge understand the shifts of power in the world which the European war of 1914–18 had brought about. He put on a course in American history, then a novel subject at any English university, and took as his theme the Civil War in the United States. I entered for that and in the course of reading for it and coaching other students in it the following year came to realize for the first time the intellectual fascination of war, which has perhaps had something to do with its high social prestige and survival as an institution. It was highly unfashionable to recognize this interest in the twenties and I did not care to admit it to myself, but it seemed undeniable. I felt it again fifteen years later when I found myself engaged as a temporary Civil Servant in the second war. In our American studies the fascination came no doubt from watching the actions of men of transcendent practical capacity, such as Grant and Lee. But I came later to think that it had something to do with the nature of military decisions. The bringing of superior force to bear at the critical point is a problem which appeals both to the calculator and the gambler in man and to both in extreme degree. However, the immediate effect of this new interest was not to make me wish to devote myself to military history but to cause me to feel that war had not been well studied by the historians who worked in England during the long peace of the nineteenth century. Surely the picture they gave of human thinking and action was to that extent untrue? This belief had something to do with my being willing to join the staff of the Historical Section of the War Cabinet Office during the second European war, despite the grave doubts about the official history of the war which were entertained by many professional historians.

My future, after taking my degree at Cambridge in 1926, was uncertain. Ill health in my final year had done much to sap my confidence in myself. Finance also ran out after that summer term. I had maintained myself largely, although not exclusively, on college and local government grants and I did not wish to continue to be a financial burden to my parents. At the same time I did not feel drawn to the schoolteaching or the Civil Service life towards which some of the closest of my friends turned. The detailed research in diplomatic history which flourished in Cambridge under Temperley's influence did not attract me. It was a difficult time and I should not care to have to swim through those dark waters again. I managed to postpone a decision and at the same time to regain some of my health by staying up for another year, living cheaply and earning some money by supervising and coaching. Gradually and painfully things cleared and I found myself walking a definite path.

This discovery of a sense of direction among distracting interests was due to a number of circumstances and my personal reactions to them. For one thing there were the public events of the time. The war was beginning to be forgotten, but social troubles were far from over. The years immediately before the war had been a time of bitter industrial relations and great strikes. With the return of peace these features of the industrial scene came back accompanied by an undertone of unrest and doubt about the economic future. I heard these events discussed as they occurred by those among my friends who were reading economics. We listened to visiting speakers in debates at the Union, including industrialists and trade unionists. I took my degree in the summer of the General Strike.

Like many others, I was puzzled and concerned by the turn public affairs seemed to be taking, while feeling that I possessed little or nothing by which to measure or to test them. I felt sure that the trade unions had made a great mistake in seeming, however unintentionally, to challenge Government and to set themselves up as a kind of state within the State, a role which they were not at all equipped to play. I volunteered therefore for service on the railways which as it turned out was not required. But it was done without enthusiasm and I felt nothing but disapproval for the fellow undergraduate next to me one evening in hall who cheerfully exclaimed, 'All miners ought to be shot!' The truth was that, from having been wholly ignorant of everything that industry implied, I was beginning to understand for the first time something of the range and complexity of industrial problems, and to think that the Government of the day was by no means without blame for what had happened.

I knew little about these things, but the development in my opinions was notable. I owed this to my friends. Cambridge was a great place for friendships with men whose background and experiences were utterly different from one's own. Two of my closest friends at Downing during these later undergraduate years came from the north of England. Norman Goodier who was reading for the Mechanical Sciences Tripos, a scientist of exceptional brilliance who later emigrated to the United States, came from Preston in Lancashire. Dennis Ward, with whom I was on even closer terms, was a student of history. Later a professor at Lahore in the present Pakistan, he was from Barnsley in the Yorkshire coalfield. These men knew more than most undergraduates did about what the industrial classes on both sides of the fence were thinking and the true nature of the issues at stake. Their doubts and indignation during the strike taught me much. They took the gloss off the official version of events. Evidently as elsewhere one should try to get at the inside story! The General Strike was soon over. It probably had less effect in Cambridge than in almost any other place in the country, except that some of us had to take our degrees by proxy that year. But it left me with a new interest in industrial relations in the next few years, when the memory of the General Strike was being driven from men's minds by the flow of later events.

My interest in economic affairs was stimulated, too, by the perfectly mundane experience of crossing London on my way to and from Cambridge every term. The London I saw east of Liverpool Street in the nineteen-twenties was still very much the London of Charles Booth and his social investigators at the end of the nineteenth century. It was less desperately poor than in Booth's day, but to me, fresh from the country, profoundly impressive in the sheer acreage of its drab streets. Many of these disappeared under the German bombs in 1940 and 1941. One would have had to be very unimaginative not to wonder, why so many poor? The question came perhaps the more sharply to members of my generation because we read much about unemployment in the papers and met casually on the streets—I am thinking of a man for whom Ward and I bought a ham sandwich in Cambridge—men who were unemployed. Why, one wondered, the waste of human resources?

No doubt it was very like young men to worry about the unemployed when they were in some danger of becoming unemployed themselves. It was like them also to criticize their teachers while remaining indifferent to the gaps in their own knowledge. The fact remained that the current history teaching at Cambridge seemed to us to throw little light on these everyday problems. We looked around for guides. In my case this meant reading Tawney.

It is difficult at this distance of time to make clear to those who never knew him or who never read his books when they were written the exceptional position held by Richard Henry Tawney in scholarship and politics in the twenties. He has been described as the best English historian of the interwar years with the exception of Lewis Namier. He was an extremely fine scholar, particularly in the field of English social and economic history of the sixteenth and seventeenth centuries. No man perhaps did more to pull down the conventional Victorian views of the Civil War and the Revolution and to try to substitute something more realistic. But he was also much more than a great scholar. He occupied as an historian a position half-way between politics and philosophy. This made him extremely interesting to young people trying to make up their own minds.

In the twenties what had been the society of Edwardian England was going sour under the influence of a terrible war, which many felt had been lost in the moment it was won, and industrial difficulties which seemed without end, certainly in the years down to the General Strike. Tawney was trying in this situation to get his countrymen to rethink their attitudes and assumptions. The whole of his remarkable personal powers were directed to this end. Of course, he failed, partly owing to the intrinsic difficulty of the task, partly to the nature of his own beliefs. As a man who was both a devout Christian and a socialist he ploughed a lonely furrow. Few of the Christians who sympathized with him were socialists, while many of the socialists were not Christian. But he certainly ploughed with a will. The late twenties probably represented the height of his public influence, although some trace of this survived into his old age.

Like many others, I felt separated from him on the religious issue, so far as I could understand his point of view. But I had begun after taking my degree to read in the field of modern social and economic history. His *Religion and the Rise of Capitalism* which appeared in 1926 was one of the books which everyone read. It responded brilliantly in typically Tawney fashion to the mood of a time of sharp disillusion and changing social values. He linked the study of history with sociology on the one side and with social philosophy on the other and asked where changes of social values in the past had come from. I found that I read the book differently from many people. He did not seem to me to be saying that Calvinism produced capitalism, although many who disliked both decided that this must be his message. He seemed rather to be saying that there was an element in capitalism which could only be accounted for in terms of the history of religious ideas. With the help of the ideas of Max Weber, he fought a war on two fronts, both against the middle-class social values he had been brought up in and against the Marxians who were becoming his most powerful competitors in social controversy.

The thirties turned out to be hostile to Tawney's idealistic socialism. On grounds of political calculation rather than of theoretical analysis, although that, too, counted, a Europe which was fast drifting towards war and civil war plumped for a moral nihilism far removed from his point of view. Why waste time on value judgements? These were nonsense statements anyway. Given the knowledge of sex and age and race, given above all class and state, a sensible man could judge at once the interests of those with whom he had to deal and decide his course of action. What need for more in a practical world? The search for human values, historical or otherwise, was moonshine. This was the activism and the harsh language of a confessional age not without terrible insights of its own. Positions were being taken up for a fight and the hard word was soon followed by the harder blow.

But in the quiet of the late twenties it was still possible to read Tawney's book and to be impressed by the power of his argument, especially if one was disposed to be critical of society, as I was. The effect with me was to make me think seriously for the first time about doing historical research. After much thought I wrote to Tawney and asked whether he would regard it as a fair test of his ideas to study the economic behaviour, the policy, the language and the ideas, of the early settlers in colonial New England? These men were strict Calvinists and they ran their communities upon lines chosen by themselves, as free as they pleased to be from the Church and State which they had left behind. Much to my surprise and delight I received a prompt and friendly reply, in which he both encouraged me and pointed out some of the difficulties in the way. On the strength of this I applied for the Joseph Hodges Choate fellowship at Harvard tenable from Cambridge University. This usually went to a lawyer for Choate had been an American lawyer and diplomat. Fortunately for me no lawyer applied that year. I sailed for the United States in September 1927.

I must not make it appear that I went to America out of research interests only. There seemed as yet no answer to the riddle of a career. I did not wish to teach in school. I wanted somehow to keep in touch with historical studies. At the same time in Cambridge and at my college, which was small and not rich, there were no prospects. I was playing for time. I was also influenced by my friendship with Dennis Ward. He was more sharply aware of international affairs than I was and had formed the scheme of going to the United States to study the history of American diplomacy in Central America. He went as a Commonwealth (now Harkness) Fellow to the Johns Hopkins University at Baltimore when I went to Harvard.

2

We sailed with a small party of Commonwealth Fellows, men and women, whose passage had been booked on one of the smaller and slower passenger liners. The United States were farther off in those days. We had ample time to sample some of the experiences of the old-time English emigrants on the North Atlantic, from spouting whales and gleaming icebergs to routine seasickness. The steerage passengers on our boat were, however, not English but French families on their way to Canada. What we were steaming towards from the first flash of the Nantucket lightship onwards was less the creation of those old English settlers whom I had come to study than of all the people, of every nationality in Europe, who had poured into the largest and fastest-growing industrial state in the world during the half-century before 1914.

One felt the sharp difference from Europe on the first hour of landing in New York. The sights, the sounds, the smells, the light and the sunshine, the accents in street and shop, many of them at that date half European, were all different. Before one had been there long one sensed another difference, too. Ten years before the United States had for the first time intervened in a war in Europe with decisive effect. She now remained anchored in enigmatic aloofness from Europe's affairs on the far side of the Atlantic. But the effects of the war in Europe and the United States had been strikingly different. The war had almost broken Europe's courage. It had taught Americans that their country was a great world power, by any standard which one cared to apply. They were not quite sure what to do about their new position and found it safest to do nothing at all. But they were amiably conscious of it. This difference of moral climate was not something one had expected. It seemed natural enough when one met it. I found myself reading the English newspapers in the light of this new and significant fact.

At Harvard I stayed two years, financed first by the Choate fellowship, then by the Rockefeller Foundation. They were on the whole happy years despite homesickness, as my years at Cambridge had been on the whole happy, often intensely so. They were certainly full of interest. For the first time I found myself working in a university graduate school and in a school of social sciences. Cambridge possessed at that time almost nothing in the way of organized teaching for those who had already taken a first degree in history or economics. The graduate schools of Harvard were well developed. Not all the teaching was equally good, but it was there if you wanted it.

I stood out, although this was not easy, against taking on a big programme of courses, on the grounds of health as well as of the interests of my research. Of even more importance than the existence of graduate classes was the borderland nature of my inquiries. This gave me entry both to the history school and to the economics department. My director of research was Samuel Eliot Morison, a New Englander and a profound student of the colonial history of the United States. He later became the historian of the American Navy in the Second World War. I owed much also to the advice and generous help of Edwin Gay, the best American economic historian of his day, now almost forgotten, but a man of remarkable personality. I found myself forced to take economics and law seriously as I worked my way into my subject. I read Marshall on economics and attended the lectures of two visiting economists, Hawtrey and Schumpeter. I visited the library of the Law

School, listened to Dean Pound and read Vinogradoff on jurisprudence.

As so often happens, the most important development was personal and unexpected. One of the first Englishmen I met at Harvard was G. T. Jones, a young economist from Cambridge, who was killed in a car crash near Paris a few years later. He was preparing to return home. But through him I met many of the young instructors in the economics department, Seymour Harris, Edward Mason, Overton Taylor and others who were to become the teachers of the next generation. Harvard economics had recently come under the influence of a remarkable teacher, Allyn Young. The effect of his broad and profound mind was to be felt all around although the man himself was in Europe, from which he never returned, for he died in London. I owed my first introduction to economics and the social sciences to a cataract of talk in the Harvard of his day.

This was a new and bracing influence. General ideas on man and society adequate to explain historical change had come to seem to some of us after three years study for the Historical Tripos the chief want of the Cambridge Historical School in our day. Impressively good scholarship was, it appeared, not quite enough. I remember the point being discussed, both during and after my undergraduate time. But we did not know the intellectual map well enough to be able to find a remedy. One could, of course, resort to private enterprise. In my last years at Cambridge I took to attending the Heretics Society, a university discussion group kept going chiefly by two young dons, the economist Philip Sargant Florence and the philosopher R. B. Braithwaite. There one heard, for example, a brilliant Polish anthropologist, Bronislaw Malinowski, expounding his philosophy of functionalism. Malinowski's concept of society as a bundle of functions with their relevant institutions, covering the whole area of human life, had been worked out by him in the course of anthropological researches in the Pacific islands. He was not interested in the history of civilized society and functionalism as he taught it was, if anything, anti-historical. It seemed to me, however, a valuable aid to the understanding of history. It freed one from the unsatisfactory basis and superstructure metaphor, and was often in my mind during the arguments about Marxism in England in the nineteen-thirties. But one Polish swallow hardly made a summer. Harvard experience suggested how necessary a well-developed school of social sciences is for a university and that history and the social sciences needed to be brought together, not kept apart. Neither could reach full stature without the other. No doubt, with or without the social sciences, history as men write it must remain what J. G. Droysen said it was, not the truth, but our surrogate for truth, our human witness that what we call the truth does exist. I determined to try to work on the relation between history and the social sciences when I got back to England, that is if I returned to England, and if I lived, for I was still much bothered about my health.

My time in the United States was drawing to an end. I was offered by Gay a place on the list of instructors at Harvard, but although much pleased and flattered I decided for many reasons to return home. One consequence of this was that the book I had expected to write on the economic and social history of early New England, considered with reference to Tawney's thesis about an older England, was never written. I showed the draft of the early chapters to an English friend at Harvard whose chief concern, it is true, was not history or economics but English literature, on which he later became a great authority. His comments on style and arrangement did not encourage me to go on. Besides, when I went back to England I was soon too busy teaching to finish what I had begun. In this way it happened that my first substantial piece of writing was not about the Massachusetts Bay and its colonists but about the English Midlands. These I had never seen when I went to the United States.

Luckily for me I visited America when I was young enough to accept people for what they were, without being anxious to study them as representatives of their class and nation. I made good friends in and around the Harvard Yard, where one met men from every state in the Union, gathered there by their common interests, at a time of life when the promise seemed endless and warmth of feeling and opinion was natural. My two Christmases I spent with Ward at Baltimore and in the South. In the summer between my two sessions I travelled with him round the United States armed with personal introductions. We saw something of the immense variety of conditions from which my friends and acquaintances came. These months of travel demonstrated the wealth and power of America in a manner all the more impressive because in those days, despite all that had happened since 1917, the difference between European standards and American was ill understood in Europe. I remember saying casually and probably in the interval between much laughing, as we travelled westward across the Texan plains after a visit to New Orleans and the Gulf, that I felt sorry for any European people who might fall foul of such a country. At that time it did not seem likely that any European country would. Surely the experience of one war had been enough?

There were fortunately other objects of contemplation besides incomes and war potential. No one had ever told us that the North American continent was beautiful. We found it to be so, although often in a wholly different manner from Europe. I was particularly interested in the strange, desert-like scenery of the south-western states, in western Texas, New Mexico and Arizona, and puzzled to account for its fascination. Charles Darwin's remark came to mind how, after the voyage of the *Beagle*, he found his mind returning more often to the empty plains of Patagonia than to the forests of tropical Brazil. He supposed that the human imagination found the distances of the plain more satisfying because it felt free in them. In California I visited someone who had been brought up as a girl in the same years and in the same quiet street in the Cotswolds where I had lived as a boy. This, too, seemed strange after so long a time.

The comparative peace of the nineteen-twenties was, however, coming to an end. It would have required a prophet to foresee the coming troubles. There seemed to be no chink in the economic armour of the United States. I returned to England from Montreal in June 1929. Some time that summer I discussed the economic outlook with my teacher Edwin Gay at his house in Boston. One would have had to be blind not to see the endless rebuilding in the American cities and I asked him where all the prosperity was coming from. He said he did not know, but he added that he thought we were only at the beginning of these vast accumulations of wealth. Whether he had the long or the short period in mind in saying this I do not know. If the long, then his remark might stand as accurate prediction. If the short, then it was lamentably mistaken. In October the New York stock market was shaken from top to bottom by panic-stricken men. The long boom was over.

I did not see the United States again for another sixteen years, when I found myself on the eastern seaboard on British government service early in 1945. By that time the conflict in Europe which had destroyed the peaceful world of my father and his generation had returned in new and more terrible form. Washington was incredibly lovely that spring, as the sunshine brought out the dogwood and the cherry-blossom. But it was the city to which the body of Franklin Roosevelt, the architect of American victory in the war, had just been brought. The streets and the trains were full of uniformed men. My old supervisor Morison was with the American fleet somewhere in the Pacific, an official historian of the war. Gay was spending his last years in California, whence he wrote me a sad personal letter. Harvard and its youthful conversations seemed an age away. Indeed they were. Youth's Eden always has its serpent waiting. The snake which had lain so quietly at the roots of our world loosed a new and infinitely menacing coil at Hiroshima a few months after I had flown back to England.

3

When I returned from the United States to England in the summer months of 1929 I found myself back in the same quiet house at Newbury, facing very much the same personal problems as when I had left it. I was, however, much more certain about what it was I wanted to do.

England seemed little changed after two years. Perhaps it was unchangeable? My future brother-in-law, Charles Hayes, was about to leave for India to plant tea in Assam, because there seemed no immediate prospects in the marine diesel engineering in which he had been trained. When we went to a restaurant in Reading it seemed to me that the members of the orchestra were exactly the same people as two years before. After the United States, this seemed strange. There many people felt they were in danger of getting stuck in a rut if they did not change their job and even their occupation once a year.

This sensation of unalterability was, of course, an illusion of mine. The unemployment rate stood high. This was itself an index of change, although of change unfavourable to Britain. Old industries were going down, new growing too slowly to absorb the natural increase of the population. I did not know this. The industrial forces which were sweeping away the Victorian past were not observable in the Home Counties. I was soon to be introduced to them where they were obvious.

It was necessary to become a genuine seeker for employment myself. I wanted to continue the researches in social and economic history in association with the social sciences which I had begun at Harvard. But how was it to be done? A visit to Cambridge that summer showed that old friends were scattered or scattering. The few who remained in college were sympathetic and delightful. But there was no opening at Downing, which was not by any means a wealthy college. I seriously considered applying for a post which I saw going at a technical college in the north, although the idea of teaching without researching made my heart sink.

Fortunately at this moment an opportunity offered. The universities in England in the late twenties were not a scene of vigorous growth. No doubt they ought to have been, but they were not. There was, however, the occasional post to be filled. I was looking, I thought, for a berth in a department of history. But when a lectureship in economic history was advertised in the Faculty of Commerce at the University of Birmingham I applied and to my surprise and joy was appointed.

My post was shared at first between the Faculty and the extramural department of the University. Only in this way, it was felt, could an appointment at three hundred and fifty pounds a year be justified. One result was that one of my earliest teaching memories is of a boy, a member of my evening class, who had just come off shift in a big motor-car accessories firm, sleeping soundly with his head in his arms while I talked about British industry. He probably thought that he knew more about it than any teacher could. This arrangement to which I owed my first permanent appointment lapsed as work grew within the University. I also came to feel that what was known as adult education demanded special teaching gifts which I did not possess.

The appointment at Birmingham marked the beginning of a big change in personal circumstances. An old circle of friends was broken, a new one begun. This process had started on the day we took our degrees at Cambridge. Old college friends, such as Alan Hitchman and Frank Lee, joined the Civil Service in London. They looked at me quizzically when I became a temporary Civil Servant myself in the second war. Frank Rosebery, an American friend of school and college days, was in Paris learning how to become a merchant banker. The break was most keenly felt with Dennis Ward. We had both enormously enjoyed the strangeness and the fun of life in America, although he had always had more energy and initiative than I had. There were some sides of his nature, perhaps a certain mixed emotionality especially, which I was impatient with and I am certain that there were things in me which he equally condemned. But our common interests were always greater than our differences. We had in three years grown up together, laughing at and approving much the same things. We both combined restless intellectual interests with temperaments and inclinations which were surprisingly conservative, in a way which was possibly easier in the nineteen-twenties than the nineteen-thirties.

Among other interests we were both sharply conscious of the swift decline of organized religion in English society. This was not a new thing, least of all in the universities, but it attracted public notice at the time because of the contrast with the conventional practices of an earlier day. The war, as in other matters, had widened a break in custom which had begun long before. We felt ourselves about equally cut off from the routine church-going of an older generation and from what appeared to be its natural successor, the religion of all sensible men. Both left us feeling extremely impatient and dissatisfied, as if we had been asked to accept something which we knew not to be true.

As young people do, we sought our own way out, pushing at the most unlikely-looking doors so long as they seemed to offer an exit. Our approach to these great problems was not, as might be supposed, philosophic and moral. It was aesthetic. Both in America and afterwards we were very much interested in Goethe. This was partly because we were trying to teach ourselves German. The German poet was also someone whom one could not encounter without being impressed. He was a man of formidable, enigmatic, perpetually fascinating powers. To young people who were finding their way about in the world, meeting new people every day, colliding joyfully or painfully with them, he posed the standing riddle of the human person. We found him an absorbing study even when in undergraduate fashion we were swift to condemn.

There was something also in his general view of life and in the guiding ideas he carried about with him which encouraged us as we tried to swim in our own way against the current of other people's opinion. We liked the way he combined, and insisted on combining, poetry with science, as if they were both necessary not opposed things. His highly eighteenth-century conception of natural law and of a world governed by law, which informed his attitude to both science and poetry, were not original ideas of his. But they were very congenial to us. So far as I was concerned I accepted his intensely personal conviction that trees could not grow into the sky and that God could not but obey his own laws, even when I found these notions puzzling and distressing. This was light in a darkened room.

Neither of us was a poet or given to writing poetry, but we also accepted Goethe's view that poetry was a natural activity of man, a kind of natural law of human nature, and that the poet was the most human of men. If there was something obviously one-sided and self-interested in these propositions, coming as they did from a poet, we found it instructive to think about human nature in this way. One could suppose that most men and women get as much poetry as their natures can cope with out of the normal experiences of life, in falling in love, marriage, birth, death and sickness. Only the exceptional individual becomes the conscious poet and there seemed nothing extraordinary about that. Most men measure and number and to the extent that it is necessary for them to do so think mathematically in the ordinary course of life. It never occurs to them to become mathematicians. If this view of human nature was correct, then painting and music and architecture, as well as drama and literature, were as sure a guide to the life of men and women, to true history, as the documents of political and economic calculation on which historians are accustomed to spend so much of their time.

We were prepared to accept the logic of that and to argue that history as historians write it ought to be about the whole of life, not some one part of it. At the same time, it must be clear from what has just been said that we had much to learn. The thirties proceeded to teach us. We were not aware what bad poets most of us are, what dreamers of terrible dreams, so that we do not know when we are writing tragedy or comedy even in our own lives. When in that decade Communism and Fascism, the two great secular myths of the age, were at grips with one another for the control of Europe, it sometimes struck me that Goethe, who would certainly have been most unhappy in that uproar, might have understood what was happening better than some political commentators. Simply because he did not regard the human imagination as a luxury or a deceit, but as the tool by which men either find their way through life or lose it, he would have grasped quicker than they did that what had built up the fabric of the civilized world had also the power to pull it down.

If I am asked what the readings of two young men in their twenties in imperfect German had to do with my proper studies, which were historical, I think the first part of an answer must be this. Goethe's love of the concrete, particular and individual, his insistence that it was only through individuals that he could think his way towards the universal all—*Individuum est ineffabile*, as he put it, quoting someone else—reinforced all my natural tendencies and prejudices. He was a great help towards continuing to regard historical studies as serious and worth while even in an age of universalizing science, for which one had a healthy respect. This was all the more important to me because of the personal position in which I found myself from early days at Harvard onwards. I was an historian working side by side with social scientists. Their work marched at every step with mine. I wanted to do justice to their methods and interests without losing faith in my own. This thinking of mine was immature, even innocent and naïve. It was far from identical with a proper grasp of the logic of historical and scientific thinking. But it was valuable as an attitude and a mood from which work could be done. Understanding of the way the work is done came later.

The other part of the answer must be that in Goethe's well-known aversion from history and historians we sensed a limitation not only in his own thought but also in that of his age. The education of humanity, which so thrilled us, was a splendid phrase of the Enlightenment. But as interpreted by the German poet and his friends it was almost wholly aesthetic in content. This was satisfactory perhaps for poets, dramatists and painters. It did not do for us as professional students of society and its history. We did not know at that time that the intellectual barrier had been broken in Germany by the generation following Goethe's own. It was in the Germany of Hegel, Ranke and Marx that men debated the proposition that the education of mankind comes through history and tried to work out, mostly in terms of the political, economic and cultural experience of western Europe, how that education had come and what its teachings were. We faced in the thirties the problems set by the German philosophies of history when we found ourselves challenged to act on our principles and forced to ask ourselves whether we agreed, on defined points of doctrine, with Russian Marxists, with Hegelians in the service of Italian Fascism, and the Rankeans, conscious and unconscious, who were ensconced in the Government offices and universities of Europe.

Young men's studies unfortunately have sooner or later to come to an end. When I went to Birmingham and Ward returned to Cambridge, where he took up diplomatic history with the encouragement of G. P. Gooch, we ceased to share this common life of reading and speculation. I missed him and his imaginative temperament greatly. He failed to establish himself at Cambridge, although he would have liked to do so. Some years later he accepted a Chair of History at the University of Lahore in the present Pakistan. We drifted in time out of touch, as men do who rarely meet. He returned to Europe after the second war, to join the allied university control in Germany, but died prematurely soon after. His was a nature which united boldness with gentleness, restless originality with a capacity to learn, in attractive proportions. Somehow he never enjoyed the permanent and intense personal happiness which one felt was his by right.

4

The Faculty of Commerce at Birmingham proved to be a small but interesting society. It had been founded at the beginning of the century, when the politician Joseph Chamberlain obtained for the University of Birmingham its charter and invited the economist and historian, William James Ashley, to come back from the United States, where he was teaching at Harvard, and devise a university course which would train men for business. As a result of this move, what would elsewhere have been a department of economics enjoyed the self-governing powers of a Faculty.

Some of the posts in it were intended to be severely practical. There was a Professor of Accounting, Martineau, who had the distinction of being both blind and an effective teacher. There was also a Chair of Industrial Law, held by a man of high legal ability very well known in his day, Sir Frank Tillyard. Both of these men retired within a year or two of my joining the Faculty. One result of their retirement was that for many years the leadership of the Faculty fell to two relatively young men of strongly contrasted character and attainments, both of whom are fortunately still alive.[1]

John George Smith was its Dean until 1947, as well as serving for many years as the Vice-Principal of the University. He was an Irishman, trained at Trinity College, Dublin, who brought the mind of a good mathematician to the teaching of economics. But he also brought much else. He was an excellent administrator, with a wide knowledge of affairs outside the university. Sceptical by nature, he was not easily deceived and would usually be found to have his own line of information on current events, whether in the university or out of it. This alarming insight did not deprive him, however, of humour and kindliness. I owed him much. As an Irishman, he had his own reasons for believing that history was important. Born a Protestant, he was no indiscriminate admirer of the English connection. Indeed, it was an education in itself to hear him tell a table full of Englishmen exactly what he thought of England's mistakes in Ireland, with a wit and good humour which made it impossible for them to be angry or even to answer back. 'Why can't you forget Cromwell?' he was asked. 'Because,' he replied, 'I happen to be the trustee of estates in Ireland the title deeds of which go back to Cromwell's day.' He did not share the convenient belief that today's forgetfulness somehow or other cancels

[1] J. G. Smith died December 1968.

out yesterday's evil deeds. He encouraged my historical inquiries, even when the growing turmoil of the thirties made me doubt the value of the work I was doing. To my relief he also left me free to teach as I pleased.

Philip Sargant Florence's influence in the Faculty was highest at a later day. Trained at Columbia after going to Cambridge, he was half American by birth, with many personal and intellectual connections and affinities with the United States. He was keenly interested in research in the social sciences and was responsible for converting the Faculty of Commerce into a Faculty of Commerce and Social Science before his retirement. At this time, in the nineteen-thirties, I knew him as an exceedingly active Professor of Commerce, who urged sociological inquiry upon economists long before in this country they were prepared to look at it. He was the kindest of friends, a sociable man, whose big house, unfailing sense of hospitality and good humour, aided and abetted by the vigour and liveliness of his American wife, Lella, swept the rest of us into endless parties and cheerful talk.

The younger members of the Faculty were very few. Hilary Marquand, who later became a Minister in the Labour Government after the war, was lecturer in economics when I arrived. He then went to Cardiff as Professor of Industrial Relations and was succeeded by Gilbert Walker, fresh from Oxford and Germany, red-haired and full of energy and fun. Throughout the interwar years Walker and I formed the junior staff of the Faculty. There was a kind of middle group formed by Donald Cousins, who succeeded Martineau in accounting, and Hugh Goitein, who followed Sir Frank Tillyard in law. Even with Smith and Florence hard at work, we were a small band. Every one of us was expected to cover a wide field in teaching and tutoring. Whatever bad effects this led to, it had at least one good result. We had to learn a great deal in order to survive.

If the Faculty was small, so, too, was the University. Physically the University of Birmingham was divided. One part was in the city, the other three miles away on the present University site, where the Faculty of Commerce had already established itself in cramped quarters. This partition, which lasted until after the second war, was not good for the formation of anything that could be described as University opinion. There was a powerful and distinguished scientific wing to the University, well represented by the chemist, Haworth, the physicist, Marcus Oliphant, the mathematical physicist, Rudolph Peierls, and the metallurgist, Hanson, in those years before the war. They were to play an important part in the researches which led to the atomic bomb. There were also men of rare gifts elsewhere in the University. The poet Louis MacNeice taught classics in the Arts Faculty, where the Wordsworth scholar, Ernest de Selincourt, and the Greek humanist, W. E. Dodds, were dominant men. These people, as in all universities, tended to inhabit different worlds.

On the other hand, the general atmosphere was friendly, almost family in tone. One met easily all sorts of people, scientists, lawyers, teachers of language and literature, philosophers, university officials. There were enmities and jealousies among our seniors, but they did not affect the life of a junior lecturer. The students of the University also became easy to mix with when the Guild of Undergraduates' Union was built. Some of us at one time lunched there regularly on certain days of the week. Just for this reason and through my tutoring work, I came to know well a generation of students, some of whose leading members fell in the second war. When they failed to return I understood at last what my old headmaster used to say of pupils of his who died in the campaigns between 1914 and 1918, that when he thought about them he ceased to know whether they had died and he lived or whether they lived and he was dead.

The University had had from its foundation many connections with the city of Birmingham and the counties which surround it. Therefore it was never difficult to meet people in journalism, the theatre and business in the city or to sense the variations in the industrial life of the Midlands. When I first went there to live in the house of a Redditch needle manufacturer, Arthur Showell, on the west side of Birmingham, the city was hit by the great trade depression of the years 1929–33. Later on in the thirties, by which time I had moved to a flat in Sargant Florence's house, it was active and prosperous. At this date, before it had been transformed by the building boom of the nineteen-fifties and sixties, it was still very much, in its architectural looks, the city of Joseph Chamberlain. It possessed few buildings of much note and was wide spreading, low built and dingy. The differences between the richer and the poorer parts of the town were sharp, even devastating. To pass, as I once did, one lovely summer afternoon, from the stifling courts and the back-to-back houses around Summer Lane to the bluebells pushing up in the grass under the trees of the big gardens in Edgbaston was to sample the extremes of English life. Clearly, the Englishman loved his home. It was less evident that he cared about anyone else's home. I felt saddened by the thought and found myself thinking of the alligators I had once watched in the zoological gardens at Los Angeles. They were cold-blooded creatures, too, indifferent to one another's fate. This was not the whole truth about a deplorable situation, but it seemed to me to be so at the time.

As time went on, one's acquaintance gradually widened and it became possible to understand something of the complicated social structure of a great industrial city. Something else happened too. Local and national politics pressed in upon us in the University, whether we wished it or not. Our private conversations and our University discussions became mixed with public controversy. This was perhaps particularly true of the members of the Faculty of Commerce. Our job was to teach economics, including the history of economic institutions and thought, in an England which was in a state of rapid transition. Both existing institutions and current policies were coming to be the centre of bitter dispute.

No one today can imagine what the want of employment meant to people who lived in the twenties and thirties. In an industrial country such as Britain had become, there was always a dearth of work of special kinds at particular seasons of the year and a more general lack at particular stages of the trade-cycle. But this interwar unemployment was something new. It was a famine of work, endemic in particular regions of the country, spreading in wider and wider circles in the early thirties with the force of the world trade depression behind it. Like famine, it seemed to possess a kind of terrible fatality, the fatality of a natural event. Only, unemployment was not a natural event. It was connected with men's knowledge, will and intention. What that connection might be became the theme of fierce argument and powerful emotion. Unemployment poisoned the life of British society, until the time came when it passed away in the economic recovery of the late thirties and in the storm of the second war, with something of the same suddenness and mysteriousness as it had appeared after the first.

I saw a little of unemployment in its worst and most hopeless form, because I knew and visited Marquand when he moved to Cardiff. Also one of my close friends in early days at Birmingham was Edwyn Isaacs, a young botanist who came from the Rhondda, but who later emigrated to South Africa. One day when the industrial depression was at its worst Marquand, who was carrying out a big inquiry into the industries of South Wales, took me to see the Cardiff Coal Exchange. This market had had its great days before 1914, when steamships were fired with coal. People who lived in the district then would tell you that the clink of coal wagons on the move on the railways between the Glamorganshire coal valleys and Cardiff docks could be heard all night. The Exchange now was dead and almost empty, except for one man who, we speculated, was more interested in selling racing tips than coal.

In a later year I went up into the Rhondda to Pen-y-greig to see Isaacs's parents and family. There I met for the first time the Welsh mining society which bred the men who had carried their rifles and their singsong Welsh accents to our quiet Cotswold town during the first war. It was a vigorous and independent society, both Welsh and non-Welsh in origin, rendered cynical by some of its experiences, but undefeated either by its surroundings or its economic plight.

The surroundings were impressive. One cold, brilliant March day Isaacs and I walked to the head of the valley and looked out north from the mountain towards a bright gleam of new-fallen snow on the Brecon Beacons and the Carmarthen Van. One could see how lovely this South Wales mountain country must have been before its mineral wealth was opened up in the nineteenth century. The view as we turned round and moved south again, towards the huge tips, the terraced houses and the pit-head gear, was very different.

More than half the men in the valley at that time were out of work. Many had been out for a long time. The results were to be seen and felt all round. One heard of men who stayed in bed in the morning, pretending that they did not need the breakfast which the children ate. The good Quakers did their best to provide some kind of interest or occupation for idle men at Maes-yr-haf. But there was a shortage of necessities as well as of every amenity in these almost completely working-class towns of the coalfield. The shopkeepers, the other important element in the community, found it hard to keep going and numbers of the shop windows were shuttered up.

There was something offensive to every human instinct in this state of affairs. It was as if the society one belonged to had chosen death in preference to life. Men felt that they had been left in a corner to rot without anyone caring. Human nature could not remain quite sane, if it was stable to begin with, under such conditions. They were paralleled in many other parts of the country, particularly where what had been the great staple industries of the past were losing ground. On the whole, it is surprising with what stoicism multitudes of men faced this terrible test of endurance. But the thirties also abounded with every form of protest, agitation and menace. An understandable hysteria made itself felt from time to time which it was difficult to keep clear of. Like gas in the mine, it was all the more dangerous when unsuspected by those who thought they were free from it.

These great movements of revolt could be studied at first hand even in the relatively prosperous Midlands. I recollect going out to Longbridge one day to tell what was understood to be a Communist cell, largely recruited from the Austin motor-car works, why I felt myself unable to accept the system of thought of Karl Marx. They listened politely and were completely unconvinced. The real leader of this group, one felt, was a woman, whose intelligence and determination held the rest together. Drab shop windows in Stirchley suddenly put up photographs of Oswald Mosley, the leader of the Fascists. A student or a member of the university staff, it was said, hovered on the Fascist line. Black shirts appeared in the Guild of Undergraduates' Union. Unromantic Birmingham businessmen studied the Social Credit scheme of Major Douglas. They would, if you let them, hold forth to you by the hour on how to control the nation's economic life, without pain to anyone, through the banks. One caught oneself wondering whether their remote ancestors had argued into the night with the same quiet-toned fanaticism in the seventeenth century about the doctrines of the 'saints'.

The waters of popular discussion flowed dogmatically in the thirties. They moved all the more swiftly because news of the execution of the first Russian economic plans was coming through to western Europe. The contrast in initiative and energy was too strongly felt to be pleasant, whether one approved of Stalin's regime or not. One has to remember that few people even among visitors to Russia at that time, knew much about Russian history or politics.

The economists were luckier than other people in this confusion of opinion, because they were discovering a new leader in Maynard Keynes. I seldom had the good fortune to see this gifted and easily bored man, with his fine lustrous eyes and his beautiful speaking voice. Perhaps I would not have liked him personally if I had met him. He had come into public notice in the dispute over German reparations after the war, but in the later interwar years was devoting his powers to an analysis of the causes of unemployment. Keynes combined the three essential qualities of a great scientific thinker. He possessed fertility in hypothesis, lively interest in any empirical investigation which would test his theories and an instinctive flair for what was important in his problems. This last quality kept him working on the main track and would not allow him to waste his time on side issues.

The intellectual excitement ran high, as he threw aside traditional positions in the early thirties and worked his way through them to a new conception of the conditions which might give rise to a chronic deficiency of effective demand. Keynes perhaps played too long with the idea of a capitalist society made stationary by the exhaustion of investment opportunities, whether this was due to reduced population growth or to some other cause. Seen from an industrial city like Birmingham, he certainly underrated the significance of the slow but fundamental structural change which was going on in British industry, although it has to be admitted that we were all slow in waking up to this. He had been trained after Cambridge in the Treasury and the City of London. He seemed to understand them and their problems, often and strongly as he disagreed with them, better than industrial England. But he did more to change economic ideas in this country than any man for a hundred years and his findings were of the utmost relevance to public policy.

He was himself no great politician, which was unfortunate, for the management of the economy is a task of extreme political difficulty. He combined the gift of understanding an argument almost before it was spoken, with a strange insensitiveness from time to time to the personality and attitudes of those he was dealing with. This made him less than the perfect diplomat. It caused him to fall into mistakes which lesser men would have avoided, as some of those who watched him at work on behalf of British interests in Washington during the second war noted. His combination of intellectual daring and public spirit was never matched on the political plane in the thirties. The country never found a man who could give a political form to the new economic thinking. This was not only a misfortune for Great Britain. It was a disaster for the democratic cause in Europe at a time when democracy was on the defensive.

The wastes of unemployment which had aroused Keynes's anger persisted down to the end of the thirties. They vanished with the coming of war, and it was only during the war period that Keynes's thinking came to be at all widely accepted, when it was discovered that his analysis was applicable to the problems of war finance. So strong was the hypnotic effect of unemployment on public opinion that most of us feared it would return when the war was over. Some years of experience were required to teach us that the world had changed in its underlying economic conditions.

The economic crisis which had terrorized the early thirties was already passing away half-way through that decade. In some parts of the country it had always been less perceptible than in others. The Midlands acquired a new and powerful industrial structure during these years which brought so much suffering elsewhere. There was, of course, nothing like the intense construction activity of the manufacturing boom of the nineteen-fifties. The city of Birmingham had not yet been rebuilt. Nor was there any inflow into the region of West Indians, Pakistanis and others, searching eagerly for the work which white people scorned to do. Plural society was what one read of in a book. It was not what one saw in the street any day. But there was much quiet prosperity about and a steady move away from the Victorian basis of industry.

In this milder social climate I turned to study the origins of the industrial society which I found myself living in. Besides, my interest had been aroused by a book published in 1931. This was *The Cotton Trade and Industrial Lancashire* by Alfred Wadsworth and Julia Mann. They demonstrated clearly what had only been strongly suspected before, that the cotton trade in Lancashire had a history going back two hundred years before the factory age. In the effort to discover whether the Midland industries had a similar long record behind them I turned over a great deal of evidence locally and elsewhere. The results were published in 1938 as a book, *The Rise of the Midland Industries*.

Seventeenth- and early eighteenth-century England proved to have been more industrial than one had supposed. It was interesting to go back to the men one had studied in the Massachusetts Bay, New Haven and Rhode Island and to retrace their steps into the Stuart England so many of them came from. Looking back at what I had done later, the rural communities of the Midlands, which transformed themselves into the early forms of industrial society, remained shadowy. They have since been patiently reconstructed, although on no great scale so far as I know for this part of the country, by the historians of population and social structure. When one reached the eighteenth century and the personal correspondence of a man like James Watt there was clearly much work to be done on the scientific background of the Industrial Revolution. But it was necessary to stop somewhere. Sir George Clark at Oxford, who was prepared to recommend the book to the Clarendon Press, thought it already too long. So much was left out which ought no doubt to have been examined.

5

By this time I was becoming strongly interested in other things besides the seventeenth century. This was the result mainly of the spirit of the times, the public knowledge that important decisions had to be taken, the keen excitement and discussion and anxiety which this awareness generated. But it was the consequence, too, of a new friendship with Keith Hancock, an Australian. He had just come to Birmingham, with his wife Theaden, to take over what was in those days the only chair in history in the university.

Keith and Theaden Hancock came to the Midlands from Adelaide. The physical contrast between the city they came from and Birmingham could hardly have been stronger, as I was to realize years later when I found myself in the hard, sunny atmosphere of the South Australian capital. But they were both born in the neighbouring state of Victoria. In those days many bright young Australians went to England to finish their education and Keith Hancock was no exception. When I met him first he was intensely Australian, equally intensely Oxford, and a Fellow of All Souls College.

Why did his friendship mean so much to me, a young lecturer in another Faculty? I remember telling J. G. Smith, when the appointment was announced, that I had 'high hopes of the new Professor.' How Smith laughed at the idea of having hopes of a man twelve thousand miles away! He was, of course, correct, but fortunately so was I. For one thing, Hancock was a trained technical historian of formidable attainments. For another, his historical interests were decidedly contemporary. In the thirties, when one was sometimes tempted to see in historical study nothing more than an irrelevant academic exercise in a world increasingly out of control, it was an education to see historical scholarship resolutely employed as a means to understanding what was going on by a man who thoroughly understood the tools he was using. Perhaps the tools were a little less refined then than now. It was Hancock's maxim that an historian must be prepared to get up any technique whatever if he found that he needed it. I was coming to think rather strongly that the historian's needs involved him inevitably in the social sciences, and the universities do not to that extent do the job of training him very well. But Hancock's own practice certainly lived up to his precept. He was engaged on a big survey of postwar Commonwealth history for the Institute of International Affairs, the final chapter as it turned out of the Imperial story. I saw a good deal of his methods and came to admire both the dexterity and resource with which he sought out material and the quality of the judgement which he brought to its interpretation.

The work went everywhere with him. One Easter, when he was engaged on the Irish chapter, I accompanied Keith and Theaden to a city of Dublin where the troubles just after the first war, the shootings of English by Irish and of Irish by Irish, were still alive in the conversation of the older people. Keith backed up his knowledge of the books and papers on Irish affairs with a series of interviews with leading politicians. I heard Cosgrave, who governed the Irish Free State from 1922 to 1932, explain the politics of his country in horse-breeding and horse-racing terms, and in the shadow of Viceregal Lodge came to doubt seriously the average Englishman's picture of a well-governed, ungrateful Ireland. Another year we took Joseph Stalin's book upon Russian colonial and nationality problems to the Austrian lakes. In the intervals of walking and swimming we debated Russian parallels with British Colonial policies and experience, only to decide that we were in a field where the argument by analogy was highly unsafe, so far as we could tell in our ignorance of it.

I read Lenin on imperialism as the highest state of capitalism at this time. He interested me so much in his views on colonial empire and the origins of the war of 1914 that I agreed to write a paper on the Marx-Lenin theory of imperialism, which was published in Hancock's second Commonwealth volume in 1940.

I was reading widely in Karl Marx's writings at the time, in an England where Marx had suddenly become intellectually fashionable. I was divided, as I had been when I first read him, between admiration on the one hand for his profound observation of European politics and the range of his mind, an intellectual far superior to that of any but a few of his critics, and on the other a settled conviction on my part that as I disagreed with him on so many of his premises, so I found many of his conclusions unacceptable.

The classical Marxian philosophy as a system, I felt, was not for me. It seemed rather the first of the world philosophies to succeed Christianity in Europe and one suspected, indeed one hoped, it would not be the last.

Marx drew attention in an unforgettable way to sides of European history of extreme importance, which the historians of Europe had, whether consciously or not, persistently neglected. He had also addressed himself to and forced us to think about problems of change and development which are among the most significant and puzzling in the field of the social sciences. I believed I had learned from Schumpeter, who was deeply influenced by the Marxian scheme, that Marx's sociology was one of a family of different possible sociological systems. His was a model of history and society in which I both recognized some of the great outlines of the world I lived in while I missed others which seemed to me equally remarkable. It appeared as something to be used, with other such models, according to the limits of its effectiveness, in empirical investigation rather than accepted whole as a social and personal creed. Marx's unqualified condemnation of the habit of treating other people as means rather than as ends in themselves, I approved, although it seemed in the thirties that the economic system of Western countries was not the only example of the abuse of human relations that one could think of. As a philosophy of history, Marx's system appeared only partially true. My generation just after the war felt sharply that it had broken with the nineteenth-century confidence in automatic progress. In the void of that age one could only hope that a wiser society than ours, and I seemed to believe that wisdom could come not only against our expectations but even despite our set will and intention, might one day discover a philosophy more true and entire than Marx's to live and die with.

Meanwhile it was interesting to try to work out in a critical manner the doctrinal history of Marxism on one of the most interesting phenomena in modern history, the domination of the non-European world by Europe. It was particularly interesting to see the way in which ideas first thrown out by the English classical economists at the beginning of the nineteenth century in the effort to understand the events of their own day were absorbed by this international revolutionary thinker, were built into the structure of his system and became transmuted into the elements of something very different.

Under Hancock's influence and my own lack of a sense of direction I might have become absorbed in commonwealth studies completely. When war broke out in 1939 I was the holder of a Leverhulme grant. This was to take me to India to make a study of rural debt and other Indian economic problems in relation to the administration of British India, as it had been influenced by economic ideas and policies in the nineteenth century. Hancock had excluded these from his scope as being too large a field to be taken in. But when I wrote in the autumn of that year to Sir Theodore Gregory, then economic adviser to the Government of India, to ask his advice, he replied that every one of the higher Civil Servants in India, without whom my inquiries could hardly be carried on, was engaged in preparations for the war and he would not advise coming out at such a time. It was the period of the 'phoney war' and the world was falsely quiet. I wondered a little whether Sir Theodore had given me correct advice. But I am glad that I accepted it, however reluctantly. The only personal debt I ever owed to Adolf Hitler was a big one. For if I had gone to India I would not have married in 1940. The best that happened to me was bound up with the worst that befell Europe in the strange way that one grows used to in life.

The course of events on the European continent was outside of Hancock's research, but very far from being beyond his interests or those of his wife. He belonged to a generation of historians too young to accept the traditions of the age before 1914. He had lost a brother in the first war. He attacked soon after coming to Birmingham the current study of British diplomatic history for what he regarded as too ready an acceptance of national interest, without further examination, as a guide to historical judgement. In his view the historian ought not to be the mere observer or recorder of public policy. He ought to be prepared to comment upon its aims and methods as well as its technical competence. All this was very congenial to me. We even made some attempt to give practical effect to these ideas and to widen modern historical studies in the university. We worked together in a joint course of teaching on the origins of the 1914 war. This paid some attention to economic and social developments and their implications, as well as to the formation of the European alliances. But it had not got very far before the second war was upon us.

6

I have referred to the sense which many people had of terrible decisions pending in the early thirties. One of the most important of these was taken quietly and hesitantly in 1935. This country began to rearm against Germany. Public opinion rose gradually to the boiling-point over the dilemmas of public policy in the course of the next few years. There was plenty of opportunity to reflect, in the Neville Chamberlain era, on the abstract proposition that historians ought to be prepared to be the critics as well as the recorders of the actions of public men.

The sense of terrible decisions pending arose from the mounting disorder in Europe. The earliest tremor of fear, it is true, came from distant Asia. It was the Japanese attack on Manchuria in September 1931 and the consequent events which first gave a sense of possible catastrophe to those who bothered themselves with the foreign news. The war in the Far East descended on us, like a clap of thunder on a man sleeping in a hay-field, after the relative peace of the twenties.

Europe remained deceptively quiet. I paid my first visit to the Continent in the summer vacation of 1931, staying with Edwyn Isaacs at Freiburg im Breisgau on the edge of the Black Forest and travelling home with my parents, brother and sister through the Rhineland. On the way to Germany we stopped in Paris. There I met Rosebery again, working in an American bank. Paris seemed an unexampled island of prosperity and peace in a troubled world. At home a financial crisis was brewing which brought the Labour Government down that August. In Germany one met many unemployed men and boys, especially in waterside Cologne. We watched raincoated citizens huddled under their umbrellas in the summer drizzle in Freiburg withdrawing their small deposits from a bank. We were sometimes puzzled by men, often middle-aged men, who marched in the evening through the streets of the town. They were, we were told, members of the Stahlhelm and Reichsbanner political groups. Who or what could they be, we wondered?

In Paris, on the contrary, serene confidence reigned. The food and the wine were excellent. American stockbroking firms were advising their clients to invest in French securities. The French, we were told, were on top of the world. One could not but agree, even if it appeared that that terrible old woman we passed lying on the pavement at night was down and out in the world she was on top of.

Sunny hours for some people and among them for us. One cannot be anxious all the time. Isaacs and I thoroughly enjoyed South Germany. There were operas to go to, films to be watched, parks to be strolled in, wine to be drunk, people to be talked to, towns and buildings to be visited. There were also plants and other things to be studied. Isaacs was delighted with the trees of the Black Forest and I equally fascinated by the living and working conditions of the peasants of Baden and Bavaria.

Yet this country in which we enjoyed ourselves so much was moving at speed towards anarchy and towards tyranny. The early thirties became the years of the Hitler fury. It is impossible to bring home to those who did not live through them the weird and terrifying atmosphere which built up in Europe between 1933 and 1939 as the direct consequence of events in Germany. It is not often that in a great society one sees an impossible state of affairs deliberately created, that is, a situation with which men cannot live, from which they must try to escape, if necessary by fighting and death.

Something like this happened, however, in Europe in those years. Perhaps it could only have happened on the basis of a great state such as Germany which had been terribly ruptured by public events, by war, inflation, unemployment, until the old forms of life were drained of all meaning for many people. Institutions survived, but they seemed to correspond to little in the day's experience of private persons. So long as economic times remained good, things somehow hung together, although one got the impression even then that many people were walking about in a void. I remember telling someone when I came back from Germany in the autumn of 1931, that there seemed to be more people there with strange personal histories and whose behaviour was to me unpredictable than in any place I had ever been. Perhaps this was youthful excitement, but it seemed to correspond to something which others who knew Germany better thought they noticed. I came to identify it later, rightly or wrongly, with the shattering effect of public catastrophe upon private personality. The pressures were mounting in Germany as economic depression deepened. Rational explanations in a broken society are at a discount. They are out of the normal context of meaning and cannot satisfy people who are used to their world finding for them what they regard as normal answers for normal questions. Bewildered, they looked elsewhere for meaning and purpose and found it in the irrational.

It seems to have been under these circumstances that the extraordinary interchange began between Hitler and the German people, not least German youth, which settled the fate of Europe. There was something neurotic about those years. A very special sort of man found a very special sort of society ready to his hand. The explosion which followed at the centre of European civilization was the work of both. A society in which social arrangements no longer correspond with ordinary human needs, where people and especially young people feel personally lost, seems to release and propagate forces of paranoia and hysteria which under more fortunate circumstances men and women can control and keep to themselves. This sense of neurotic drive at the heart of events, using reason as its tool and allied to remarkable political abilities, made those years hard to live through. Every political problem that came up in Europe in those days could be defined and measured in rational terms. But one soon came to feel that this was not the true dimension. The Alice through the Looking Glass dimension was correct, because this was the one desired at the centre of power. Perhaps this is why at the end of the thirties, as many people must still remember, the news of war, terrible as it was, came almost with a sense of release. One had come to feel that war could not, or more accurately would not, be avoided by Hitler.

I was on the Continent for short periods every summer whenever possible during these years, I was a believer, no doubt, in a Europe that was a dream, for I was a collective security man among people who trusted for the preservation of their rights and even for survival upon nothing but the strength or the weakness of themselves and their friends. I was therefore a looker-on in an age when civilized man in Europe, caught in a terrible trap of his own devising, knew no better than the animals he had so successfully preyed on in the past how to escape from the fate he had prepared for himself. In 1933 I visited Germany again with two Cambridge friends, Dennis Ward and Reg White. We were in the Rhineland once more. It was fermenting with all the enthusiasm of the National Socialist revolution. Two years before Isaacs and I had been deeply impressed by the forlorn hopelessness of the unemployed graduate in South Germany, for the curse of unemployment was even greater in Germany than at home at that time. Now much of the energy of youth seemed to have been swept into the Brown Shirt movement partly by the promise of work, partly by the hope of glory. We met some of these new recruits to the party. It was impossible not to be struck by their youthful idealism and by their utter vagueness in matters of practical politics. They lived off slogans. The emotional temperature was fantastically high. We saw a performance in the theatre of one town of the play *Schlageter*. This glorified a hero of the resistance to the French in their occupation of the Ruhr. The entire audience rose to its feet at the end and went wild with delight. The excitement was so extreme that we were glad to find ourselves in the quiet street again unharmed. Propagandist films against the Communists, intellectually beneath contempt, were solemnly watched and absorbed by huge crowds.

In this furnace of feeling all sorts of elements were being melted into the Nazi metal. One could meet a middle-aged railwayman, an old Social Democrat one felt sure, now expecting the world of his dreams from the National Socialists. Or a sailor from Hamburg, a former prisoner of war in Britain in the first war, who had been led into the party by the hope of never again being without work. But the chief impression was of the way the National Socialist party, both radical and violently nationalist, contemptuous of other nations and of Germany's own past wherever it did not understand that, had successfully captured German youth and above all uneducated youth.

We watched one day Brown Shirt youths pour out of the Brown House at Bingen. I thought I recognized something personal to me behind the German voices and the uniforms and was startled by the resemblance to boys of my first school. The ill-fed bodies and the neglected minds behind the eager undeveloped faces were the same. Youths like these were the foundation of every state in Europe. They got as raw a deal in Germany in the thirties as elsewhere and at the hands of their own countrymen. In the course of the next few years one saw them fed with dreams of glory and empire by men who sought first their own power, then flung into battle to die. The fact that they listened willingly to that savage rhetoric and died fanatically did not to my mind excuse this crime on the part of their Government. It was all of a piece, I thought, with European history since Sarajevo. The dying Archduke Franz Ferdinand was said by Austrians to have muttered to his dead wife, 'Sophie! Sophie! Wacht über die Kinder!' Who in Europe since 1914 had looked after the children?

The next summer in 1934 I happened to be in Italy with my sister before she went to India. We were on the Ligurian Riviera, then at Pisa, Florence, Perugia. The German frenzy appeared to evaporate on the line of the Alps. Outwardly Italy was very calm. Photographs of Mussolini were everywhere and slogans painted on the houses declared that he could not go wrong. This seemed absurd. Many Italians certainly thought so. The trouble with them was that, unlike the naïve and cruel idealists one met in Germany, they were often cynical about politics. When there were the children to play with and jobs to be done, why bother one's head with that man in Rome? This attitude of the Italians, one felt, must be very old.

But even the Alps could not keep out the sound of confusion elsewhere. This time it was a shot in Vienna. Towards the end of July I had gone with my sister to Assisi for the day. We read in the bus coming back the news of the murder of Engelbert Dollfuss, the Austrian Chancellor. He had seized power with violence that spring, after fierce street fighting in the Austrian capital. No one who had watched relations between Germany and Austria was surprised that the Austrian crisis had entered on a new phase. Still, a shocked stir of opinion was perceptible in Italy. A swift and extremely unpleasant vision opened up. Austria's future, one could see, was in the balance and with it Europe's. Whose turn would it be for trouble next?

Italians who prided themselves on some military knowledge were probably discussing the strength of garrisons on the Brenner by the time our holiday came to an end and we took the train home. The Austrian trouble did not, however, materialize that summer. Hitler did not occupy the country until 1938. Two years after Dollfuss's murder the coast seemed even clear enough for an Austrian holiday. For a short while in July 1936 I was staying with Keith and Theaden Hancock at a small mountain hotel above Schwaz in the Tyrol. We were making the best of a wet summer. Even here, amid mushroom picking in the woods and swimming in the cold pool of the hotel, the stresses and strains of central European politics occasionally broke surface. One spoke to people who feared their personal fate or that of their relations and friends. When we English visitors were bored or needed to buy something, we would spend an hour or two in Innsbruck, drinking coffee, eating pastries and reading the newspapers. It was while picking a way through these in our favourite café that one realized that civil war had broken out in Spain. Never mind! It was the other side of Europe. Not at all, approximately next door. Austrian newspapers carried the news with a studied reserve which put the reader on his guard. It was clear from their demure statements that not only Spain's affairs but the Continent's politics generally had taken a wholly unwelcome turn. Two great military and ideological powers, Russia and Germany, had been offered by this revolt a golden chance to intervene in the affairs of other states. For if they took a hand in Spain, and rumour was swift to suggest that they would, where else might they not meddle? The Austrian journalists swallowed their fears as best they could, but they were obviously unhappy about their own country. Meanwhile coffee grew cold and even the delicious pastries seemed less appetizing as one tried to absorb the news through imperfect German. The political outlook appeared as unpromising as the weather. As one watched the heavy clouds move above the valley of the Inn and the mountains appear and vanish again in the mist, that seemed to be saying a lot.

How unpromising the outlook was one did not quite grasp until one had returned to England. Spain was understood to be a country separated by physical nature and history from the rest of Europe, isolated behind the famous Pyrenees. But no event of the interwar years more effectively demonstrated the underlying unity of European life than the Spanish war. At home for the next few years it was continuously with us. No other happening had such a dividing and inflaming effect on British public opinion. This was because of what were understood to be the issues of the Spanish Civil War. The clash of extreme doctrines and parties, Falange, Communist, Anarchist, in Spain mixed at once with the leading issues of British politics, with persistent unemployment and the deep mutual suspicion of classes, so steadily denied, so constantly present between the wars.

There was, too, about the civil war an air of political romanticism, almost refreshing to a generation brought up on the disillusionment of the twenties and the bitterness of the great depression. I met very briefly one or two of the men who went out to help the Republic and who died, Julian Bell and John Cornford. There was an attractiveness about them, which one hesitates to describe as charm. Perhaps they were somewhat like the hopeful young men of Tawney's generation who volunteered in the early days of the 1914–18 war.

The romance soon died out of this war, as it did out of the earlier one. One or two young Spaniards, quiet and reserved political refugees, whom one met in Birmingham on their way elsewhere, gave the impression that they felt their problems were not easily understood by men and women from other parts of Europe. This was no doubt true, but the trouble lay deeper than ignorance. Europe neither understood nor cared. In the playground ruled by bullies which was the European scene of that decade it was unwise to start a fight even for the best of reasons and in the most secluded place, if one did not want one's troubles to be exploited for their own ends by alert watchers elsewhere. This was what happened to the Spaniards. Their calamities were first exploited with the rest of Europe looking on, then forgotten before they were ended. There were, after all, new and more exciting fights elsewhere, with the possibility of a general free-for-all always round the corner.

In the meantime one had to grow used to the fact that, just as there were Englishmen who had acquired a kind of second citizenship in Russia, so there were others, often men of wealth, intelligence and education, who trusted Hitler and Mussolini rather than their own countrymen. It was a painful discovery to make. The England which went into the first winter of the second war was a divided country and the events in Spain had helped to divide it.

7

As Europe became an armed camp in the late thirties it became increasingly difficult to make visits to the Continent without being regarded by one's friends as slightly mad or without wondering oneself what the chances were of surviving a European war in a concentration camp. Travel was from time to time uncomfortable. There were 'prohibited areas' of military preparation where visitors were not allowed. Men wearing steel helmets and carrying weapons made it extremely clear just where the car should be turned right round and driven fast in the opposite direction. Even the most peaceable and remote districts, perhaps these in particular, began to contain surprises.

Europe's business, whatever it was in those days, was not the tourist trade. Add the growing hopelessness of people—'Have you come? Then there will be no war!' was the inspiring welcome one of us received in Heidelberg—and a visit to the Continent had ceased to be an amusement. The tired face of a Belgian sentry standing by a bridge on his country's German frontier, seen at night in the gleam of the car lamps and the light reflected from his rifle, is the sort of face which one associates with the Europe of those days. The impression was perhaps misleading. Many men thoroughly enjoyed the state of affairs which existed. The sentry, whoever he was, paid for their pleasure.

The Continent drew one, however, with a painful interest of its own. One did not like to let it pass unvisited if possible. In 1938 and 1939 I had the chance to travel with John Hawgood, who was then Reader in the School of History at Birmingham. He knew Germany well and spoke the language perfectly. The summer of the first year, the year of Munich, we went through Germany to Czecho-Slovakia and Austria; the summer of the second, the year of war, to Italy and France.

In 1938 I had a surgical operation at Whitsun, following an accident, then went swimming in the Avon with a party of other people before I was fully recovered. As a consequence I passed a most miserable summer, physically and mentally. But once abroad somehow it was different. With new things to see, old pains and sensations could be forgotten. One's own situation in any case looked small compared with the enormous shadows of approaching trouble in pre-Munich Europe.

Going to Germany by this time was a little like entering a prison. The naïve National Socialist enthusiasm of 1933 was over. The whole country was firmly held in the grip of the Party. The arrogance of what was loosely described as race was unbelievable. Currently it expressed itself in an outrageous and stupid form of the old contempt of German for Slav. We visited in Leipzig a National Socialist of our acquaintance. He was a well-educated man who had made a special study of British affairs and was supposed to understand our national approach to politics. We asked him what would appear to him to be the correct, the most desirable relation, between Germany and Czecho-Slovakia. He answered, 'The same relation as between British India and Nepal.' This sort of analogy, making equal nonsense of European and Asian history, dominated a long and pointless discussion. When we came away, after urging on him the danger of war, we asked him how children should be brought up in the Europe that we all knew. He made a gesture, for he was a family man, not without feeling, and said, 'Bring them up tough. There is nothing else.'

With this message of hope for civilization still ringing in our ears we set off through the Sudetenland, then bitterly in question between Germany and Czecho-Slovakia, for Prague. Czech tanks and soldiers were on the move. The men looked hard-bitten and concerned. They had need to be, for they had few friends in Europe. The Munich agreement in September, only a month or two later, showed that the few were scarcer than their statesmen had thought. At the Austrian frontier, by this time under Hitler's control, we were treated, as visitors from the despised Czecho-Slovakia, with official contempt. We were instructed to get out of the car and to cleanse our shoes with antiseptic. The excuse was that there was foot-and-mouth disease on the Czech side of the frontier. This was, we suspected, simply a way of being disagreeable to Czechs.

Revisiting Vienna was a strange experience. One of us had been there a few years before, when it was still the capital of an independent Austria. At that time, it was a city of immense fascination. Walking through the Hofburg or driving round the Ring, it was not difficult to imagine that one might meet at the next corner the old man, Franz Josef, who until his death in 1916 had been to his subjects Austria incarnate, whether they loved or hated him for that. There had been unemployment and hunger in the city in those days, along with the famous municipal flats, and a child medical care institution which was one of the showplaces of Vienna. I had the good fortune to see these creations of the city's government in the company of friends from Birmingham, Dorothy and Philip Styles, who were curious to see them. But I remember also our taking a meal at an open-air restaurant. When the waiter cleared the table he handed a half-eaten roll to a woman who was standing in the shadows a little beyond. She neither spoke nor moved, but ate the bread in a way one had never seen anyone eat before. She devoured it silently like an animal. I found it difficult to get her out of my mind even among the many amusements and distractions Vienna had to offer.

The Vienna of 1938 had by contrast no longer the air of a great European capital. The buildings were the same, but the people were different. Vienna had become a provincial city in a German empire. We went to a café which John Hawgood remembered from old days as a haunt of artists and other interesting people. It was strangely, uncomfortably crowded. Light dawned when we discovered that it was one of the few public places where Jews were allowed to congregate. We viewed it not with the pleasure we had anticipated but with something like horror and pity. By that time there were worse things in central Europe than hunger.

We returned to an England full of the fear of war as the Czech crisis approached. People were hard at work digging air-raid shelters in their gardens, including Highfield garden. The tension was extreme. Much which the Chamberlain Government after Munich took for gratitude and public understanding of its policy was simply emotion released when the tension induced by the prospect of war came off. There was gratitude and approval no doubt, but many, perhaps most, people were merely glad not to have to face war within the week. I was acutely conscious that I shared their cowardly emotions.

The summer of 1939 looked even less cheerful politically than that of 1938. The Munich agreement had been torn up by the German dictator. Czecho-Slovakia had by this time disappeared. The impossible situation in Europe looked as if it was approaching the time when someone would fight. If not some great nation, then perhaps some small nation; if not some prudent nation, then perhaps some imprudent nation, might turn and defend itself. But this had not happened yet. Italy was a country more safe than some others to visit. She was politically on the right side of Hitler and despite Mussolini's rhetoric it was not at all certain that Italy would go straight into a European war at Germany's side.

I was friendly at the time with a young Italian student, Carlo Ruini, who had been writing his thesis in economics at Birmingham. Hawgood and I arranged to look up Carlo and his parents where they were summering in the Dolomites. There was a vaguer plan to visit Naples and the Neapolitan philosopher and historian, a severe critic of the Mussolini regime, Benedetto Croce, whom I greatly admired. Croce was known to Ruini's father. Both were public men living under police supervision.

The first part of the scheme went well. We found the Ruini family staying in a comfortable old hunting lodge in the Alps, where tradition had it Bismarck had once stayed to shoot. Carlo had a bad cold, but rose from his bed to receive us. I was astonished at the political freedom of the conversation in an unfree country. The Italians lived, however, under a less savage regime than the Germans. They had much less to be afraid of from their Government. A poorer people than the Germans, they were in some ways more politically sophisticated. Perhaps they were more civilized.

It was while staying in the Ruini house that the first thunder-clap of the coming European storm reached us. News of the Russo-German pact came through and promptly drove out every other subject of talk. It was generally assumed at the time that only respect for the military power of Russia prevented the German Government from going to extreme lengths against Poland. The comment of the family was immediate: 'This means war.' We had to decide what to do. We resolved to go on, but to turn back if worse news followed. We were influenced by the obvious Italian reluctance that summer to be drawn into war. But we had reckoned without the speed of Hitler's action against Poland and the decisiveness of western Europe's expressed hostility.

In Verona, walking in the street, we read over an Italian's shoulder the headlines in his newspaper. They announced the full mobilization of the French Army. John took the car round to a garage at once and filled up with all the petrol he could buy. We left very early the next morning for Switzerland, leaving a note under the door of another Englishman in the hotel, an elderly man paying his first visit to the Continent. We told him that everything looked like war and that we were going home.

To announce one's intention of going home was easier than to carry it out in a Europe more full of men answering their call-up papers than at any time since July and August 1914. Our first attempt to cross the Swiss border and to sleep on the neutral side of it miscarried. The political and economic outlook was so utterly uncertain that the Swiss in Lugano would not accept our English money. We had to recross and sleep one night more in Italy at Varese, then go through Switzerland in a day. In France we became involved in the French mobilization, which choked westward roads with traffic. We were impressed by the pedantic efficiency of the French. They must have been much less impressed by us. The eyes of a high French officer, motoring slowly in review of an immensely long line of military lorries, popped out as he passed a touring car, undeniably English, hopelessly stuck in the middle of the column.

These were the armies which were so terribly smashed in the next summer by the force of the German thrust. I only knew one man who foresaw that their efficiency might prove to be only on the surface. This was Alexander Baykov, a Russian and an exile from his own country, who had recently joined Birmingham University from the Charles University at Prague. A good economic statistician, he had taken some trouble to study and compare French and German industrial production. He had come to the conclusion that for a war in which tanks and aeroplanes were likely to play a great role, the French were ill prepared. He was less surprised than most of us when the worst happened and the French Army collapsed in the first great fight of the war.

But that experience belonged to a different world. Meanwhile John and I had to get home, and we did. I went straight to Newbury and was still asleep the next morning when my father walked into my bedroom and said, 'We are at war with Germany.' So self-enclosed are we and so unimaginative, or so at least am I, that it never occurred to me that he must have spoken almost exactly the same words to my mother in the old house at Cirencester on another summer's day twenty-five years before. For him and for his generation it was not a new quarrel, but the fatal continuation of an old.

8

With the outbreak of war my life was gradually but completely transformed, like that of everyone else who was of age for national service. But not at once. The universities were not suddenly denuded of students in the Second as in the First World War. On the contrary, student numbers kept up and there was plenty of work to be done. Then, in the summer of 1940, the big military blows arrived with the fall of Belgium and France. The months that followed were filled with the sensation, equally new and sinister, of being a member of a nation which was alone in a Europe controlled by formidable and merciless enemies. After the incredulity of the first winter of the war a national mood of immense sobering up arrived with these disasters. As autumn and the winter of 1940-1 approached the first air-raids began.

The life of a big industrial city shifted on to a new basis. There was a phrase coined by the Home Secretary in the Churchill Government, Herbert Morrison, which was often quoted in the big munitions effort. 'Go to it.' Birmingham went to it. Special buses for the factory workers ran along the road in which I was living at the time. As the weeks and months passed one could see the men and women who sat in them growing greyer and older. If one needed further reminders that a war was on, they were delivered more or less nightly that winter. The house shook to its foundations with the concussion from anti-aircraft batteries and the near-by bomb.

Despite my horror at the policies which had led to the war, for which I felt the nation to which I belonged carried some responsibility, I did not see why men should have Hitler's ideas of justice and Goebbels's notion of truth thrust down their throat by force. So I sought for ways to join the war effort myself.

I had put my name down at an early date on the register for temporary Civil Service work, as the only form of national service in which I thought that I might be of some use. In the early spring of 1941 I joined the Ministry of Shipping in London as a principal officer. I spent the first days at their central offices in Berkeley Square struggling with a cold in the head and a sense of utter ignorance of the work in hand. The business at that stage of the war in my section of the Ministry was the requisitioning of ships. I was fortunate in working under the extremely able direction of W. O. Hart, who became Clerk to the London County Council after the war was over. Our function was to take ships over for Government service and to reach agreement on terms and conditions with their reluctant owners. Most of this work had already been done under the Liner Requisition Scheme. But as the war spread in the Far East in 1941 and 1942 a mixed bag of ships from Hong Kong, Shanghai, Singapore, Penang and elsewhere fell into our net, to say nothing of unconsidered trifles snapped up in New Zealand, the Falkland Isles, Cyprus and Madagascar. This work was done by wireless signal to the ship's next port of discharge, followed by interview and correspondence about the charterparty with the owners. Sometimes they were men who had only just escaped from the advancing Japanese by the skin of their teeth. In the long and technical discussions men who, one knew for a fact, had recently lost someone in the war far more dear to them than the expensive capital instrument known as a ship, would argue fiercely down to the last penny. It was an education in the strangeness of human nature. Other people provided the ships we took over with cargo and sailing directions. We liked to imagine that what we were doing had some relevance to the war.

Gloom mounted in the Ministry with the full tide of Japanese victory. The winter months of 1941–2 were very dark. Then the war entered a new phase with Hitler's attack on Russia and the emergence of the Russian alliance. When I left the Ministry (by that time, of War Transport) for the War Cabinet Office in 1943 many of its officials must already have been busy, as one learned later from the course of events, with the first plans for the invasion of Europe.

We were a highly mixed staff in the Ministry. Gerald Finzi, the musical composer, worked in a room almost opposite to mine. There were architects, logical positivists, poets and translators to be met at work and in the canteen. The two strongest elements in the body of men and women which called itself 'the Ministry' were the professional Civil Servants and the shipping men. These latter were brought in mostly from Glasgow, Newcastle and the City of London. There were some obvious failures among them and one or two black sheep, but on the whole I came to develop a great respect for the abilities of the ship-owners. The strong suit of the businessmen was their willingness to take a decision and their confidence in their own ability to retrieve a mistake. The Civil Servants did not possess in the same degree this capacity for improvised organization. But as professional administrators they did know how to make a huge machine swallow daily an incredible amount of work. They made it move with reasonable smoothness and without too much inhumanity.

Life does not cease to be comic even in wartime, and a section of the Ministry which contained Hugh Boyle and Sonia Orwell was not without its lively side. Sometimes one could be amused simply by looking up from one's desk. My first office faced the establishment of Norman Hartnell, the great couturier, on the other side of the street. One summer evening when the temporary Civil Servant was working late, he was surprised to see a wonderful creation of a hat, all light and feathery, float out of an upper window which had been left open by someone in the hot weather. Carried by a light breeze, it descended with the utmost grace into the street. This was wholly deserted, bathed in evening sunshine and silence. For someone who was far enough away to feel there was nothing he could do, there was keen enjoyment in watching the appearance on the scene of a woman who was on her way towards Regent Street. From the solemn windows of the Ministry one could see her amazement at the discovery, the swift glance up at Hartnell's, the firm step towards the door, the uncertain retreat, the resolved glance round at an empty street and her final disappearance, carrying the hat.

There was a strict limit to the number of ships on the British register available for requisition. In the middle years of the war, when the war fever of public opinion was at its height, I found myself seriously underemployed. In a London where the streets were crowded with the soldiers and sailors of many nations, a city which felt itself to be for the time being the headquarters of the war against Hitler's Germany, there was for me too little to do. After first trying in vain to effect a transfer to the new Ministry of Production, I accepted in 1943 an offer from Keith Hancock to help him at the War Cabinet Office with the official history of the war.

The section of the official history of which he was in charge was civil, not military. It was concerned with the social and economic history of the war. Hancock took as his own share the overall picture of the economic conduct of the war by the Central Government. He also advised on numerous monographs. Michael Postan from Cambridge looked after the history of war production. I assumed the supervision of the record of the fuel and power industries in the war. The coal industry I took as my own subject and in doing so found myself back, metaphorically speaking, in the Rhondda.

For the civil history of the war was the record of the transformation of British economy and society, law and state, by the war. The war history of the coal industry was the story of a part of British society and industry which had already passed through an immense and painful transition in the nineteen-twenties and thirties. Coal had been for generations the centre of the nation's industry. Much of the interest of its war history lay in watching the process by which that centre continued to shift away from coal-mining towards other sources of fuel and power. In the war coal declined further from its old dominating position, although it remained essential to the war effort. The interwar years were still alive in the wartime coal industry. Its traditions included memories of the General Strike, in which the miners had played a leading role.

I became deeply interested in the story I was telling and continued to work at it after the war. It was a section of British industrial and social history in an age of national change and decline. The wartime history of coal was published as a part of the official history in 1951. The other sides of the fuel and power industry I had to leave for other hands to finish.

For some years I had been back at full-time teaching in the university. The war against Hitler was over. By many of those who had thought about it and acted in it with such passion it was already beginning to be forgotten. This was a natural reaction. Men began at once to conceal from themselves and others the nature of the experience through which they had passed, as the price of getting on with the business of living. Like most people at the time, I felt tired of six years of war and more than willing to turn to other things. Besides, who would not but be appalled by the scale of events? The fire which had burst out in Europe in my father's day, in the summer of 1914, at Tannenberg and on the Marne was still burning itself out, most literally, thirty years later in 1945 in the ashes of Berlin.

At the same time it seemed unwise and dangerous to forget too much and too soon, never to look back or try to make sense of the past. As a child I had been brought up at a time when the existence of profound poverty on a great scale among the advanced nations of western Europe was thought by good observers to be the foremost social problem of the age. To Alfred Marshall, the ablest English economist of the early years of this century, it was 'the problem of problems'. For the greater part of mankind it still is an evil of that huge magnitude. But after the two European wars it appeared that the 'problem of problems' had a formidable competitor for scientific and political attention in the institution of war with its huge demands upon scarce resources and its growing threat to civilized life. It is hardly likely that the problem of poverty or that of war will ever vanish so long as either remains present in society. It is more than likely that power in the world will ultimately go where there is or appears to be the capacity to solve the double riddle.

For this reason, if for no other, I thought that one day if the opportunity occurred I would return, although not as an official historian, to the extraordinary age just over, when the European peoples had first risen with the aid of their new populations and their added resources to an unrivalled position among men, and had then descended from it again, not as a result of the course of inevitable events, but as a consequence of the decision of the leading nations among them to find a way out from their deep antagonisms by going to war. To that purpose they had devoted, for ten years out of thirty, the immense resources which an industrial age had given them. But for a long time the opportunity to do this did not offer itself.

My first task after finishing the study of the coal industry in the war for Hancock was to complete at the request of the Cambridge University Press a manuscript, a short economic history of Britain, which Sir John Clapham had left unfinished at his death. I accepted the task, partly out of gratitude to a former teacher, partly because it seemed an opportunity to think out if one could one's own position. The North of England Liberalism in which Clapham had been brought up and Tawney's Christian Socialism were beginning to look remote in the after-war years, although British social democracy, it seemed to me, owed a good deal to both. The task looked easy but became difficult, for the sequel turned into a separate book. Clapham's volume, prepared for publication by John Saltmarsh of King's College, Cambridge, came out in 1949, mine in 1954.

9

In the years before the war I sometimes met Tawney and discussed, most imperfectly as it seems to me now, work and plans with him. At his cottage above Stroud I got his characteristic blessing on the proposed Indian trip. 'You may not get to know India. You are sure to learn more about this country!' Coming from a man who had published a brilliant book about China a few years before, this was enough for me. He had liked the Midlands book and I looked forward to the history of seventeenth-century England which he was understood to be writing. But I felt that my interests were gradually turning away from seventeenth-century England and from colonial New England. I do not think that he was surprised at this change, for he followed the events of the day with great keenness and perception.

Sometimes I reflected on the religious difference between us, for his religious faith was central to his work, even as an historian. I had a great admiration both for him and for his great friend, whom however I never met, William Temple, one of the theologians and churchmen of his time. I could not take, however, an Anglican view of the world and by contrast with these two excellent men felt myself to be a Christian only in a sense that would have been held to merit burning in most centuries of the Christian era.

I never ceased to deplore this lack of religious faith as a serious personal inadequacy. There were a number of reasons for this. I neither felt myself to be religious, as these men were, nor could persuade myself that religion was to be written off as something outgrown by mankind. On the contrary, judging by the enthusiasm with which many people in the thirties embraced political faiths which seemed to be substitutes for religion, it had a living function in society, along with art, politics and economics. For myself I felt that I needed a mystery religion in a world which, once one tears the veil of familiarity off it, is mysterious anyway and does not grow less so as we learn scientifically to understand and control it. Why the flux of events which we call the world? Why our ability to understand it and our faith that it can be understood? Why, for a piece of final strangeness, should the freedom of human action lie in obedience to natural law? These questions seemed to me to need answering and I was unable to adopt the attitude common to many of my contemporaries that one way or another they answered themselves. In my personal life they did not appear to do so and I doubted whether they did in other men's lives, strictly examined.

A Canadian friend of mine at Harvard was once accused of growing more silent as he grew older. This was, of course, the attack of one young man upon another. He admitted the charge, but said that as he grew older he found himself more occupied with his own thoughts. Perhaps something similar happened to me in this matter of religion. I suspect that I was like many of my contemporaries, both impatient of conventional piety and sceptical of conventional doubt. When one had reached that point, there seemed less to argue for and more to think about than one had at one time supposed.

What was impossible to avoid in the thirties was the question: what standard did one live by? This was raised directly by the politics of the age. The thirties were a cruel and persecuting time. For or against Germany in Europe? For or against the working class in the State? These were the questions of the hour. They were held to justify any amount of bloodshed, according to the temper and disposition of the questioner and the nature of the reply.

In this storm of fury the ideals of the German Enlightenment to which two young men had looked up in the twenties seemed far away. A visit to Weimar in National Socialist Germany was a strange and disillusioning experience. Not that I felt like turning my back on Goethe and his friends although perfectly willing to own that Hegel and Marx saw in some respects much further than they did. There was something great about the endeavour of these dramatists and poets, whatever the quality of their achievements. Above all they possessed by nature and cultivation an inextinguishable sense of human personality and of what goes with it, a sense of human right. That seemed worth clinging on to in a Europe where men assigned absolute and overriding value to the interests, supposed and real, of their nation or their class and where they were disposed to sacrifice everything and everyone to them. The war cry of the Enlightenment, 'Humanize humanity!' seemed as good a cry as any one heard in Europe in the thirties and better than most. But it was not what anyone wished to hear. Men wanted a different kind of war cry and a different sort of war.

There was no need in those days to argue about the problem of human right in the abstract. It walked in at the door on two feet. Sometimes the feet were Russian. They could not carry their owner back to Russia, because he fought in his ignorant teens on the wrong side in the Civil War, worse still had fought on both sides, and had never been forgiven by the regime. Sometimes they were Italian. They were apprehensive of what might happen at home as the Rome-Berlin axis revolved and were inclined to emigrate to the United States. More often they were German and Jewish. Their owner's prime offence was that his or her nose was the wrong shape. Such was the grandeur of the State and the wisdom of statecraft in Europe in the thirties.

The extent of the evil seemed all the worse if one suspected that it was not German nature or Russian nature which was alone at fault. Men of other nations could act just as badly, given the opportunity and the temptation and the excuse, pushed hard enough by their own weakness and by the fate which we call history. Simple goodness in these circumstances came to seem one of the rarest commodities of life. Unlike other scarcities, this one could not be overcome by the mechanism of the market or by the direction of the State. The Stock Exchange did not obviously mark their prices down, or for that matter up, when men and women died unjustly. As for the State, it ordered the killing.

In thorough revolt against what a contemporary poet called 'the cadence of consenting feet', I found myself going back to a literature which as a boy I disliked and never opened unless compelled. This was the Old Testament. What I came to admire, however, was not its historical books, but those strange and vivid dialogues of which the books of Job and Jonah are such wonderful examples. In these, the men of the old Palestinian cities, goaded by the outrages and oppressions of their time, turned upon their god in heaven and called upon him to account for the intolerable spectacle of the world he had created. The old writers left the dialogue unfinished, their dilemma unresolved. This seemed at least honest and it did not, so far as one could tell, impair their faith. I could not share their direct and simple beliefs. But one could feel the depth of their disillusion, the force and passion of their search for justice in an unjust world. Compared with them, the literature of Victorian England which one had been brought up to admire seemed the amusement of a leisure class, not intended to be taken too seriously.

I was bound to feel grateful to these old Hebrews for putting in my head thoughts which otherwise would not have been there. How otherwise could one have found oneself brooding above the waters of an Alpine lake, some time in the summer of 1939, about the distinction between justice and revenge? Justice and vengeance, it appeared, were not, as many men supposed, the same. On the contrary, they were so far apart in nature as to be almost entire opposites mutually excluding one another. If this was true, then there must be something fraudulent in the rule by which civilized Europe lived. Because the doctrine then ceaselessly preached and generally accepted was that the law of life and the supreme good of society were best served by doing all the good one could to the friends of one's nation or one's class and all the damage one could to their enemies. Any other consideration could be safely brushed aside as a guide to conduct.

The sudden blazing conviction that this was wrong and the root of Europe's misery came, I suspected, from men who first thought the matter out under wholly different circumstances, the distant ancestors of the Jews who were now the victims of this very rule of conduct in central Europe. How odd it would have been to meet them, if one could meet them, those old writers! What mutual mystification, sharing not a word in common, only a faith! How odd, too, it occurred to me later to ask, if the uniformed men who had given rise to this train of thought had appeared round the corner of the path, armed with the usual weapons. How would my conviction have stood up to that grim test? One was always wondering in those days how soon one might be called upon to justify one's beliefs.

I would say now that this was, to say the least, a somewhat simplified version of what had actually happened in Europe. But such as it was, it was my vision of the thirties as they drove towards their disastrous end. No one, of course, appeared round the corner. We were after all some way from the Austrian frontier. The forest path was empty and silent. As usual, I had allowed myself to be left behind. I was able to catch up with my companion and to return to England, to war, and to something which for me was more important than either. I had written to an old student and friend, Audrey Brown, then living and working in York at Rowntree's to say that I was going out to India in the winter of 1939–40 if there was no war. This news, I had understood, although she had been born in India, would be a matter of profound indifference to her. It proved somehow or other to be less indifferent than either of us had imagined. We were married in March 1940.

It was a lovely spring that year. Military plans, like the flowers, the oxlips and the wild daffodils in the fields on the way to Racedown, matured early. We were staying just after the wedding in Dorset when one day the news of the German invasion of Norway came through. The army officers residing in our hotel disappeared overnight. We knew then that the fighting in the west had begun. It would not be long before we, too, were drawn into it. Nothing that one could do or say would alter that, either for us or for those other people whom we could look towards but not see, somewhere far out there in Europe, beyond the sea haze and the glitter of Lyme Bay.

2 The Years 1914–1918 in British Economic and Social History

I

The conflict of the years between 1914 and 1918 was the first to make such extreme demands upon the population and resources of the fighting nations as to force men to doubt whether the institution of war, in the sense of the armed struggle of sovereign states, could any longer be reconciled with the survival of state and society in Europe, in the forms which these had assumed throughout the centuries of her modern history. This was the first unmistakable emergence of a problem with which every European has since had to live and still lives. It is also the supreme practical reason for studying the history of the war.

The war's economic burden was not, it need hardly be said, its most fateful aspect. For a vast number of men and women, both of those who fought and died in it and of those who lived through it, the war became a personal tragedy, the source of loss and sorrow if also of new fellowship, comedy and intense boredom. No such waste of human life, especially young lives, had been seen in a war since men first pushed into and settled the European wilderness. For Europe as a whole the war was a catastrophe of the first order. European society discovered barbarism at the heart of its civilization. The results spread far beyond Europe. The failure of that society, at a time when it stood at the centre of the world's affairs and governed one half of mankind, either to contain or resolve the conflicts of nations and classes within its own borders, was felt throughout the human community. The consequence will last long after the war and its great battles have been forgotten, as they have been except among the few for whom these events were once a part of their life.

Within the limits of the economic history of the war it is the British experience which will be considered here. This is not to assert that the peoples of the British Isles, although they were in the war from start to finish and endured its full weight, suffered more of its hardships and miseries than others. The price of the war was higher to other nations. Of all those who took part, the Russians were almost certainly the heaviest losers, both in terms of absolute loss of life and the breakdown of their economy, in those days only partly modernized. It could fairly be argued that the French, the Germans and the nations of the Austro-Hungarian Empire suffered more than the British from the immediate disasters, brought about by enemy occupation, blockade, the collapse of supply and communications, and the sheer physical destruction involved in continuous fighting on a vast scale.

The interest of the British experience lies in the effects of the war upon a strong national economy, a democratic state and an advanced industrial society. The British industrial system in 1914 was the oldest and most powerful in Europe, in terms of the ready access to developed resources both at home and abroad. If the British suffered less than some peoples from the hardships of the war, this was due partly to their fortunate freedom from invasion, partly also to a national income which was greater than that of other nations to begin with, although within the country extremely ill distributed. The straits to which Great Britain was driven to meet the war's demands out of resources which were regarded at the time as great, the penetration of every part of her economic, social and political life by the stresses and strains of the conflict, demonstrated as no earlier event had the immense change which was coming over the institution of war. For Europe was more highly organized, politically and economically, than ever before and had reached a stage in society when the most systematic and unremitting attention was paid to scientific and technological advance.

2

In approaching British economic life between 1914 and 1918 we have to remember the change which has come over our general view of the war and its place in European history since the armistice of November 1918. At that time, certainly to much British opinion, the war recently over appeared as a huge and isolated event. It was a phenomenon without antecedent or successor which had broken unintelligibly the peaceful progress of Western civilization. The war's isolation would be apparent, men felt, when the world settled down and the conditions of former days reappeared. We know that this settlement did not occur. The European war of 1914–18 was followed by another, no less terrible, in 1939–45. The twenty years between were full of disorder. In a perspective unforeseen in November 1918 the first war appears as a gateway through which European society entered upon thirty years of crisis.

What appeared an event over and done with in 1918, when the air was still full of confusion, proved to be the beginning of a protracted phase in the history of Europe marked throughout by organized violence. It is the nature of this phase which needs understanding. One can only point out here one aspect of the change which has come over our views. It happens to be closely related to the duration of events. At the time of the war of 1914–18 and just afterwards the causes of the war were usually sought in the diplomatic relations of sovereign states. Much attention was paid to foreign policies on the eve of and in the generation before the war. This was proper, since the war, whatever else it was, was undoubtedly a conflict of states, although much of this thinking was a search for scapegoats. But diplomacy is dependent upon conditions which are not themselves created by diplomacy. In the light of the experience of the interwar era it appeared necessary to probe deeper for explanations.

Many men began to think that the explanation of the war lay on a different side of social life. They were impressed by the contradiction in the history of the nineteenth century between the nationality movements which did so much to shape European politics and the process of industrialization. The latter brought into existence a common economic and social organization, with a unity and problems of its own, in many parts of Europe. This seemed far more significant than nationality. Economics, they concluded, should form the basis of any analysis of the development of European politics before the war.

Most certainly the demographic and economic revolutions of the nineteenth century transformed the conditions of European politics. They entered both into the situations out of which the war arose and the conditions which sustained it for more than four years. But this doctrine in its simplified form, which identifies the process of industrialization with the accumulation of capital and the conflicts to which the latter gives rise with the origins of the war, must be rejected. It is not adequate to the scale and complexity of the events which have to be understood.

No one nowadays[1] would think of accounting for the course of

---

[1] The transformation of views can be seen coming in the lectures on the 1914 war delivered at Oxford in 1929 by Elie Halévy, a philosophic French historian of

events between 1914 and 1918 in terms of what was said and done in foreign offices or of the policies and strategic interests of the states which were known as the great European powers, even when the widest possible interpretation is being given to what diplomacy means. The general underlying cause of that time of troubles is to be found in the instability of European society itself. This gave rise both to war and revolution. The lack of unity arose out of the conflicts generated in the course of the development of a great civilization between the mighty and half instinctive collective forces of nationality and class and a structure of political authority in Europe which was in many respects disastrously ill fitted to direct and control them. The struggle between two great currents of social action—misdirected no doubt, but the very prevalence of misdirected tendencies in society proves the misdirection of prevalent tendencies—and the existing centres of political power produced problems which were intensely characteristic of the time. They were also incredibly difficult to deal with, if only because more than one set of social forces was at work. The dual stream of conflict in Europe's life accounts for a singular feature of the history of the years between 1914 and 1945. General wars tended to become civil and civil wars general, according as nationality or class took a hand.

The more the conditions of Europe sixty and seventy years ago are studied, the more deceptive will the relative quiet of the years before 1914 appear. The materials of a great crisis in European society had existed for years and had been known by good observers to exist. What could not be foreseen was the unique path of events, of decisions and acts, by which the conflicts so far held in check by the established arrangement of things broke surface and erupted into violence. Here the motives of persons and groups came into play. The crisis came in the

---

British and European affairs. *The World Crisis of 1914–18* (Oxford 1930). Halévy might be said to have raised the question, whether there was a war in 1914? Was it a war or a revolution? Did both arise out of the strife of the age? Halévy did not develop his opinion systematically, but he pointed out that the great cluster of events associated in our minds with the European war of 1914 and the Russian revolution of 1917 could not be understood in terms of diplomacy only. He argued in effect that nationality and class provided the correct general categories of analysis for that age of confusion. He was not prepared to accept, as many men did, that the war was the simple consequence of the blunders and crimes of individuals, however powerful, or that it belonged to the realm of abnormal psychology. Halévy was not, of course, contending that diplomatic history could be discarded from an explanation of the war. Some of the best of the diplomatic historical writing came after his day with W. L. Langer's *The Diplomacy of Imperialism 1890–1902* (New York, 1935) and L. Albertini's *Le Origini della guerra del 1914* (1943).

Balkans, where wars and rumours of wars had prevailed so recently as 1909, 1912, and 1913. As everyone knows it was a young student idealist, Gavrilo Princip, who on the 28th June 1914 shot the heir to the Austrian throne and his wife at Sarajevo. This was a demonstration of defiance of Austrian authority on behalf of the South Slavs, planned by a small group of nationalist revolutionaries calling themselves the Young Bosnians.[1] Six weeks later the five states, Russia, Austria-Hungary, Germany, France and Britain, which controlled the greater part of Europe's population were at war.

How do these general reflections upon the European crisis bear upon the economic history of the war? They bear to this extent that they ought presumably to condition the kind of questions that we ask about it. To the economic historian, primarily interested in the effect of economic change upon the management of resources and of means upon the ends men set before themselves, it might seem reasonable to ask, in the first place, what the relations were between the organization of resources in prewar Europe and the emerging ambitions of nationality and class as these affected the balance of European society as a whole? It might seem necessary to ask, in the second place, what were the main decisions taken during the war which affected the use of resources between alternative ends, whether for military or civilian needs? What gave those decisions special shape, how were they carried into effect and with what consequences? Finally, he might ask what was the effect of those same decisions taken during the war upon the situation immediately after the war. Was Europe as a society left better or worse off economically speaking to deal with those fundamental antagonisms of nation and class out of which war and revolution arose?

These are questions far easier to put than to answer. But they are worth asking, even if only the most imperfect answers can be found. No attempt will be made here to answer them for Europe. But we shall try to carry them in mind in considering the economic history of Great Britain. The Government of that country joined the war at midnight between the 4th and 5th August, when the ultimatum which it had sent to the Government of Germany expired. From that moment a new and incalculable factor entered into all public and private economic decisions.

---

[1] Vladimir Dedijer's *The Road to Sarajevo* (1967) gives a description of these men. By setting them in relation to the country they lived in, at a stage of development when they longed for a choice between old and new, he makes them intelligible, whatever one may think of what they did.

3

In the ten years before the war Great Britain was herself a striking example of the immense disturbing powers of nationality and class in a country which in those days presented to the world a dignified face of law and order, riches and authority. 'The age of the Forsytes' was very real at least so far as wealthy upper-class people in England were concerned.[1] This should not deceive us into taking the part for the whole of society. These years saw a significant increase in public disorder. This was particularly true of the last five years of peace. It is these troubled years, as well as those of war which followed, that require to be explained.

One way although not necessarily the only way to approach the changes of the time is to look at it through the eyes of those who held the positions of authority in central politics and administration, the relatively small élite who governed the country. From the Cabinet papers and other public records of the day now available it is possible to see the situation as it unfolded before their eyes and those of their advisers. We can perceive what they thought had become or were becoming the main problems of current economic and social policy. The point of doing so is that in these years the pressures at work without and within British society were beginning to force on choices between alternative lines of conduct which even an uninstructed public could understand. Informed men were anxious and their concern was beginning to affect, if only through the conflict of their opinions, public policy and finance. In considering their view of the resources of the country and its commitments, it is interesting to see what things worried them, what things worried them not at all, and what things ought perhaps to have worried them more than they did.

Men of the Balfour, Campbell-Bannerman and Asquith administrations between 1902 and 1914, and their professional advisers in Whitehall knew well enough that their problems had come to them mostly through the vast social changes of the previous century. They were also aware that they were confronted by something new, although what gave it novelty and how this should be dealt with was a subject of deep and bitter dispute.

Great Britain was the smallest great power in Europe among the five

[1] John Galsworthy's novel of wealthy English commercial and professional society *The Forsyte Saga* was published in 1922. But it begins with the generation which lived before the war.

states which held that they had a right to use the title. But her small area supported a large population and a formidable industrial, commercial and financial activity. These resources, capably governed and defended, were the basis of most of her power and influence in the world. According to the last prewar census, in 1911, the population of England, Wales and Scotland was 40,831,000, or if one includes Ireland, which was then part of the United Kingdom, 45,221,000 persons.[1] This was three and a half times as large again as the size of the British peoples when they had gone through the Napoleonic wars a century before.

This much larger British society was also, in an aggregate which one must confess meant nothing to individuals, much wealthier than that of a hundred years earlier. The growth of capital and income had more than kept pace with an extremely rapid growth of population. This was owing to the enormous changes which had taken place in world markets, communications and technology in the nineteenth century. Great Britain had been both the leader in these developments and the chief beneficiary from them. A fortunate conjuncture of events had placed her temporarily but very decidedly at the centre of the world's economy for most of the century. By 1900 net national income in the United Kingdom per person was more than double what it had been in the eighteen-fifties.[2]

This was an astonishing change. In a small and crowded island, without great land reserves or natural endowments, with the significant exception of coal, the increase of income had only been made possible by largely abandoning the old economic base of society in agriculture and handicrafts and going over on a large scale to industry. Much of this was export-oriented, with more than a quarter of total British production going abroad just before the war.[3] The British who fought the French under Napoleon in 1811 had drawn something like a third of their gross national product from agriculture and allied pursuits. The British who were to declare war on Germany in 1914 were overwhelmingly industrial. They took less than ten per cent of their incomes from the land and lived mostly by mining and manufacture, trade and transport.

They were also thoroughly urban. When the census of 1851 showed that one-half of the population of Great Britain lived in towns the news

[1] B. R. Mitchell and Phyllis Deane, *Abstract of British Historical Statistics* (1962), pp. 6–7.
[2] B. R. Mitchell and Phyllis Deane, *op. cit.*, p. 367.
[3] W. Schlote, *British Overseas Trade from 1700 to the 1930s* (translated Henderson and Chaloner) (1952), pp. 75–8.

had been received with surprise. By 1911 about three-quarters of that population lived in towns of one sort or another and a large number, about one-half of them, in great cities.[1] More than half a dozen cities or, as a later age was to call them, conurbations, in south-east Lancashire, the west Midlands, west Yorkshire, Merseyside, Tyneside, Clydeside and London, with a total population of over sixteen millions, increasingly settled the economic and political climate of the country. Much of the history of modern Britain is city history.

This was the national community, part of an industrial civilization new to the world, burdened with the consequences of the swift social changes of a hundred years, the centre of a vast international trade and a great colonial empire, which presented its urgent domestic problems to prewar governments. These problems were becoming more and more complex, as relations continued to alter, in an age of rapid transition, between classes within the nation, between the nation and its neighbours in Europe.

4

One question was largely missing from the mind of prewar Liberal Governments which we might perhaps have expected to find there. Economists and historians have rightly given it much attention since, for the conditions surrounding it were far from simple. This was the problem of Great Britain's long-term economic position. The dominance of Victorian Britain in the world's economy was a thing of the past in 1914. The continued economic development of western and central Europe and of North America had thrown it out of date in little more than the lifetime of a generation. International economic competition had increased immensely since 1880.

This aspect of the nation's position certainly received attention before 1914. It would have been difficult to support down to that date the proposition that Great Britain had suffered serious loss in foreign trade from the industrialization of the rest of the world.[2] But particular industries in particular markets suffered, especially around the turn of the century. The short-term effects were painful to British industry. So

---

[1] B. R. Mitchell and Phyllis Deane, *op. cit.*, p. 19.
[2] *Industrialization and Foreign Trade* (League of Nations, Geneva, 1945), p. 119. See also the detailed inquiry by S. B. Saul, *Studies in British Overseas Trade 1870–1914* (1960).

there had been a great deal of debate, whether so much should have been yielded to foreign competitors and what the economic and political costs and benefits of protection might be if protection were adopted. All this became part and parcel of public discussion and party politics as early as 1903. The Free Trade versus Tariff Reform dispute then rose to the rank of first-class politics.[1]

Foreign competition as a result of industrialization in other parts of the world was not quite the same as the problem of Great Britain's long-term economic position as it would now be understood. The debate of the early nineteen hundreds was only a first stage in the approach to the bigger question. This was just beginning to enter political consciousness and the area of public policy. Long-term issues, almost by definition, take a long time to declare themselves. A later age has concerned itself much less with the relatively minor issue of tariffs and commercial policy than with the problem of the best use of Britain's resources. Granted that the use of resources in other parts of the world was altering fast before 1914, owing to changes in transport, production and markets which seemed vast to contemporaries, what was the correct course for Great Britain? What was the best handling of her material and invisible assets in the way of savings and capital, science, design and technology, labour and management, to enable her people to earn more of the income they required for their private and public purposes? This was the true issue of the long-term position, as it began to emerge before 1914 and became far more apparent in the years after the war.[2]

---

[1] The controversy was the occasion of two remarkable economic writings: Alfred Marshall's *Memorandum on the Fiscal Policy of International Trade*, printed as a parliamentary paper in 1908, and Arthur Balfour's *Economic Notes on Insular Free Trade* of 1903. The restricted area of the argument is evident from their titles.

[2] It was known before 1914 that real wages had ceased to rise. See W. T. Layton, *An Introduction to the Study of Prices* (1912), ch. VIII. But the essential measurements of national income and expenditure were not available until after the war. It was A. L. Bowley, *The Change in the Distribution of Income 1880–1913* (1920), who first made it clear that the growth of the national income as a whole had been checked after 1900. He pointed to the fact, but did not go into explanations.

Economists in the past forty years have made a determined effort to fill the gap. Explanation has been influenced, very properly, by later experience. Unemployment between the two wars and the Keynes-Hayek controversy on capital formation had something to do with the form and direction of the investigations of A. K. (later Sir Alec) Cairncross, *Home and Foreign Investment 1870–1914* (1953), and W. W. Rostow, *British Economy of the Nineteenth Century* (1948). The decline in the rate of growth of exports and its effects on industrial investment suggested a further line to W. A. Lewis, *Economic Survey 1919–1939* (1949), and D. J. Coppock,

The question of the size and stability of the national income in the light of the use of resources may well seem to us a problem affecting everything else, from the economic welfare of classes to foreign policy and military strength. This did not make it a first-class question of public policy before 1914. For men brought up in the thoroughly commercial society of Victorian and Edwardian Britain occupying positions of authority in the early nineteen hundreds, the market, not public policy, ruled economic matters. The market had done wonderful things for Great Britain in the past century. They were inclined to think that it would go on doing so. They thought it was for the market, not for Government, first to call resources into existence, then to indicate where they should be set to work, and finally to reward them. They had not yet seen world markets settle down in the nineteen-twenties to leave in any given year one-tenth, sometimes more, of the British work force always unemployed.

There was another reason apart from doctrine why these men were unworried. National resources were fully employed. To unemployment as a periodic thing people were well used. The Liberal administrations from 1905 onwards saw with relief and pleasure that the resources of the country were becoming more fully employed than for many years. Idle men and machines were for them a short-period problem, born of the trade cycle. After a spell of sharp depression in the early years of the century following the South African war, markets and investment were once more on their way up. In the remarkable period of industrial activity which followed between 1905 and 1913 unemploy-

---

'The Climacteric of the 1890s: a Critical Note', *The Manchester School of Economic and Social Studies*, vol. xxiv, No. 1 (January 1956). But events in the fifties moved discussion away from investment aggregates and the export proportion towards innovation, technical change and management and their influence on industrial structure. See E. H. Phelps Brown and S. J. Handfield-Jones, 'The Climacteric of the 1890s: a Study in the Expanding Economy', *Oxford Economic Papers* (New Series), vol. IV, No. 3 (October 1952), and J. Saville, 'Some Retarding Factors in the British Economy before 1914', *Yorkshire Bulletin of Economic and Social Research*, vol. 13, No. 1 (May 1961). For a more recent view, H. W. Richardson, 'Retardation in Britain's Industrial Growth 1870–1913', *Scottish Journal of Political Economy*, vol. XII, No. 2 (June 1965).

That the check to real incomes was mainly the consequence of a decline in the rate of growth of the national economy is now agreed, although it is less easy to decide whether this was in the nature of a decline to be expected or the result of a failure of private and public initiative. The analysis of aggregates has probably been carried as far as it can go. A large industrial society can exhibit decidedly contradictory tendencies. Recent research tends to concentrate rightly on the region, the industry and the firm.

ment, in the limited number of trade unions which collected figures and give us our only source of knowledge, sank after a bad patch in 1908 and 1909 to just over two per cent. This was in 1913, at the height of the boom. There had been no years so free from unemployment for fourteen years.

Thanks to the staff of the Board of Trade and the curiosity of some politicians, the course of the prewar boom from 1911 on was watched by the prewar Cabinets in a series of reports which show a considerable degree of knowledge of what was happening to incomes and employment.[1] They also had before them the broad outlines of what was going on in the United States, Germany and France. They knew that their country was passing through a phase of expanding industrial activity which was world wide. Englishmen were used to an economy which had grown to an unusual extent in response to the demand for British capital and goods abroad. The investment boom of the Edwardians and the first Georgians was very much a boom of this type. Almost one-half of the savings of the country were going overseas.[2] The general activity was sparked off by the exports of a few large and well-established industries, of which coal, engineering, shipbuilding and textiles were the chief. But whether the boom was old or new in character—and the industrial structure described in the Census of Production of 1907 was largely a nineteenth-century product—it was deeply satisfactory for a Government which wished to hear no more of depression and unemployment. This trade recovery could solve many problems.

Many, but not all. For as time ran on it became clear that a contradictory situation existed. The business community was passing through the longest burst of investment and productive activity which it had known for years. Judged by familiar standards, the nation was occupied and prosperous. But it was also politically unhappy and discontented. Its tendency to become so mutinous as to threaten to be ungovernable seemed to increase with its prosperity. This mood created dilemmas for the policy-makers in Cabinet and Parliament. Full employment, it appeared, was no remedy for a new state of mind.

The prosperity and the discontent rose from the same economic root. The foreign investment and export business of those years was there largely because the primary producers of the world, in their exchanges

---

[1] These reports exist from 1911 onwards. They are noticeably lacking in any analysis of the boom, which they take for granted. They were perhaps written largely to serve the purposes of those who advised Government on labour problems.

[2] A. K. Cairncross, *Home and Foreign Investment 1870–1913* (1953), p. 121.

with the industrial nations of Europe and North America, were benefiting from relatively high prices for foodstuffs and raw materials. They expanded their output accordingly and wanted capital to do it with.[1] This was a position far more favourable to those who lived by interest and profit in Great Britain than to the wage-earner. Foreign investment organized by the City of London might in the long run bring the cost of living down by cheapening imports. Meanwhile, many people had to work harder to make their income go as far as before, with the prices of clothing and food well above, just before the war, their 1900 levels. The long investment boom provided wage-earners with an incentive to work which, from their point of view, was indistinguishable from a necessity.

Rising prices helped to force on the national strikes and the formidable industrial discontent of the years 1911, 1912 and 1913, as the boom worked up to its height. The Government's chief industrial adviser thought in the summer of 1911 that a general strike might be just round the corner.[2] There was much bitterness among those whose wages came upon the public budget, such as postmen and the sailors of the fleet. People had something to complain about. One has to remember that anything resembling a working system of industrial and Civil Service arbitration was only just coming into being.[3] Important industries such as the railways remained without recognized collective bargaining machinery until just before the war. Modern inquiries into consumer expenditure in the period between 1906 and 1914 suggest that the boom brought no advantage to the ordinary consumer, beyond more regular employment.[4] It was a time of great economic activity which did little or nothing to improve real wages.

---

[1] Sir Alexander Cairncross, *op. cit.*, p. 195, and table on p. 206.

[2] In a memorandum on 'The Present Unrest in the Labour World', 25 June 1911, Cab. 37/107 (1911), No. 70 (P.R.O.). The writer was George Askwith, chief industrial conciliator of the Board of Trade. What he had particularly in mind was the tendency of coal-miners, railwaymen and transport workers to concert their policies. His report alarmed the Home Secretary, Winston Churchill, who drew new instructions for the police that August. Cab. 37/107 (1911), n. 97 (P.R.O.).

[3] Two men who were helping to build it up have recorded their experience. See Lord Askwith, *Industrial Problems and Disputes* (1920), and Lord Amulree, *Industrial Arbitration in Great Britain* (1929).

[4] A. R. Prest, assisted by A. A. Adams, *Consumers' Expenditure in the United Kingdom, 1900–1919* (1954), pp. 7, 9.

5

The bulk of the nation, between 1906 and 1914, had a considerable and justified quarrel with its weekly income, whether expressed in terms of money or goods. But the discontent was older than the boom and went well beyond a failure of wages to rise fast enough to match prices. This will not of itself account for the extraordinary scale, intensity and speed of development of the social movements of the time.

From about 1909 onwards these movements of opinion turned to an increasing extent upon the position of a minority of the nation. They were the people who, in what was at that time a new phrase, 'fell below the poverty line'. This meant that even when continuously employed, and many of them at any given time were not employed,[1] they did not earn enough to buy food, shelter and clothing adequate to keep themselves and their families in the state of health required for ordinary working efficiency. How much was enough was a cause of dispute. But since the beginning of the century the size of the group had become known. The inquiries of the statisticians and social surveyors, Charles Booth, Seebohm Rowntree and Arthur Bowley, which were beginning to be sufficiently well known by 1914 to be quoted by politicians and the Press,[2] suggested that it included from twenty-five to thirty per cent of the town-living population of Great Britain.

What made poverty a political problem was not its scientific measurement. The failure of recruiting in the South African War, blamed by many people upon the bad physical condition of the city populations, did much to bring it to the forefront of politics. The drive towards full democracy in British politics after 1884 did even more by its insistence upon the equal rights of all citizens. This belief was transforming the Liberal and Conservative parties; while it created the Labour Party, after 1906.

Most people were interested in poverty because most people were poor. More than three-quarters of the persons in England and Wales in

---

[1] This lack of work was the result not only of seasonal or cyclical fluctuations of trade but of the underlying structure of the labour market in relation to the economic growth of the country. Before 1914 much employment in Britain still showed the casual, periodic and irregular characteristics, which nowadays we tend to associate with undeveloped economies. R. C. O. Matthews, 'Why Has Britain had Full Employment since the War?' *Economic Journal*, vol. LXXVIII (1968), pp. 564-7.

[2] The rising politician, Winston Churchill, read Seebohm Rowntree's study of York, *Poverty: a study of Town Life* (1901), and pressed the book upon his friends.

1912, if sold up for everything they possessed, would have been found to be worth less than £100.[1] Some sixteen million people out of between eighteen and nineteen million who were aged twenty-five and over owned no more than they stood up in or sat down at[2] and unknown numbers of them were constantly drifting in and out of debt. These were the great mass of the families from among whom the soldiers, the sailors and the munition workers of the war were largely drawn. A substantial part of the population lived always near the poverty line. They were acutely aware, in talk among themselves and in moments of solitary worry, that if their chief wage-earner died or became unemployed, if another child came or when sickness or old age arrived, they could hardly hope to maintain themselves. If their income became broken beyond the power of relatives and friends to help, then they would become objects of public charity. That involved a loss of social status and of the right to vote right down to the end of the nineteenth century.

It is not possible to turn over the literature of the 'social problem' as it was coming to be called in the decade before 1914 without being impressed by the huge proportions and complexity of the situation. Primary poverty, want of the elementary necessities of life, then existed on a scale which has since become rare in Great Britain. Incomes which after a century of fast economic growth were not high enough for a decent life for most people were bad enough. But it soon appeared to an aroused public opinion, as it continued to worry at the question, that the conditions complained against were not merely bad. They were also self-perpetuating and most unlikely to disappear of themselves. Closely examined, the poverty problem seemed to reach into every branch of the national life. It became clear that many people had no chance of breaking out from conditions which made them poor workers and indifferent citizens without the most drastic and permanent changes in the houses they were brought up in, the schools where they were educated, the size of their families, the medical services they enjoyed, the markets where they sought work and the other major institutions which supported the customary pattern of their family and working life. These things seemed to call not only for much hard work and goodwill from individuals but also for public action and investment over a long period of years. They were likely to make great demands both on finance and administrative ability. Many questions arising out of the

[1] H. Clay, *The Problem of Industrial Relations* (1929), Table III, p. 291.
[2] A. Abrams, *The Condition of the British People 1911–1945*, Table IX (a), p. 110.

existence of deep poverty in town and country, left in the past to the local community, were now held to demand national solutions.

But were incomes the whole problem? It appeared not, to judge by the depth of emotion released. This boiled over in many directions. Men and women were concerned with something as real to them as cash. They were involved not only with their income and what seemed to go with it, the ill health, the ignorance, and the other constraints which effectually prevented them from bettering their condition, but also with their relations with other people and with their own selves.[1] They felt compelled to wear the badge of inferiority because of their poverty. It was not the economic system only, it seemed, which they were up against, but a society which lived by it and moulded so many of its values upon poverty and wealth. To the problem of income in an industrial society was added the question of social status, both in industry and outside of it.[2] Many people wanted more money. But they also believed that they had a right to esteem, their own as well as other people's.

The combination of two criteria of equal citizenship, income with status, raised finally a problem of authority. The disadvantaged could not see themselves getting what they wanted from existing authority, which they distrusted. Therefore they demanded power, in the State, in industry and in society.[3] This demand can be seen making its way in the State through a new political party, the Labour Party. In industry, where there was a great expansion of trade unions, distrust of trade-union officials, industrial managements and the State created the 'ourselves alone' movement called Syndicalism.

It may seem strange to see, all growing together, the women's

[1] A vivid sense of the breakdown of traditional relationships comes through in the newspaper reports which the novelist and journalist H. G. Wells wrote at the time. H. G. Wells, *Journalism and Prophecy 1893–1946* (ed. W. W. Wagar) (1965), pp. 42–53.
[2] The emotions roused by status and the contemporary shift of social values were not wholly on one side. I once expressed to an old lady, who had herself been a considerable member of the servant-owning class in 1911, my perplexity at the wealthy ladies employing domestic servants who said they would never stamp their insurance cards, under the National Insurance Act of that year. The amount of money involved appeared paltry. 'My dear,' she replied, 'it was not the money at all. It was the idea that somehow or other Mary in the kitchen could be regarded as the equal of Elizabeth in the drawing room.'
[3] The essentially complicated nature of the inequality which was complained against in Britain between the wars has been explained by W. G. Runciman, 'Relative Deprivation and Social Justice' (1966). It was certainly no less so before 1914.

suffrage movement, the democratic socialism of the Labour Party, the syndicalism of Tom Mann, the Marxism of the Central Labour College, and many other movements, often contradicting one another and from time to time themselves. They arose, however, in a perfectly natural way out of a situation in which large groups and classes found themselves, as they saw it, matched against the economic and social system in which they lived, the law, the police, and the Government of the day.

The State's policy in these circumstances had to breast a mounting wave of popular interest and passion. Nothing can be more striking than the contrast between the relative stationariness of the British economy in the boom before 1914 and the speed with which a social crisis developed. While due in no small measure to the failure of the boom and a slowly changing industrial structure to increase incomes, this also reflected the problems of welfare created by a century of industrial growth in the towns, where the greatest victories of industrial society had been won and where its greatest diseconomies were to be found. A sober historian wondered twenty years later whether, if there had been no war, 'an undistracted concentration upon home issues would itself have bred some kind of revolution'.[1] Some of the men who had to make policy at the time were much concerned with what one might call the law-and-order aspect of all this. This was sensible enough. There was violent and irrational behaviour, as well as remarkable attempts on the part of many people to work out new ways of acting morally and rationally in a situation which was both novel and confusing.

The main issues went deeper than law and order. They were as European as British, for they were coming up everywhere in Western industrial countries in the thirty years before the Russian Revolution of 1917. It is difficult to pick out the more important British events in the period between the appointment of the Poor Law Commission in 1905 and the National Insurance Act in 1911. Something more important happened in those years than the supersession of private charity and local relief by centrally administered finance. What occurred was the recognition in British law of a new class of citizen rights. These were social rights as distinct from the civil and the political rights which people already had.[2] They were rights to medical aid, an income in old

[1] R. C. K. Ensor, *England 1870–1914* (1936), p. 557. Phelps Brown raised the same question from the industrial side, *Growth of British Industrial Relations* (1959), pp. 344–8.
[2] The sociologist, T. H. Marshall, *Citizenship and Social Class* (1950), put it that citizens of the English State acquired civil rights, in and through the courts of law, in the seventeenth and eighteenth centuries; political rights, in central and

age, some provision against unemployment in the industries most liable to it, and so forth.

This new system was still growing when the war broke out and with every step that was taken it became clearer that there was further to go. The original intention of such legislation as the Trade Boards Act, 1909, which introduced the principle of a minimum wage, was to enable men and women in some industries to earn a decent living on the market. But to correct the standing primary poverty of the cities required much more. It needed great programmes of building, public investment on houses, schools and environmental amenities, far beyond anything that local communities could afford. This implied an increasing and permanent commitment of public finance and economic resources, including those decidedly scarce factors, political and administrative talent. All this could not take place without a deep shift of social values, no less important than social institutions.

The true economic or opportunity cost of the European war of 1914–18 to Great Britain, as distinct from its human cost, which was strictly immeasurable, was that for four and a half vital years the problems of profound urban poverty and the modernization of the industrial structure which had to support both social and defence policies had to be neglected. How much, but for the war, the taxpaying classes of those days would have been willing to see diverted out of their income and out of available resources towards social transformation it is impossible to say.[1] The question was less one of taxable capacity than of willingness to pay the taxes and to endure the legal regulation which an effort on this scale requires. The war helped to break down some inhibitions. But the fact remains that it was not until the mid-twenties when her national income was back at its prewar figure that Great Britain's governing circles thought she was in a position to take up the programmes required to fulfil the aims of her prewar policies. They had lost an invaluable decade.

Meanwhile, the pre-1914 impact of new social policy on British public finance was immediate. Government expenditures in the United

---

local government, in the nineteenth; social rights in the twentieth century. It is not necessary to assume that each grew out of the other inevitably, although there was a kind of logical progression.

[1] Taxpayers opposed to the rise in social expenditure in 1909 complained that to raise income tax to 1s. 2d. in the pound was to 'encroach upon a war reserve'. The income tax rate had never been higher than 1s. except in time of war. Sir Josiah Stamp, *Taxation during the War* (*Carnegie Economic and Social History of the World War*) (1932), pp. 136–7.

Kingdom on social services, central and local, towards the end of the nineteenth century, in 1890, had been running at twenty-seven million pounds. They were up to over one hundred million by 1913. This was a rise in the values of the time from just over twenty to thirty-three per cent of all public expenditure.[1]

6

The simultaneity of disparate decisions is an important part of history, especially when they happen to call upon the same pool of resources. While these innovations were going forward in social politics others were being made, sometimes by the same persons, sometimes by others, in the wholly different field of national security. If the one set of concerns arose out of the difficult problems of class, the other sprang from the no less real consciousness of nationality, its shared experience and its fears.

The influence of nationality upon British policy was complex. The United Kingdom both dominated over other nations and feared domination by them. Within her own borders, as they were defined in those days, she faced in Ireland what was probably the most acute nationality problem in Europe outside of the Austro-Hungarian Empire. The Asquith Government in the summer of 1914 feared civil war there. An armed rising came, under different circumstances, two years later, in 1916. It was a matter of surprise for English official and public opinion when the act of national resistance which broke the European peace in June 1914 came from Sarajevo. These men had expected the lightning to strike in the western quarter of the sky. But the Balkans! There was probably no part of Europe which, by their historical traditions and habits of mind, they knew less of or were more ill fitted to understand.

While the Irish question, at once economic, social and political, was unsettled and remained so until 1922, Great Britain was herself deeply involved in a rivalry with Germany. This, one of the new things of the century, became one of the underlying conditions of European politics for its first fifty years. It was a rivalry of a special type, closely bound

---

[1] Social services here cover education, health services, pensions, national insurance against sickness and unemployment, poor relief and housing. A. T. Peacock and J. Wiseman, assisted by J. Veverka, *The Growth of Public Expenditure in the United Kingdom* (Princeton, 1961), Table A15, pp. 183–6.

up with the political unification of Germany and the immensely rapid rise of the German industrial system after 1860. Had Germany remained the three hundred petty states of Napoleon's day or had Bismarck's German Empire never industrialized, Englishmen would presumably have never discussed before 1914 the problem of their relations with Germany. The collaboration of economic with political events created a new situation.

The mere existence of power on the new German scale upset the balance of the European state-system or constantly threatened to do so. It is with reference to this fact that the two world wars can be described, as they have been by a German historian, as the last of the wars of national hegemony in Europe.[1] The real possibility of German dominance in Europe arose as that of Spanish and French dominance had arisen in earlier times. Englishmen were particularly sensitive to a change of this sort, because of the vastness of the power which was concentrated in their hands, from their economic, naval and colonial position. So arose a context of which trade rivalry, though an important part, was only a part. It was a competition throughout the world for power, influence and wealth between two great European nations. The debate had its vital ideological side, too, for it was immensely sharpened and aggravated by the difference in political values and institutions of the two peoples. The leaders of the one regarded themselves as in some sort heading the popular democratic forces; those of the other treated themselves equally seriously as representatives of the more conservative elements in European society. How these two great causes fared at their hands, it is not our purpose here to inquire.

National competition on a great scale might not have been, and was not wholly, a bad thing either for Great Britain or Germany. The rise of American industry and power which took place at the same time similarly affected the British economic and political position. But it did not lead to war. Both American and German competition was industrially healthy for Great Britain.[2] A competition for power was a different matter, given the special and intense conditions of European political life. It carried a logic of its own, in a continent containing independent and highly armed sovereignties.

[1] Ludwig Dehio, *Germany and World Politics in the Twentieth Century* (trans. D. Pevsner) (1959).
[2] The economist, Alfred Marshall, had an acute sense of what Britain could learn from both her competitors, as his *Industry and Trade* (1919) shows. See also S. B. Saul, 'The American Impact on British Industry, 1895–1914', *Business History*, vol. III, No. 1 (1960), pp. 19–38.

The tragedy of the European peoples was that they had never, throughout the centuries of their history, discovered either how to protect the rights of a nation except by force or how to make the common interest prevail. National rivalries in the past had led to war. But war was accepted as one of the institutions of society. By European historical tradition, the problem of relations between nations was to balance power with power. How to balance the power of 'the tremendous group'[1] composed of Germany and her allies and how to do this without precipitating a general European war became, after 1890, the dominant problem of European politics. It was also the problem which European political wisdom, including British wisdom, failed to solve. Bethmann Hollweg, who guided the destinies of Germany between 1909 and 1917, said later that he believed the vast accessions of material power to Germany in his lifetime had not been good for the judgement of the nation he governed, since it led them to overrate their ability to control events. That basic mistake was shared by men in all the great capitals of Europe before 1914.

A situation grew up in which Great Britain felt herself to be a leader under challenge, while Germany was the challenger.[2] Before 1900 this was mainly a matter of trade rivalry. Germany gave a lead in new science-based industries such as electricity and chemicals. She developed an economy which, unlike the American, depended heavily for its standards of living upon imports of food and raw materials purchased by industrial sales on world markets. After the turn of the century a new and more dangerous competition sprang up in the field of armaments.

The race in naval weapons between Germany and Great Britain was the first of the great arms races of this century. The foreign policy of the two states, without being determined by the race—rather determining it—had to adapt itself to the new rigidity of long-term technical programmes.[3] It was fed by all the inventiveness of the time, at work on

---

[1] The phrase used by Lord Haldane in his conversations in Berlin with the Kaiser and his Chancellor in February 1912 at the height of the naval race, as recorded in the diary of his visit. Cab. 37/109 (1912), No. 32 (P.R.O.). The men concerned did not decline the compliment.

[2] I have applied to the situation as a whole the phrase employed by Alfred Marshall to describe the economic situation. See his *Industry and Trade* (1919), ch. V. It looked that way to many men both in Britain and Germany, not least to the naval architects and sailors who designed and built the German High Seas Fleet.

[3] Thus the argument over the British naval estimates in 1909 was essentially a discussion of relative naval power in 1914. By 1912 the experts on both sides of the North Sea were making calculations to cover the next five years, even to 1920.

the problems of the 'ultimate deterrent' of those days, the enormous floating gun platform known as a battleship. This was, of course, in the technical era before the submarine and air warfare. It has sometimes been supposed that British industry before 1914 was increasingly out of touch with scientific and technical development. But the First Lord of the Admiralty, submitting draft naval estimates for 1913–14 to the Cabinet on 11 January 1913, said, 'The Navy is passing through a phase not merely of expansion, but of swift and ceaseless development. It is in fact a vast scientific business of ever-growing range and complexity, stimulated and governed by inventions and improvements in every sphere of applied mechanics, forced without cessation to enter upon new paths of research and application, and fanned to the highest point of activity by the rapid advance in every direction of rival Powers.'[1] But much of this work was done under conditions of secrecy in a field apart from normal peacetime demand, although the Navy's interest in oil technology, aircraft and radio rubbed off in time into other spheres. Meanwhile something resembling the famous military-industrial complex of a later day had already taken shape in both countries, to be developed further after 1914 under wartime conditions. It was civilized Europe's dubious gift to the world.[2]

All this could be justified from the standpoint of the assumptions of contemporary British thinking in Whitehall and out of it. Men accepted the possibility of war, even from about 1904 that of a war with Germany. They accepted also the growing relationship in the new century between science, technology and defence. But the new defence had its economics as well as its technology. It had to be paid for. Along with growing social problems, a more expensive defence policy brought about a revolution in public finance after 1890. The current costs of defence rose from nearly thirty-five million pounds in that year to over ninety-one million pounds in 1913 or from 26.7 per cent of total Government expenditure to 29.9 per cent of the increasing total.[3]

Total Government expenditure both central and local was rising in those prewar years faster than gross national product, after the long Victorian period in which the one had been a fairly constant proportion of the other. In 1890 it stood at nine per cent of the whole; in 1913, at

[1] Summary of 'Draft Navy Estimates 1913–14', Cab. 37/114 No. 11 (P.R.O.).
[2] The naval race has been the subject of excellent studies, e.g. E. L. Woodward, *Great Britain and the German Navy* (1935), and (using German documents) J. Steinberg, *Yesterday's Deterrent: Tirpitz and the Birth of the German Battle Fleet* (1965).
[3] A. Peacock and J. Wiseman, *op. cit.*, Table A–15, pp. 184, 186.

between twelve and thirteen per cent.[1] Defence and the social services accounted for the greater part of the expansion. Together they required 202.1 million pounds out of Government outlays of 305.4 million pounds, or nearly sixty-three per cent of them.

Increased Government activity and a growing commitment of resources to the public sector of the economy were the reaction of British society to the anxieties of the time. But those anxieties created as much conflict as agreement. The decisions embodied in the new public finance were not reached without the imposition of new taxation in 1909 and again in 1913. This led to bitter political controversy. Battles developed both in public opinion and in the inner circles of Government between exponents of the two fastest-growing sectors of expenditure. In March 1909 the First Lord of the Admiralty, Reginald McKenna introduced his naval estimates to Parliament with the words, 'No matter what the cost the safety of the country must be assured.'[2] But he had to defend increased spending on the fleet against the protagonists of the social services, who were the Home Secretary, Winston Churchill, and the Chancellor of the Exchequer, David Lloyd George. This quarrel divided the Cabinet.[3] Four years later it was the turn of Winston Churchill, now a First Lord who had been profoundly impressed by the implications of the German Navy Law of 1912, to be attacked by the same Chancellor of the Exchequer, Lloyd George, because of rising naval costs in the plans and estimates for 1914–15.[4] The earlier of these two Cabinet crises, since a solution depended on finding the money both for armament and social expenditure, led directly to the 'People's Budget' of 1909. This in turn created political trouble and a constitutional crisis.

No easy solution to the problems of public finance was possible for a society such as Britain. She was deeply divided on class lines, herself unstable in an unstable Europe. The prewar pressure of public commitments turned out to be the first thrust of a long-term dilemma, wholly characteristic of the new century, arising out of the urgent need to counter antagonisms both within the State and without and to bring out of conflict a new community of interests. There is an extreme interest about these years, when not only Britain but also European society moved away from the temporary balance they had reached in

[1] A. Peacock and J. Wiseman, *op. cit.*, Table A–5, p. 164.
[2] S. McKenna, *Reginald McKenna 1863–1943* (1948), p. 60.
[3] See the account in Violet Bonham Carter, *Winston Churchill as I Knew Him* (1965), pp. 168–74.
[4] R. S. Churchill, *Winston S. Churchill*, vol. 2 (1967), ch. 17, 'The Naval Estimates Crisis'.

the nineteenth century. Under the impulse of many kinds of change, they inclined towards a future which combined new promise with immense risks.

Whatever view we take of the Anglo-German fleet rivalry and of the causes of the quarrel between the two peoples and their governments, it must be agreed that it was a calamity for Europe when they allowed themselves to become involved in a situation which substantially increased the risk of war. Yet European war did not come out of the fleet rivalry nor out of the endless search for deterrents. This competition had a rationale of its own, which it is hard to appreciate unless one keeps constantly in mind that Europe was fundamentally without law. In a situation where neither law nor good custom were strong enough to govern the relations of nations without breaking down periodically into war, any sort of force, prestige or bluff which was reasonably cost-effective in increasing protection had a purpose. But the Anglo-German arms race was only one of the symptoms of a dissolving peace. General war came out of the emergence of the fully organized alliance system after 1907 when the power of Germany and Austria-Hungary was matched by the countervailing power of France, Britain and Russia. It came out of the nationality movements active within the Austro-Hungarian empire and the assassination at Sarajevo. Finally, in the month of July 1914 it was the result of the attitudes and policies of the leading European states, including Russia, towards the problems presented by the peoples living in the Continent's eastern half. These policies, both self-centred and superficial in their pursuit of what were judged vital national interests, permitted a new Balkan conflict to transform itself within six weeks into a European and a world war. When this happened, every existing financial commitment of the British Government as of other governments had to be looked at again, in the light of the probable demands of such a war upon all available resources.

7

What were the expectations with which British society entered the war? What especially did men think of the economic effort which might be required? The economic problem of any society is no doubt fundamentally the same in peace and war.[1] It is a question of the allocation of

[1] This was the argument of Lord Robbins, *The Economic Problem in Peace and War* (1947), writing after his personal experience in the second European war.

resources between alternative ends. War, if only because it simplifies all ends, enforces a different allocation. But the difference between war- and peacetime arrangements may be very great. It is necessary to consider what shape the expected war took in the minds of those whose duty or business it was in prewar Britain to calculate the contingencies ahead.

This was a question of strategy. Strategy is a choice of military priorities, and economic priorities in war time follow strategy. If we examine the discussions and conclusions of the relatively small body of men who from their position in society, or as elected political leaders, or as Civil Servants, soldiers, sailors, and financial advisers, found them- selves taking the vital decisions in defence and weighing policies for the nation as a whole, we shall soon find that their economic views pro- ceeded not only out of such economic doctrines as they knew but to a much larger extent out of their estimate of the military and diplomatic conditions of Europe.

The 'strategic-diplomatic factor'[1] was most uncertain, but there were some assumptions that could be made. Men's minds tend to be condi- tioned by what they have been accustomed to. British governments had a long experience, extending back over three centuries, of military intervention in Europe. Their traditions of strategy were those of a naval, colonial, commercial and insular power, turning to account both its strength and weakness towards the end of victory.[2] The Committee of Imperial Defence, which was charged with the duty of advising the Cabinet on military problems and had been meditating almost since its inception in 1904 the implications of war with Germany, framed its plans accordingly.[3]

Their first choice of weapons was naval. They expected the role of Great Britain in a European war, as the possessor of the most powerful fleet in the world, to be played mainly at sea. The fleet would in the first place protect the island from invasion, so preserving the indispensable base for all further operations. It would in the second place retain for

[1] Both the phrase and the concept belong to M. Raymond Aron, *Paix et Guerre entre les Nations* (4th ed. 1962), ch. I.
[2] C. R. M. F. Cruttwell, *The Role of British Strategy in the Great War* (1936). See also P. Guinn, *British Strategy and Politics 1914–18* (1965), pp. 1–31.
[3] The prewar discussions and recommendations of the Committee, which possessed no executive power of its own, have been described, a little too compla- cently, by its secretary, Lord Hankey, *The Supreme Command*, vol. I, ch. V–XIV (1961). The papers of the Committee, which are available in the Public Record Office, present, as one might imagine, a less tidy view, more exposed to the moods and pressures of the time.

Great Britain her freedom of action in choosing a point for an attack on a Continental enemy. Command of the sea would cover any military expedition that might be necessary to invade Europe or to carry on war in other parts of the world. The fleet would blockade the enemy's coasts, capture his colonies, so depriving him of naval and military bases and of valuable elements of economic strength. It would interrupt and break off his trade, inflicting the maximum commercial and financial damage. There might be a great naval action, such as actually took place at Jutland in May 1916. On this the main issue of the war might largely depend.

The United Kingdom possessed no land frontiers. Therefore British society in modern times neither had nor thought it politically desirable to have a large army based on conscription such as existed in many Continental states. Military intervention on the Continent and elsewhere might and almost certainly would be necessary. But in British strategic conceptions the military effort was secondary to the naval. Plans devised in 1911, when there had been a serious war scare following the collision of French and German policies in Morocco, made this clear. It was understood that in the event of Great Britain going into a European war on the side of France an expeditionary force, small but highly trained and equipped, would be sent at once to the Continent. It would take up its position on the left flank of the French Army. The main military effort would be left to the armies of France and Russia.

The economic aspect of the war was remarkably little discussed before 1914 either in Whitehall or out of it. It seemed to follow from the strategic conception. The economy would have to do two or three things at once. It would have to find out of national income and output the finance of the war and supplies for the forces. It would maintain the civilian part of the population, which would be by far the largest part of the nation. Finally, out of Britain's balance of payments, which in those days was extremely favourable, it would give whatever assistance might be necessary to Continental allies. Subsidies would replace foreign investment.

No untoward strain either on the industrial system or the machinery of public finance appears to have been expected. There might be differences of opinion as to whether national income was growing as fast as it ought. There could hardly be any on the scale of the resources available for war if it came, at the service of the State to tax, borrow or requisition. But these powers, it was assumed, would be exercised in a traditional way. There seemed to be no economic problem at home or abroad which the market could not tackle as it had in previous wars. Great Britain's financial and economic strength had been an important part of her war-making equipment since the early eighteenth century.

How did these assumptions come to be falsified, so that large-scale economic problems of a most unexpected kind began to emerge from the first days of the war? Largely because the fundamental strategic conception was mistaken in two highly important respects. The first of these was the assumption that war, if and when it came, was likely to be short. This was axiomatic to pre-1914 European military thinking. It was known to British soldiers that the leading military advisers of the great states on the Continent did not expect a long war. They expected a conflict enormous in scale, terrible in its use of force, but short. The plans of the German Army's Great General Staff since 1905 contemplated a decisive military operation first against the French and their allies in the west, then against the Russians in the east, for the Germans had to be prepared to fight, if war came, on two fronts. The western campaign, it was hoped, would be substantially over in forty days after general mobilization.[1] The war in the west which the Germans actually fought lasted for nearly four and a half years. It was not only the German plans which were upset by this switching of all expectations into the long period.

The other British assumption relevant to the economic shape of the war was that their army's part would be limited in what for Englishmen was the classic manner. The commitment of the British Government to France was for six army divisions or 160,000 men. This force was landed on the other side of the Channel at the beginning of the war and shared the earliest fighting. It took part in the retreat before the advancing Germans and the subsequent counter-attack. But the entire expeditionary force had not been landed and the Germans had not even begun to retire from the Marne before the whole of the prewar military plan on the British side was scrapped.[2] The formula for the war had to be restated in new, and to British ears, most unfamiliar terms.

This was a result of what British soldiers discovered in France when they got there. The German Army Staff had taken the initiative at the outset of the war by concentrating their main military strength in the west. They invaded France with one and a half million men.[3] The great

---

[1] M. Stone, 'Moltke-Conrad: Relations between Austro-Hungarian and German General Staffs, 1909–14', *The Historical Journal* vol. IX (1966), p. 209.
[2] *History of the Ministry of Munitions*, vol. I (1922), Part I, p. 8.
[3] Liddell Hart, *A History of the World War 1914–18* (1934), p. 78.

turning movement through neutral Belgium which they had designed to roll up the French armies, drive them back on Paris and defeat them in eastern France failed. But by leaving German forces in possession of a large part of northern France and Belgium it did much to determine the course of the war. When the Germans dug themselves in on Belgian and French soil and defied the Allies to throw them out, this was the beginning of the Western Front, the long line of field fortifications extending from the Channel to Switzerland, which until March 1917 never moved more than ten miles in either direction. This front absorbed the largest part of the fighting forces of France and Great Britain down to the armistice in November 1918.

Weight of numbers could, it appeared, only be answered by weight of numbers. The war began at once to wear that appearance of a competition of populations which it carried to the end. But behind the German armies the British soldiers found not only population but also engineering resources employed in support of a new kind of war. Novel weapon systems endowing the defence with extraordinary fire power, above all German superiority at the start in heavy artillery and machine-guns, created the trench-war system of the next few years. Trench war evolved on both sides a technology of its own, which could only be maintained with the aid of elaborate systems of communication and supply.

A vastly enhanced military participation in the war did not exhaust the war's novelty to British minds, as it actually emerged in the summer of 1914. The war developed out of a whole way of life created in Europe by the economic, social and political changes of the nineteenth century. The demographic and industrial revolutions shaped it and so, too, did other things. Above all, population and resources in Europe became united in the service of an idea. This was the belief that only the nation, that is, its adult manhood trained and equipped for war, could properly defend the national interest.

The conception of the nation in arms replacing the small professional, often mercenary, army of earlier days, went back to the French Revolution and Napoleon. Napoleon's military doctrines had been founded upon it. The nation supplied the massive military force with which the fighting strength of the enemy, as the first aim of warlike operations, was to be sought out and destroyed. But the social developments of the nineteenth century, especially between 1860 and 1914, had given to the French revolutionary concept an altered form, mainly at German hands. The military objective of war remained victory in the Napoleonic sense, the destruction of the enemy's army and of the State's will to fight. But the constant growth of population, industrial organization and technique, not least of the organization and administrative capacity of government, which had gone hand in hand with the increase in the productive powers of society, made it possible now to mount gigantic blows. These disposed of organized violence far beyond the levels of Napoleonic times. They were in their nature blows delivered by one society upon another. It was the whole national society, organized for victory, militarily, economically, politically, psychologically, which lay behind them. Fighting forces became the indispensable cutting edge of this tremendous and extraordinary weapon.

War on this scale raised problems, as the next few years were to prove, which went to the root of nineteenth-century military and political thinking. To defeat an army, which was the military intention of war, it now became necessary, it seemed, to destroy also an economy, a society and a government. What then became of the political object of war, if war became subversive and destructive to this degree? The ultimate aim of war in Clausewitz's words was the pursuit of policy by other means, the use of violence to alter the political will of another. What happened to that objective, indeed to that will, in the moment of total military victory in a total war?[1]

The war which had now begun raised the problem of a radical contradiction of aims in the most acute form. But if the true nature of a thing is what it develops towards, then the European war of 1914–18 was not total to begin with. It took time for the conception of the nation in arms, manned and equipped according to the scientific and technical standards of the new century, to show its potentialities. Without this conception, however, we cannot hope to understand the structure of action of the war. This holds for the British as for other people. They adopted the principle of the nation in arms in August–November 1914, in order, it might be said, to fight it. This step prepared the way for a wholesale repudiation of all earlier estimates of the probable cost of the war.

[1] In what has been said above of the idea of the nation in arms, the place of victory in the Napoleonic theory of war, and of politics in Clausewitz's interpretation of Napoleonic doctrine, I have followed the writings and lectures of M. Raymond Aron. The writings of Clausewitz, whose book *On War*, first translated into English in 1873, became classical theory for the soldiers of Europe before 1914, deserve to be compared for intellectual distinction with Adam Smith's *Wealth of Nations*. Two books more opposed or more characteristic of the experience and attitudes of the two nations who produced them can hardly be imagined.

8

What would now be called the escalation of the war, the ascending scale of military effort, was extremely rapid. The House of Commons voted provision for the addition of 500,000 new recruits to the Army on the 6th August 1914. This limit was soon abandoned. A second vote for another 500,000 men was taken on the 10th September. On the 16th November the House of Commons voted for another million men. Three months later, on the 10th February 1915, the maintenance of land forces to the total of three million men was authorized. The first million men were recruited before November 1914. In July 1915 a total of two million recruits had been reached.[1]

Voluntary recruitment failed to provide all the military manpower that was required. In the middle of the war conscription had to be resorted to. There were many attempts to avoid an institution regarded as antipathetic to British political and social tradition, all the more because it became linked with the deep class hostility and suspicion of the time. The idea of conscription for the Army, it was feared, might lead to the conscription of labour to supply the Army. Industrial conscription, strongly opposed by the trade unions and the labour movement, never arrived. Military conscription was voted by Parliament in May 1916. In the first eighteen months of the war 2,532,684 men were raised for the armed forces by voluntary enlistment. In its last thirty-three months another 2,438,218 men were raised under the compulsory system.[2] The whole number taken for the services was, therefore, 4,970,902 men.

This was a formidable call-up, out of a total population for the United Kingdom in 1914 of 46,048,000 persons. The entire male-occupied population in 1911 was 12,927,000 men and boys.[3] The call-up created a manpower scarcity which lasted for the rest of the war. This was the most important of all the war scarcities and in a sense the root of every other. For in addition to fighting and renewing the fighting line it was indispensable that labour should equip, clothe and feed the armed forces, provide the civilian population, much of it engaged on munitions, with food, heat, light, clothes and transport, and keep exports at a level which would earn exchange for essential imports. The island population could not feed or keep its industries going for a week

---

[1] *History of the Ministry of Munitions*, vol. 1 (1922), pp. 9–10.
[2] Lord Hankey, *The Supreme Command*, vol. 2 (1961), p. 477.
[3] B. R. Mitchell and Phyllis Deane, *op. cit.*, pp. 10, 60.

without exchange with the rest of the world.[1] Much of the economic history of the war could be written in terms of the shifts and devices by which, outside and inside of the armed forces, every man and woman had to be persuaded or compelled to do the work of one and a quarter or one and a half persons.

The growth of the Army from six to thirty divisions, which became the target of 1914, then from thirty to seventy, which was the aim in 1915, presented a major economic problem in the matching of military demands with supplies. This difficulty was heightened by the constant changes in the standard of equipment and the rapid development of new and elaborate weapon systems. A war of fixed positions on the Western Front proved to be a war of material, to an extent and in a sense that no army staff in Europe had expected.[2] This logistic effect had results on military thinking and generalship which are still disputed among the historians of the war. But the consequences for the prevailing economic doctrines and policies were no less interesting or momentous.

How could war of this intensity and scale be reconciled with the prewar size and pattern of incomes, expenditure and output in Great Britain? By far the greater part of the national income in peacetime went immediately into consumption to satisfy the urgent needs of a poor population. Was this consistent with the devotion of a large part of the existing resources to supplying the Army and Navy? How could public and private needs best be brought into balance? By cutting down on the personal consumption of the greater part of the population? By neglecting to renew capital equipment? By using up stocks on hand? By increasing output per head in a diminished labour force?

These are sensible questions to ask about the economics of any large-scale modern war. They were actually asked and answered by those concerned with the management of the British war economy in 1914–18. An English banker and temporary Civil Servant, trying to explain in September 1917 to an American audience what was being done in Great Britain, calculated in rough figures that just before the war, in

---

[1] Humbert Wolfe, *Labour Supply and Regulation* (*Carnegie Economic and Social History of the War* (1923), p. 2.

[2] For some technical comment on the supply problem in 1914–18 see Colonel G. C. Shaw, *Supply in Modern War* (1938), pp. 90–2, 133–4. He points out that some of its principal characteristics arose from the fact that this was still largely an unmechanized war, not least in transport. This appears among other things from the number of horses employed.

1907, the British gross national product could have been valued at about ten thousand million American dollars. Of this amount over seven thousand million dollars, by far the greater part, had gone into immediate consumption. A little more than eighteen hundred million dollars were invested at home, about one-half in new capital, the other half in maintenance. Investment outside of Great Britain took five hundred million more. Stocks in hand absorbed three hundred and twenty-five million. How was the war being paid for out of incomes which ten years before had been used in this way? The owners of the incomes were in the first place cutting out all foreign investment. This was being replaced by loans to Continental allies, mainly Russia, France and Italy. Then they were refraining from the normal expansion of capital, in the form of houses, factories and equipment, except where new investment was essential for the war effort. They also dropped normal maintenance of buildings and machinery. Stocks as well as equipment were being run down, except where indispensable for the war. Above all, personal consumption was being reduced. This was done at the point where it depended on imports. Before the war Great Britain imported fifty-five million tons per annum of goods required for consumption. Now she imported no more than thirty million tons as a total. Of this amount, ten million tons was munitions of war, leaving twenty million tons for imported foodstuffs for the civil population.[1]

This statement, made at a late stage in the war, defines the central problem of the war economy. This was the allocation of the national resources in a way to make war production grow fast. The economic logic of the war was mathematical. It has to be remembered, however, that this way of looking at the economic problems of the war grew largely out of the war itself. The type of economic analysis required to think effectively about national income and outlay was only just coming into existence before 1914. Very few people thought about the war economy in this way, even among those whose professional business it was to do so. A distinguished economist of the interwar years, J. M. Keynes, who served in the Treasury throughout the 1914–18 war, said later that he never heard inflation discussed in Whitehall in the first war in the terms of analysis which became common in the second.[2] This is not surprising. Neither the statistical nor the theoretical tools, which

[1] The banker was R. H. Brand, later managing partner of Lazards Bank. His address to the American Bankers Association, unpublished at the time, found its way into J. M. Clark, W. H. Hamilton and H. G. Moulton, *Readings in the Economics of War* (Chicago, 1918).
[2] J. M. Keynes, *How to Pay for the War* (1940), p. 70.

Keynes himself did much to create, were to hand.[1] The war itself caused men to study the allocation of resources with a new intensity.

It does not follow that if national resources had been better known and analysed in advance they would have been more successfully employed.[2] Flexibility in the transfer of resources from one use to another had often to take place between 1914 and 1918 under conditions of overwhelming uncertainty. The deliberate creation of uncertainty is a necessary part of war. The decisions of private persons and public authority in Great Britain about the use of resources during the war were far from autonomous. They were only part of a system of interdependent decisions,[3] taken as the war went on in five great capital cities, London itself, Berlin, Vienna, Paris, St. Petersburg (the later Leningrad), and Rome, with Washington striking in as an unexpected partner to the European game both before and after 1917. In this war game it was of the utmost importance to defeat the expectations of one's enemy and compel him to use his resources not as he wished but in a way to serve, or at the least not to hinder, one's own ends.

The great economic choices of the war followed the political and the military. Two of the largest transfers of resources of the war were forced upon Great Britain by enemy decisions. The British could only react to them in what seemed an appropriate way and hope for the best. One was the wholesale movement of industrial resources into the equipment of a Continental-size army. This became necessary when the British were presented in the summer of 1914 with the spectacle, which powerfully impressed their imaginations, of a German army on the coasts of the Channel. The other was the change of British policies in food and shipping forced on by the German decision, taken early in 1917, to starve the islanders out and drive them out of the war by the weapon of unrestricted submarine warfare. There was a third case. This was the change of British arrangements in finance, shipping and

---

[1] No satisfactory set of figures for national income and expenditure survives from the war years. Brand was forced to refer to 1907, to the year of the first Census of Production. The development of adequate national income and outlay statistics was largely the work of A. L. Bowley and Colin Clark at a later date.

[2] See the comments of E. A. G. Robinson on another war, *Lessons of British War Economy* (National Institute of Economic and Social Research, ed. D. N. Chester) (1951), p. 41.

[3] The interdependent nature of wartime decisions has been discussed by T. C. Schelling, *The Strategy of Conflict* (Cambridge, Mass., 1960). He insists at the same time that the type of game-theory devised by economists to illuminate the nature of economic decisions in peacetime has its strict limitations in trying to understand the nature of war.

imports brought about by the decision of a neutral people, the Americans, to enter the war as a belligerent later that same year. Their sending of troops in strength to Europe began a new transformation of the war.

Immense risks could be attached to the transfer of resources on this scale from peacetime to war purposes. The ruin and collapse of the overstrained and violently assaulted society of Russia half-way through the war proved it. This was not only a matter of the size of the transfers. It was also a question of the haste with which these movements had to be executed, under conditions the most unfavourable the enemy could devise.

War transfers conflicted, just because of their great weight and speed, with the general limits of the economy. Different limits were reached at different times. Thus in the early months of 1915 the economic problem for Great Britain was one of finding the factory and workshop capacity and the labour to equip the new armies which were springing out of the ground. In the middle years of the war it was a question of freeing shipping space and building enough ships to move troops and their constantly increasing supplies to France and other parts of the world, while maintaining essential imports and exports. Round about the same time an alarming limit appeared in a different direction. British officials in Washington and at the Treasury in 1916 were pointing out that the problem of finding dollars to purchase food and munitions in the United States was rapidly becoming insoluble. This scarcity of exchange was caused by the emergence of a highly unfavourable British balance of payments. Sooner or later it must compel the Allies to modify or scale down their military effort. So men of great ability and experience thought. The next year the United States entered the war and the limit of the dollar exchange disappeared, for the American Government stepped in to finance Allied purchases. An urgent food and shipping problem followed. Men on both sides of the Atlantic wrestled with the need to find ships to transfer two million American troops to Europe with all their equipment at a rate of 225,000 men a month,[1] in preparation for the campaigns of 1919. They were acutely conscious that they had somehow or other to maintain at the same time food imports for Europe's crowded civilian populations.

Both the scale of the wartime allocations of resources and the extraordinary conditions under which they had to be carried out, with one scarcity pursuing and conflicting with another, raised intolerable issues

---

[1] *American Industry in the War: a report of the War Industries Board* (March 1921), Bernard M. Baruch, Chairman (New York, 1941), p. 15.

of priority. Such conflicts also arose in peacetime, but they were settled in the market by the scale of preferences behind effective money demand, whether coming from consumers or producers. Within a few months of the war's beginning it was clear that no money offer on the market however high could call out supplies large or fast enough to meet the State's urgent need to train, equip and maintain by July 1915 an army of two million men.[1] But if prices on the market were to be abandoned as a means of bringing supplies and demands into balance, how was this to be done? Who was to settle the order of demands to be satisfied and the remuneration of those who did the satisfying?

9

The transfer of real resources on a vast scale was the central domestic problem of the war economy. Transfer had to take place in a particular society, with its own fixed arrangements and ways of doing things, its known traditions and values. The problem resembled to some extent that which faces countries which have undertaken to modernize their economic life. Such countries find that the transformation of their economy, for whatever purpose, requires the modification of their social and political structure also. Conversely, the desire to escape from intolerable social and political conditions may be the chief incentive towards economic change.

So it was here. Once war had begun the menace of German military power in Europe, aptly illustrated for British opinion by Belgium's swift loss of her independence in August 1914, created a political problem for which men felt that they had to find a solution at any price. All other ends in society became subordinate to the intention to survive and to win. Economic action was therefore inseparable from the general course of the war. The hopes and fears aroused by this played the main part in building up the war economy. Men and women were driven on by some of the most powerful emotions they had ever known, surrounded as they felt themselves to be by powers and intentions which they could imperfectly comprehend and measure. It is not possible to understand what was done economically, except in the light of the sense both profound and lively in 1914 and 1915 of unbroken, almost untouched, German military power not far away upon the Continent; of the growing, sombre realization of the enormous sacrifices that

[1] *Official History of the Ministry of Munitions*, vol. I(1922). p. 10.

would be necessary to break it in 1916 and 1917; of the sudden panic, still perceptible on cold paper, when the German Army turned furiously in March 1918 in a last attempt to overwhelm its enemies in the west, as it had already done in the east, and for a brief moment looked like doing so, until it appeared that this final effort had exhausted its strength. Observers at the time noted[1] in this situation of constant anxiety and emotional tension and the pressing need to seek relief from both that men and women proved capable of doing what would have been pronounced impossible in peacetime and what they were not prepared to do under other conditions or from any other motive or incentive.

The management of the war economy cannot be separated from the management of opinion. The moral tended to vary with the military factor, but it had a life of its own. To understand why many things happened, why they had to happen in that way and no other, it would be necessary to know where people picked up information, what its sources were, and what they did with it in their own minds and actions. This is partly the history of Fleet Street, the centre of the one great mass communications industry of Britain in that era. But it would also be necessary to consider other sources and sorts of opinion, not only the solid information of the day but also its myths and rumours. These latter were significant because they were an essential part of the symbolic popular thinking of the time.

Allowing for the tremendous emotional drive generated by the war, it was still true that not all things were possible. The war economy had to be carried on through the fixed channels of existing institutions or by building up, against time and difficult conditions, new institutions which would stand the strain. The two relevant organizations were the market and the State. Men had strong views in 1914 both as to the roles which these did play and those which they felt they ought to play. Industry, Whitehall and the City of London went into the war with attitudes towards economic activities powerfully influenced not so much by economics as by certain practical axioms with all the prestige of Victorian and Edwardian success behind them. They were mainly two. First, the allocation of the resources of the nation and of its incomes was the business of the market. Second, the prime economic function of the State was to maintain the value of money. This was a division of labour, it was argued, in which each institution supported

---

[1] A somewhat clinical and biological but interesting essay upon the social psychology of the war was published during the war itself, in Wilfred Trotter's *Instincts of the Herd in Peace and War* (1916).

the other. The State bought what it wanted in the market. When its wants were urgent it outbid its subjects and if necessary drove them out of the market, as it had in the Napoleonic wars. By maintaining a stable currency the State provided the market both with a standard of value and a means of payment. This made its own purchases possible.

These were the inferences of practical men from their experience rather than doctrines of the economists. British economists before 1914 were beginning to develop a critique of the market, under the influence of social reform. They seriously doubted whether the market was an altogether perfect device for satisfying wants. They wondered whether the incomes it created were either so large or so stable or so well distributed as they ought to be.[1] But these criticisms had not affected the convictions of businessmen and administrators. It was in the empirical process of tackling one by one during the war the great scarcities and the connections between them that citizens revised their views of the roles they might be called upon to play both as actors in the market and subjects of the State.

The greatest challenge to accepted views in the first half of the war came in the supply to the Army of munitions, that is artillery, small arms and ammunition of every sort. At the beginning of the war the State armed itself with money like any private citizen, which was not difficult to do, for there was idle money in the City of London, and hurried into the market. It soon became known that the service departments, the War Office and the Admiralty, were buying against one another in the classic style of competition. The economic problem seemed to be a matter of price. The higher the price and the more the freedom allowed to the contractor the greater would be the supply. Resources would follow the price. But it soon appeared in the winter of 1914–15 that supplies of guns and shells on the scale and at the time required would not be forthcoming, whatever the money offered.

If the Government of the day wished to see the industry of the country organized to meet this need and to buy the product at something less than the full scarcity price exacted by suppliers it had to act in the confidence of its own superior knowledge of the situation, arm itself with the necessary administrative powers and take away from the market as much of its function of resource allocation as might be necessary to satisfy the requirements of the armed services. Their needs would not wait.

The break with tradition came with the foundation in May 1915 of

[1] A summary of the opinions of A. C. Pigou, *Wealth and Welfare* (1912).

the Ministry of Munitions directed by Lloyd George. Almost the entire output of the engineering industry was virtually requisitioned and most of the iron and steel supplies available were turned to war purposes.[1] National factories were built, raw materials taken over and distributed at fixed price. Manufacturers were not left free to produce munitions if they pleased and at any price they could obtain. If the Army needed shell they were required to produce shell, instructed in the methods of production and paid a price based on cost.

This was the start of a munitions organization which spent a total of two thousand million pounds over a huge range of trades and industries and employed at the end of the war a staff of more than 65,000 people. But it was only a beginning of State intervention in the use of resources. The Ministry of Munitions covered one part of the Army's requirements. Many other things were wanted besides munitions. The production of munitions drew on the steel industry and the engineering trades. Other Army supplies had to come from the food industries, the textile and clothing trades, the leather, boot and shoe industries. In the long run, the Army needed to be able to feed and clothe over four million men all the year round and under a vast variety of conditions. It was an immense task to secure supplies at a price which the State was prepared to pay. The broad result was again an enforcement by Government of war priorities over all others.

To clothe the Army at the height of the war at a time when world wool production was falling, the War Office decided in June 1916 to purchase and arrange for the distribution of the entire wool clip of the British Isles. They went on to follow this up, since the British clip had satisfied only one month of the British consumption in 1915, by arranging a few months later to take over the whole of the Australian and New Zealand wool clips as well.[2] The private sale and shipment of wool in those two countries suddenly ceased by arrangement with their governments. When the wool was bought its prices were fixed and its distribution organized according to priorities laid down by public authority. It went first to Government contractors for the war, secondly to manufacturers for export, thirdly to essential home requirements.

Somewhat similar steps were taken by the War Office in the same year, when supplies of leather and hides for boots and shoes were growing scarce. The British boot and shoe industry was trying at the

[1] E. M. H. Lloyd, *Experiments in State Control* (*Carnegie Economic and Social History of the World War*) (1924), pp. 23–5.
[2] E. M. H. Lloyd, *op. cit.*, pp. 118–19.

time to fill vast orders not only for the British but also for the Russian, Italian, Belgian and Serbian armies. Stocks of leather and the entire output of the tanneries at home were requisitioned at fixed prices. The import of hides was organized on Government account.[1] The State's officials, who were usually businessmen taken temporarily into Government employment, arranged the distribution and fixed priorities for use.

The allocation of resources by central authority continued to extend throughout the war, under the pressure of the lack of shipping and foreign exchange for imports. From 1914 to 1917 the chief economic task of the French and British governments was to find the arms to match their military manpower. Their munitions effort reached its maximum in the middle years of the war. Mines and factories, fully organized, provided the overwhelming masses of material, deceptively victory-winning, which were used to try to break the deadlock on the Western Front, in the unsuccessful campaigns of 1916 and 1917 on the Somme and at Passchendaele. Every contemporary observer testifies to the influence which war production was by this time beginning to have on the military conduct of the war. It was a phenomenon in itself, even if transient.[2] But by this time, partly as a result of the success of munitions output, partly as a result of the losses of men, the balance of resources was changing. From 1917 on the manpower of Great Britain and France was waning. Their soldiers were, however, relatively well supplied. When the United States came into the war in April 1917 it brought new and large armies. These were dependent for an important part of their supplies in 1918 on the munitions industries of the Western allies.

By that time the business of central resource allocation had become

[1] See especially, in the *Carnegie Economic and Social History of the War*, the study of control at the War Office and Ministry of Food by E. M. H. Lloyd quoted above, Salter's 'Allied Shipping Control', Beveridge's 'Food Control', and H. D. Henderson's 'Cotton Control Board'.

[2] A tank officer, D. G. Browne, so describes the ten-mile long bombardment which opened the third battle of Ypres (Passchendaele) in 1917; '. . . . the apotheosis of the artillery barrage, although no one suspected it then: the greatest blast of gun-fire ever concentrated at once on any battlefield, and, so far at least as the British Army was concerned, the last of its kind.' He and his tank-crew were so fascinated by the spectacle that they forgot for the moment to start the tank. (Guy Chapman, *Vain Glory* (1937), p. 452). The use of artillery to break up field fortifications was a passing influence, because the aeroplane, radio and above all the tank were on the point of restoring some degree of movement to the war and compensating for the absence of men. Winston Churchill, when Minister of Munitions, applied a brief but significant cost-effectiveness analysis to the use of tanks at the battle of Cambrai in November 1917 (*History of the Ministry of Munitions*, vol. 2 (1921), Part 1, pp. 99–100).

international. This was a singular and ironic development. European nations were not used to working together. Everything in their historical traditions and a great deal in their physical and social conditions in the early years of the present century forbade it. There was much talk of unity of decision and action between the Allies which was in the nature of propaganda. It was designed to reassure civilians and soldiers under stress. The war started with no common policies at all, military, political or economic, between the Allies. It was only gradually that joint working measures were concerted out of sheer necessity. They were accepted with foreboding and reluctance.

With Great Britain's industrial resources, command of finance and uninvaded territory, it was natural that in the first half of the war, before Russia went out of it in 1917 and the United States of America came in, she should become the chief supplier of munitions to the Allies. Large credits were placed by the British Government at the disposal of the Russian, Italian, Belgian, Serbian and Portuguese governments.[1] As British war production grew, large quantities of munitions were supplied by her out of her surplus. She also became a great purchaser in the United States on Allied account, long before that country became a belligerent.

There was a great deal to be discussed about supply transactions on such a scale. This was done to an increasing extent in 1915 and 1916 by conference between the Allies—there were more than thirty such conferences, often of much current importance, between August 1914 and March 1917, usually called in London, Paris or other French cities[2]—and by the formation of *ad hoc* administrative bodies. But as the war went on the difficulties increased. They compelled a more permanent and all-embracing organization. The events of 1917 especially forced on a change. The unrestricted submarine campaign and the consequent world shortage of ships and supplies brought home to the three European Allies, Britain, France and Italy, in the most unwelcome way, their interdependence. This made necessary schemes to economize both shipping tonnage and materials. The withdrawal of Russia from the war in the same year assisted the trend. With her increasing military and administrative confusion, that country had become a highly inconstant factor in the calculation of requirements.[3]

[1] *History of the Ministry of Munitions*, vol. 2 (1921), Part VIII, p. 47.
[2] *History of the Ministry of Munitions*, vol. 2 (1921), Part VIII, pp. 86–7.
[3] An example arose early in 1917. A statement of required war materials was put forward by the Russian Government totalling thirteen million tons of munitions. Experts who analysed this figure decided, after a scrutiny of Russian ports

At the same time, Britain and France had to prepare to meet the demands of an American army in Europe. It was expected to rise to eighty divisions in 1919. This could not be done without joint planning. The movement and supply of so vast an army could not be arranged without affecting the shipping and import programmes of all the Allies.

It is hard to understand the dimensions of the problem and the magnitude of the stakes which were being played for without figures. When the shipping position was examined in March 1918 it was found that tonnage under Allied control, excluding American, fell short by some ten million tons of the import requirements of the three European Allies, Britain, France and Italy.[1] But British imports included high-priority munitions and munitions material to an even greater quantity than foodstuffs. A most serious conflict developed between the movement of troops and munitions, especially from the United States, and the elementary need of food for the civil population. In the light of what was known or could be estimated, a decision was taken, just before the war came to an end, to give priority for six months to munitions over food.[2] This was in preparation for the campaigns of 1919 and for the leading part which the American armies were expected to play.

The urgent need to prepare and keep moving elaborate programmes for shipping, food and munitions accounted for the coming into existence in the last phase of the war of international bodies such as the Inter-Allied Munitions Council, the Allied Maritime Transport Council, the Inter-Allied Food Council and their subordinate committees. The initiative of the Americans, their national habit of thinking about resources on a Continental scale, even their dislike and distrust of Europeans, played a leading part in the building up of these organizations. This would presumably have gone much further had the war continued. As it was, the international organizations had a short if crowded life. They did not play, however, either in the transition from war to peace or later the creative role which some men, including some of those who had worked hard to construct them, had hoped.[3] For when men became sick of blood and the end of the war came into sight

---

and railways and other relevant conditions, that four and a half million tons would be an optimistic estimate of the amount which could be absorbed by Russia in a year (*op. cit.*, vol. 2, Part VIII, p. 29).

[1] *op. cit.*, vol. 2 (1921), Part VIII, p. 36.
[2] *op. cit.*, vol. 2 (1921), Part VIII, p. 36.
[3] There were traces of this hope on the American as well as on the British and the French side, among the temporary war administrators. Arthur Salter and Jean Monnet became examples of the influence of the hope in Europe.

the international economic institutions came to symbolize for some that practicable unity which civilized Europe had never known, but had, after all of its great wars, always longed for. They were too clearly, however, the instruments of a transient purpose to survive, once conditions of war scarcity had passed or were seen to be about to pass. In bringing them into existence, men had done from fear of an enemy what they would not otherwise yield even to their own self-interest. Once the danger of a German conquest was over, Americans and Europeans alike willingly turned their back on economic arrangements which they had regarded a short while before as their life-line.

10

The British war economy was essentially a hybrid. It combined features of what was often called at the time war socialism, by which seems to have been meant simply the central allocation of resources, with other characteristics, inherited from the powerful capitalistic and market-using economy of prewar days. If central allocation was almost wholly new, so there was much that was new about the market and the conditions under which industrial managements and labour had to work in it. This was largely due to the vast scale on which public finance was deployed in order to hold out incentives to both capital and labour adequate to attract them into war production and away from the satisfaction of civilian demand.

Total Government expenditure as a proportion of gross national product was relatively modest before 1914.[1] From the first day of the war it began to grow, until the public sector of the economy, that part of it which existed to satisfy public wants, came to dominate all others.

Gross public expenditure on the fighting services in current prices rose from £361,156,272 in the budget year April 1914–April 1915 to a total of £1,415,523,534 in the comparable period for 1918–19. Gross public expenditure of all kinds, including sums for loans to allies, food, ships and so forth, increased over the same financial years from £559,638,585 to £3,146,475,568.[2] As early as October 1915, when a strong dispute was going on between leading members of the Govern-

[1] Not more than thirteen per cent of the whole. This measurement includes transfer payments, involving payments for past wars, among Government expenditures (A. T. Peacock and J. Wiseman, *op. cit.*, p. 166).

[2] Sir B. Mallet and C. O. George, *British Budgets 1913–1921* (1929), Table III on pp. 392–3. These were amounts voted and expended, not voted only.

ment whether the country would afford an Army of seventy divisions and meet at the same time the needs of her fleet and her allies, a young Financial Secretary to the Treasury, Edwin Montagu, made a name for himself nationally by informing the House of Commons that every citizen ought to be prepared to spend one half of his income on the war.[1] By the end of the war total public expenditure on current account, which in 1914 had been running at a little under one-twelfth of the national income, had in fact risen approximately to one-half of all incomes. Most of this expense was war caused, directly or indirectly.[2]

Public spending on this scale reversed the prewar trend of the trade cycle. The first impact of the war on employment was to throw men out of work, as markets and credit became disrupted. Then a huge new effective demand, expressed in Government contracts and financed by generous advances from the banks, which lent money both to Government to buy and to industry to supply, transformed the situation. Unemployment in those of the trade unions which collected the numbers of their unemployed members reached about seven per cent late in 1914. There was some serious distress in these early months. Then unemployment sank to boom levels, to less than one man in a hundred, and remained there for the rest of the war.

The years 1915 to 1918 represented in the history of the British economy a new cycle of activity. This contrasted strongly with the flagging industrial employment of the period after May 1913.[3] It was also unlike the prewar boom. The industrial expansion of 1905–13 had developed out of a great phase of home and foreign investment by private persons. Foreign lending and export business generated at that time personal consumption and capital spending at home, as orders and money flowed in from abroad. The wartime industrial expansion of 1915–18 had a very different root, but a similar mode of growth. It arose out of public expenditure and the growth of production to satisfy it. The public sector of the economy had been increasing in size before the war. Now it took an immensely sharp upward turn. As contracts were placed and money flowed out into the pockets of contractors and their salaried and wage-earning employees two things

[1] S. D. Waley, *Edwin Montagu* (1964), p. 78.
[2] E. Victor Morgan, *Studies in British Financial Policy 1914–1925* (1952), p. 105.
[3] See Wesley Mitchell's description, The International Pattern of Business Cycles, 22nd Session, International Institute of Statistics, the Hague, 1934, quoted in W. A. Brown, *The International Gold Standard Reinterpreted*, vol. 1 (New York, 1940), p. 179.

began to happen. A wide movement of labour into the war industries set in and prices started to rise.

The labour market remained technically free, although it came under increasing regulation as the war went on. Men retained to begin with the right to choose their occupation, as also to spend their incomes as they pleased. The first effect of Government spending and the mass creation of new incomes which it produced was to transform this market.

In July 1914 there were some 13,886,000 occupied persons[1] in Great Britain. Of these, 3,276,000 or about twenty-four per cent of the whole were women and girls. In four years of war, 4,896,000 men and boys, or forty-six per cent of all persons earning an income in July 1914, left civil life for the armed services, mostly for the Army. This was an enormous drain on the manpower of the nation, although less heavy than some other countries had to sustain in the war. But despite it, there were still 13,015,000 persons employed in July 1918. The net loss in occupied population was no more than 871,000 persons. The total occupied population, the producers of goods and services of all kinds, had been well maintained.

How was this done? Contemporary opinion was most impressed by the flow into industry of an additional 1,659,000 women and girls. It was certainly one of the most striking features of British society in the war. By the summer of 1918 women and girls, of whom about 400,000 had been domestic servants before the war, formed thirty-eight per cent of the whole labour force of the country. But more surprising in some respects was the movement into industry of an even larger number of men and boys, including many who had left industry before the war or were newcomers to it. They numbered 2,366,000[2] How far the women and the girls or for that matter the men and the boys were as efficient as those who had joined the Army, it is impossible to say. Taking old age, youth and simple inexperience into account, it is probable that productivity per person fell, but not by so large an amount as might perhaps have been expected, considering the size of the movement of labour.

[1] 'Occupied population', for Board of Trade statistical purposes, included all main groups of workers in the United Kingdom, except those engaged in agriculture in Ireland, domestic servants, dressmakers in very small workshops, some minor forms of employment, and all those working at sea, whether in the Merchant Navy or the fishing industry. Employers and persons working on their own account were also excluded (*History of the Ministry of Munitions*, vol. VI (1922), p. 4).

[2] *History of the Ministry of Munitions*, vol. VI, p. 19.

Even more remarkable than the general movement into new occupations was the concentration of labour in the great war industries. The munitions demand of Government in industry fell mostly upon the chemical and the metal trades. But the coal-mining, wool, clothing and food trades tended also to be drawn into the public sector. Of all the persons employed in production or distribution, those working for the British and Allied governments rose from one fourth of the whole in July 1915 to about one-half in July 1918. In industrial employment the concentration was even higher. Approximately three-fifths of the staff of all industrial concerns were by July 1918 employed on Government orders.[1] By the end of the war some 3,400,000 people were engaged directly or indirectly on the production of munitions. In Government establishments in the metal and chemical trades, which were the chief munitions trades, there were 2,046,000 men and boys and 825,000 women and girls, or a total of 2,871,000 people at work. They formed more than a third of the workers in all the industries of the country.[2]

This was the labour force which made possible the vast munitions programmes of the later years of the war. These reached a climax in 1917 and 1918. In the latter year the programme for guns and gun ammunition, already great, was half as large again as in 1917, the aeroplane programme had been tripled, the programme for chemical shell was two and a half times the 1917 programme. The Admiralty shipbuilding programme in the same year was doubled. Since purchases from the United States and Canada were by that time being curtailed to save foreign exchange, almost the whole burden of these programmes had to be met out of national production. At a time when it was expected that ten million tons of steel would be available in British industry in 1918 (the actual amount forthcoming was considerably less) they were allocated as follows:[3]

Admiralty (including shipbuilding)	2,000,000
Munitions (including 700,000 tons for Allies)	5,400,000
War Office, India Office, etc.	600,000
Steel for France (imported from U.S.A.)	500,000
Construction, machinery, civilian services	1,500,000
	10,000,000

The dominance of war production was complete.

[1] *History of the Ministry of Munitions*, vol. VI (1922), p. 44.
[2] *History of the Ministry of Munitions*, vol. VI (1922), p. 63.
[3] *History of the Ministry of Munitions*, vol. II (1921), pp. 94–5.

II

Something resembling a new society had developed in Great Britain in the short space of four and a half years. It was formed of new groups of people. The four most important groups in it were the fighting men, the munition workers who kept them supplied with weapons and necessaries of war, the export workers who maintained exports for the sake of indispensable imports of food, materials and munitions, and the small but powerful circle of administrators and politicians who directed the whole. The rest of the nation fell into a residual group being without obvious war functions. Such was an industrial society fully organized for war according to the conditions of the early years of the present century.

The swift assumption of new, strange roles by a multitude of men and women was made possible by a sudden revolution in social values and attitudes. All public ends were resolved temporarily into one, the winning of victory in the war. Both State and economy became the servants to that purpose. The impression common at the time that the new state of society had been created by Government was an illusion. A powerful democratic State was certainly necessary for its creation. But so, too, was a new kind of social compact, a crude temporary national agreement upon ends and means. The fears and the hopes of the war, the risks of the time, provided the mould in which this was formed.

To very many people this emergence of a sense of common national purpose was a welcome relief. They compared it with what had seemed to them in peacetime the confusion and conflict of political aims, and in particular with the sharp class divisions and the national industrial disputes of the years immediately before the war. The unity was real, especially in the early years of the war. The sense of nationality had temporarily risen above and submerged the sense of class. But the experience of 1914–18 demonstrated that a high degree of self- and mutual-deception entered into this intense and novel state of mind.

Social emotions, including some of the most gentle and refined as well as the most savage and primitive, drove people along. But the drives of organized society at an advanced stage tend to express themselves in terms of money. The most powerful motives at work were not measurable in cash. When they were so measurable, it soon became clear that the wartime society was still in its main structure, its underlying values and standing dilemmas, the society of Edwardian and

Georgian Britain. No doubt it was in process of rapid transformation, but it displayed the same differences of income and property, status and authority, as before the war. It also suffered from the same profound sense of insecurity and injustice, hard to define but sharply felt by many people, which had generated the social politics of the prewar decade.

The tough and enduring quality of industrial problems made itself felt early, partly as a result of the munitions effort, partly of something else which went with it. This was a change in the measuring rod by which motives were measured. The altering value of money was as characteristic of the war years as the central allocation of resources. Both occurred for the same practical reasons. To make the war economy expand and grow fast, it became vital for Government to take away from the market many of the functions which it possessed of distributing and rewarding resources. It was also necessary to use money in a way and to an extent which was completely inconsistent with the maintenance of its former value. Inflation became a weapon of war.

In the early days of the war it was fashionable to deny that inflation existed. But in the sense of a tendency for the volume of money incomes to grow faster than the quantity of goods on offer, it was there from the first. This was so, as soon as the resources thrown out of use by the outbreak of war had been taken back into production. The rapid increase of effective money demand at that time was a consequence of the financing of the war and of the speed with which public spending was turned into military channels. Soldiers in constantly growing numbers had to be paid and soldiers' wives given a separation allowance. At the same time, in order to arm the soldiers with a mass of equipment such as no previous army had possessed, labour and industrial managements, even where they fell under strict Government control, had to be given financial incentives. These again had to be sufficient to bring them whole-heartedly into the war effort. It was necessary not only to pay for goods on the market and for the labour and organizing ability to make them, but also to advance capital out of public funds as an essential part of war contracts. The weapons and war material required were often of a type that demanded new equipment to produce them or to manufacture them on the requisite scale. Much of this capital equipment would be valueless in peacetime. Manufacturers could not be expected to shoulder the whole risk of installing and housing it.

Industrially the war was a boom publicly financed. The leading sector of the economy was war industry, just as other booms at other times had arisen out of demand in export markets or from home demand for houses and durable consumer goods. It was subject to the usual limitations of a rapid upturn in production. The first of these was that the volume of outlay on new investment must not exceed the quantity of new savings available for that purpose out of personal incomes. If it did, then the banks would have to be called in to make up the difference. The resulting inflation would be, at least to begin with, in some sort of rough proportion to the overemployment of capital and labour. This sort of inflationary economy, with both Government and industry borrowing actively from the banks, began to grow swiftly after the first year of war. It moved towards its full height between September 1915 and June 1917, as war production was built up to the physical limits of manpower and industrial capacity.

There were, of course, other elements besides the influence of heavy public spending at work in the great rise of prices. The limitation of imports in a country where the general standard of life depended on them and the huge pressure of military demand on resources played their part. But the trend of public expenditure was a powerful influence. The official index of the cost of living showed in the autumn of 1917 that the prices of all the goods in most common demand were on their way towards doubling compared with July 1914. A year later they had more than doubled.[1] This brought home to the least observant the reality of inflation in the midst of the boom.

The first of the British war inflations of the present century was relatively mild compared with some later European inflations. But it gave rise to much discussion in 1916 and 1917 among those who were not too busy with the day's work to think about public affairs. The mere existence of a tendency for money to lose its value raised first-class issues.

Prices rising fast were to the injury of the interests of the Government waging the war as well as of private citizens. This development greatly concerned the Government's financial advisers. Their preoccupation with monetary stability and their conflicts of opinion have left many traces in the official and personal papers of the time. Official anxiety was connected with the existence in the City of London of strong banking conventions, of which the Bank of England was the

[1] The index rose by eighty points in the first three years of war, by another twenty or twenty-five points in the next twelve months. See the index reproduced in E. V. Morgan, *Studies in British Financial Policy 1914–1925* (1952), p. 284.

repository. These laid down what ought to be done by financial institutions in the money market in the inflationary stages of a boom to restore what was deemed to be the rational relation between the amount of credit and currency in use and the real resources of the country. There was also a well-established and highly stable British monetary standard. Of this, in the last resort, the Chancellor of the Exchequer, acting for the Government of the day, was the guardian.

What men close to the Government feared was that the constant growth of State borrowing at home and abroad for the purpose of fighting the war would end by undermining both the public credit and the value of money. But out of their discussions no first-class analysis of the new war economy arose. Policy, both of the banks and the Treasury, remained without theoretical guidance and had only a set of precepts. These were of more than doubtful use under the changed conditions. How could one expect the central bank to reduce the volume of effective demand in peacetime style by throwing men out of work? For the Bank of England to behave so in the middle of the munitions drive would have been a novel kind of treason. Nor could the Chancellor of the Exchequer be expected in wartime to press economic considerations upon the Cabinet with the same vigour as in peace. Other ministers, more closely engaged with the military and political struggle, might and did retort that monetary disequilibrium was the very least of the troubles they foresaw. Besides, as they pointed out, there were other measures, more easily taken in war than in peace, which were in some sense an alternative to traditional procedures.

The public and official discussion of inflation illustrated most vividly the difficulties of a society used to measuring motives in money and to trust to market forces to get things done, in adjusting to war conditions its outlook and its style of action. Some inflation of money incomes could be defended with great force as inevitable. Even the most effective taxation could not possibly keep up with war expenditure. But in addition a certain measure of inflation and monetary instability appeared definitely favourable to the war's economic effort. There were two reasons for this. First, the free creation of money incomes, even of incomes which fell a little in real value every twelve months, formed a system of rewards and incentives necessary to bring over industrial managements and labour into war production. The war was not being fought by slaves accustomed to obey orders and to do as little as possible. An all-out effort was wanted. To persuade men and women to change their occupations and pace of working they had to be addressed in the language they understood. That language comprehended many other things besides money, but it certainly included a wage and a profit. Second, if a free choice of occupations was one of the bases on which the war effort was bring mounted, then the logical correlative of that must be, it appeared, a certain freedom to spend as one pleased the income earned in the chosen occupation. It was only gradually, as war scarcities multiplied, that it became clear that a complete organization of industrial society for war was deeply hostile to these assumptions.

Much of the debate took place in the first half of the war. At that time the exchange of peacetime for wartime occupations and of one income for another was still new. It was also the period when a nation, many of whom had always lived on an extremely poor standard and had seen no improvement in it for some years before the war, were spending their money on consumer goods which were still uncontrolled.

Inflation was the price that had to be paid by a commercially minded people, accustomed to dominate their Government rather than be dominated by it and hostile to the direction by the State of labour and capital, for bringing supplies and demands into balance. The creation of the great war sector, in an economy which in 1914 had no war industry worth speaking of, was its achievement. But the price of that achievement was extremely high. It would have been less wasteful and less unjust to have retained the system of money incentives and rewards, while adopting deliberate and drastic methods of taking away from the citizen, by taxation and other devices, part of his money income as he earned it, as was done in a later war.[1] To some extent this was done. Many controls both of capital and labour were, in fact, adopted. The windfall profits to which the system gave rise were partially annexed by the State, from 1915 on, through the Excess Profits Duty. But this was done to pacify working-class opinion, justifiably angry at the amount of money being made out of the war, rather than out of any clear vision of the workings of inflation or of possible ways of controlling it.

Inflation put up the cost of the war to the nation and created an internal war debt larger than was necessary. It placed the main rewards in the hands of entrepreneurs and left the wages of the wage-earner chasing the cost of living throughout most of the war. The discontent

---

[1] This was the criticism of the economist, J. M. Keynes, looking back upon 1914–18 from the beginning of a second war inflation (*How to Pay for the War* (1940), ch. IX).

caused by high prices, especially for food, led to serious popular discontent at a critical phase of the war, in 1917.

If aggregate working-class consumption was surprisingly well maintained, this was due to two circumstances, neither of which were among the objects of public policy. On the one hand, the war created conditions of full employment, favourable to continuous earning at rising levels of pay. On the other, the shipping shortage after 1916, due partly to German sinkings, partly to the worldwide scale of military operations, drove home the lesson that war production must be pursued at the expense of civilian consumption. This applied especially to imports. The price control and rationing schemes which came in for clothing and foodstuffs took away from the higher incomes the advantage which inflation had given them. They enforced some sacrifice all round. The success of British agriculture in raising its output was another among a coincidence of contingencies which helped to correct the consumption situation. The year 1917 was otherwise the worst of the war for the civilian and industrial population. Inflation was one of the strong causes of its troubled state of mind.

12

To manage an economy is to do so on all of its great sides, whether the decision taken is to control or to let alone. From this point of view, the handling of British war finance between 1914 and 1918 was wasteful and ineffective. In offering money incentives to war production it acted without due measure. It allowed the resulting inflation of incomes to have too uncontrolled an impact, until late in the war, upon relations in industry and between the different classes of the nation. Inflation raised important questions of social equity. They were dealt with too late and with little sense of the interrelations of things, until it was found by experience that the great war scarcities could not be overcome so long as people thought themselves to be unjustly treated. They would not then give of their best.

The influence of unstable prices and uncertain money incomes was strongly felt by a society already in transition when the war broke out. After 1906 a rapidly growing trade-union movement had begun to challenge the whole conventional structure of industrial wages.[1] From August 1914 the war's devouring need for manpower began to raise the

[1] Henry Clay, *The Problem of Industrial Relations* (1929), ch. 1.

scarcity value of labour higher than ever before in the nation's history. Once unemployment disappeared the bargaining power of industrial labour was relatively great. By the spring of 1915 this was clearly apparent in the demand for skilled men for munitions work. By that time the first rise in cost of living and the early windfall profits had had time to make themselves felt and observed. Discussions took place at the Treasury[1] in February and March 1915 between members of the Government headed by Lloyd George and representatives of the trade unions. They concerned the terms on which the latter would agree to take part in a greatly enlarged munitions effort, not only for that spring but for the duration of the war. The unions in the munitions industries, in particular the engineers, agreed to waive their rules, which protected the interest of the skilled worker in his trade by regulating entry to the trade and output, on condition that excessive war profits should be taxed.

These discussions and this agreement, translated into practical terms by the Munitions of War Act, 1915, by the introduction of an Excess Profits Duty in the September budget and by a gradual change in industry at shopfloor level turned out to have a significance well beyond that of a bargain over restrictive practices on the shop floor. The unions henceforward stood in a special relation to Government. Backed up by a general popular feeling that the war must be won, the pact inaugurated a temporary but extremely effective wartime working arrangement between the unions, industrial managements and the State. This became the firm foundation in industrial relations of the war effort, the indispensable industrial underpinning of the wartime political coalitions.

The State's role of intervention in industry continued so long as the war was on. The vast expansion of the labour force, achieved by handing over much of the work of skilled men to less skilled men and to women, was supervised jointly by Government, employees and employers. To keep pace with prices and the cost of living, a long series of official awards raised wages on a national basis. This was done in frank disregard of many old regional and group differences. The war brought a new authoritarian element into the distribution of wealth which was not there before. The State also found itself called upon to set new

[1] The discussions of 1915 and the subsequent working of the Munitions Acts were described later by G. D. H. Cole, who was adviser to the Amalgamated Society of Engineers at the time, in his *Trade Unionism and Munitions* (*Carnegie Economic and Social History of the War*), 1923. The official record of these affairs is in the first volume of the *History of the Ministry of Munitions* (1922).

standards in health, industrial feeding and welfare, not least where women were concerned.[1]

If the State's powers in industry increased, so did those of the unions. Trade-union membership rose, in the war as before it, and for the same reasons. Continuous earnings provided the subscription and a rising cost of living the cause. The change was more than a strengthening of collective-bargaining organizations. The status of the worker, as well as his wage, was enhanced by the wartime demand for his services. This was seen on the shop floor. Full employment and the rapid influx of new labour increased the authority of the shop steward and the workshop committee. At the other end of the scale the alteration of social values was seen in the rise of trade unionists, such as Arthur Henderson and George Barnes, into the coalition administrations and the War Cabinet. They became men holding office and some power.

It was said by an acute observer of British industrial relations, G. D. H. Cole, that the war changed nothing basically in them. This was in a sense true. But the war forced important developments in a system of relationships which was already on the move. The institutional assumptions of prewar wage theory were gradually being eroded. The theory was that in a highly traditional system of wage rates important but relatively minor changes had to be made from time to time by collective bargaining. All that appeared necessary was to strengthen the weaker bargainer. This was done by the formation of unions and after 1906 by new law favouring their activities. But the boom of 1909–13 and the fierce industrial bargaining which followed had begun the process of sweeping away in a drastic fashion Victorian standards of industrial remuneration. The war carried the erosion of the structure much further by State intervention and collective bargaining on a national scale. Both arose out of the underlying scarcity of labour, the basis of all these changes.

13

The maximum domestic effort of the British economy between 1914 and 1918 was not enough. One-fifth of the resources needed to fight

[1] There is an enormous mass of information, from the official side, about these aspects of wartime policy in the fifth and sixth volumes of the *History of the Ministry of Munitions*. For a lawyer's view of the wage awards, Lord Amulree, *Industrial Arbitration in Great Britain* (1929). See also Henry Clay's studies of wage structure and wage policy in the war quoted above.

the war had to be purchased overseas, mainly from North America.[1] Canadian and American supplies were always marginal compared with home munitions production. They were also expensive. But they formed the margin on which it might be said the war was won. The importance of North American supply can be measured from the costs and risks Great Britain was willing to suffer in order to obtain it.

The war in the West was between industrial societies. It was one of the advantages which the naval power, Britain, possessed over her antagonist, the land power, Germany, that she was able to cut the other off from the resources of the world. She did more; she diverted them to her own war effort. This position was only gradually achieved and not without heavy sacrifice.[2]

When the war began the most powerful of all industrial states, the United States of America, deeply divided in her European political sympathies and preoccupied with her own development, declared her neutrality. The war in Europe proved, however, more hostile to the traditional conception of neutrality than any previous conflict. This was because in the nineteenth century, with the industrialization of western and central Europe, men had begun the process of knitting the whole earth together by trade, transport and investment. The economic unification of the world, added and adding to the new productive powers of Europe itself, helped to make possible a war of material on a prodigious scale. It also threw obvious difficulties in the way of peoples and governments anxious to avoid becoming a party to the European dispute.

But to begin with all was well. No serious obstacle arose to prevent the United States continuing to trade with Great Britain, except for the cruiser operations of the early days of the war and the irksomeness to American producers and merchants of British naval control in its efforts to maintain a distant blockade of Germany. American trade with Britain had always been considerable. British citizens in 1914 owned large investment properties in both Canada and the United States and made large imports from them. As a market for British goods, the United States was rather less important than Germany.

The prewar pattern of activity, after the first interruptions, was soon

[1] A. J. Brown, *Applied Economics: Aspects of the World Economy in War and Peace* 1947), p. 52.
[2] Nothing was said in the lectures on which this paper is founded of the extremely important and complicated story of the blockade of Germany, or of the counter-war against British trade and sea communications which was Germany's answer.

transformed by a colossal demand for war material from Europe. Great Britain was the chief consumer. Munitions purchased in North America were costly compared with British prices and costs, but there was no doing without them. Britain became largely dependent on the United States for propellants and explosives, shell steel, copper, aluminium, railway material, machine tools, farm machinery, but especially gun ammunition, above all the heavy artillery ammunition which played such a dominating part in the Western war.[1] Great Britain also became a big purchaser on behalf of her allies. Her position as the dispenser of credit to Russia, Serbia and Italy, her investments and credit in America, even allowed her to exercise some control over their buying.

The American economy was of huge capacity. It had been moving through a period of strong growth before 1914, although the boom of that phase of expansion was over when the war broke out. Under the influence of European purchases, together with the many opportunities for investment latent in the country, temporarily unemployed resources came into employment again. The years 1914–18 saw the number of people out of work fall. Gross national product, output per head and consumer expenditure all increased. The effect of British and other war demands were particularly marked in the most developed part of the American economy, the manufacturing and mining districts of the eastern seaboard between the Potomac river on the south and the Ohio on the west.[2] A war economy was beginning to grow strongly in the United States even before she entered the war. With the communication of European war demand to North America, to Canada and the United States, went the spread of war inflation. Even before the American declaration of war the cost of living became the subject of complaint and public inquiry in New England.[3] But it was not until after that date, well on in 1918, that American society and Government found themselves facing the issues of priority in production and of

[1] In December 1917 British expenditure in the United States on munitions account included fifty per cent of total British copper requirements, fifty to sixty per cent of propellants, ninety-two per cent of acetone, eighty-three per cent of sulphur, forty per cent of aluminium and so forth (*History of the Ministry of Munitions* vol. II, Part III, p. 82).

[2] The Mid-West also contributed importantly to Allied supplies of foodstuffs and munitions. It was said of the Anglo-French loan raised in the United States in October 1915 that sixty per cent of the proceeds were spent in the Mississippi Valley (T. W. Lamont, *Henry P. Davison a biography* (New York, 1933), p. 186.

[3] Report of the Commission on the Cost of Living (State of Massachusetts), February 1917, *Edwin F. Gay Collection* (Hoover Memorial Library, California).

public intervention in the economy which Great Britain had had to begin to resolve several years before.[1]

The place of the American economy in the history of the years 1914–18 needs to be looked at in relation to the wide-ranging economic war. Both of the contending parties tried to wrest into a shape to suit their warlike designs the pattern of world trade which had sprung up mainly since 1870. This pattern was largely centred on Europe. The Allies' naval blockade of the central empires was pursued with increasing severity through the early and middle years of the war. It was intended to cut off their opponents from the food and raw material of the rest of the world. Against this, the Germans mounted their submarine war, a counter-blockade directed especially at the food and munitions ships moving on the North Atlantic. It was aimed to secure that if Germany was isolated from world trade, so should her enemies be. The economic struggle, carried on by both protagonists with a growing disregard of neutral opinion and international law, justified by both out of necessity, brought the great neutral, the Government of the United States, into dispute with the Governments of Great Britain and Germany from the first.

The North Atlantic food and munitions trade possessed a complicated and dangerous administrative and political history. This was especially so in 1916 and 1917, when the war was becoming one of exhaustion and both sides were resorting to every weapon to hasten the end. American exasperation with British methods of controlling international trade in the interests of blockade rose higher than British public opinion has cared to remember. Americans perhaps have forgotten how thoroughly they themselves, once in the war, entered into the spirit of a game they had formerly disapproved. As for the Germans, they had to decide whether they would let themselves be slowly strangled or whether they would resort indiscriminately to submarine war—defying in doing so the United States—to force an end to the

---

[1] A sketch of these problems as they arose is to be found in Bernard M. Baruch, *The Public Years* (1960), ch. 3 and 4; more than a sketch in *American Industry in the War: a report of the War Industries Board* (Washington, 1921). Baruch was chairman of the War Industries Board which settled war-production priorities. Much valuable information about its activities is to be found in the Bernard M. Baruch Collection at the Firestone Library, Princeton University. The Harvard economic historian, Edwin F. Gay, who had first-hand knowledge of the wartime economic controls in Washington, proposed at one time to write a history of them. It is unfortunate that the plan was abandoned. Some of the material he collected survives in the Edwin F. Gay Collection, in the Hoover Memorial Library, Palo Alto, California.

struggle. Or would they, as a third alternative, attempt by diplomatic means to enlist the interest of the American Government in general peace negotiations, with the threat of unrestricted submarine war in the background?[1] What in the light of the situation which existed early in 1917 was really possible between Germany and the United States we cannot here decide. It is enough to record that when the American Government declared war that April, following renewed German attacks on shipping, it was not only the security or the value of the war trade which brought them in. The decision taken was on a balance of considerations. In its general nature, it resembled the British decision of August 1914. The United States came in because the balance of power in Europe and the issues which hung upon it proved to be far more important to her than American public opinion had believed possible three years before. It is true that American economic development since 1880 had done much to bring the country to the point where a world role in politics, however novel, came to seem to American judgement unavoidable. If the United States intervened in the European war, she cast herself irrevocably for no less a part.[2]

The need of North American resources profoundly altered the international economic position of Great Britain. Two countries, Canada and the United States, which before the war supplied a little more than one-fifth of British imports, were by 1918 supplying nearly a half. Purchases from the United States were in that year nearly forty per cent of all British purchases overseas.[3] Both were countries with which Britain before the war ran an adverse balance, importing more from them than she exported to them. The balance could be looked after by the favourable account with other countries. The swift rise of a large debit balance with North America, especially the United States, combined with the wartime reduction of British exports to most markets to produce an acute payments problem. How to meet it soon became a major question in the management of the war economy.

In October 1916, when the tremendous battles of men and material

---

[1] The debate in the circles of the Imperial German Government late in 1916 and early in 1917 is described in K. E. Birnbaum, *Peace Moves and U-boat Warfare* (University of Stockholm Studies in History: Stockholm, 1958).

[2] The fullest discussion of the motives and actions of the Wilson administration between the outbreak of the war in Europe and April 1917 is in Arthur Link's *Wilson: the Struggle for Neutrality, 1914–1915* (1960), and *Wilson: Confusion and Crisis, 1915–1916* (1964).

[3] E. V. Morgan, *Studies in British Financial Policy 1914–25* (1952), p. 310 and Table 43.

on the Western Front were making American supplies constantly more necessary and more expensive, British and French financial experts reported to the Chancellor of the Exchequer on the scale of the dollar problem. In the five months from May to September 1916 British expenditures in the United States had amounted to $1,038,000,000. They had been running at the rate of $207,500,000 a month. These expenses had been met as to three-fifths by the sale in the United States of gold or British-held American investments. The other two-fifths had been covered by American loans. In the coming six months, from October 1916 to March 1917, dollar expenditure was expected to rise at a conservative estimate to $81,500,000 or $250,000,000 a month. Only one-sixth of this could be met with gold or bonds. The rest must be paid out of loans. By this time, of the £5,000,000 which the Treasury had to find every day for the war, nearly £2,000,000 had to be found somehow or other in America. The doubt was not whether the money could be borrowed but whether it could be had in time. Some money could always be discovered somewhere, but there was a difference between that and meeting the whole demands of the war.[1] If payments could not be met, then the military operations of the Allies in Europe would have to be curtailed, with what effects on the outcome of the war could not be foreseen.

No contrast could have been stronger than that between the tone of this debate on the dollar problem in 1916, although confined to financial experts and politicians and little known or heeded by the general public, preoccupied as always with the day's events, and the inclination only a year or two before, in 1914 and 1915, to boast the financial power of the City of London. There was a wide difference between the sense of freedom of action with which the decision had been taken to go to war and the new fear that British policy in the conduct of the war might be compromised by the growing reliance of the British economy upon the American, or as it was put in the terms of reference of an interdepartmental committee, the dependence of the British Empire upon the United States of America.

What the consequences for Great Britain and her allies might have been if the German Supreme Command had not decided to attempt a swift end to their difficulties through the submarine campaign and if the

[1] Report on the Anglo-French position in North America, October 1916, by British members of the joint Anglo-French financial committee, Bradbury Papers T 170/95 (P.R.O.). See also the earlier memorandum on the allied financial position, 29 August 1916 (by R. H. Brand and F. Perry) reprinted in R. H. Brand, *War and National Finance* (1921), pp. 284-7.

Americans had never come in, is one of the might-have-beens of the war. It will always remain insoluble if only because, as we have seen, there were from the German point of view more than two ways out of the situation. As for the immediate British problem of laying hands on dollars, the stream of events was already modifying its shape when it was being discussed. American output had supplemented British in all classes of munitions, except for heavy artillery, in 1915 and 1916. The home munitions effort grew faster than had been expected. It became possible late in 1916 to reduce or cancel American orders, first in light shell, later for other products. The big irreducible element was heavy shell. The expenditure of this in the Somme battles of 1916 had been far ahead of home production and hence the heavy buyings in the United States in the spring of 1917. The question raised by the dollar crisis of the winter 1916–17 was whether these, too, could be reduced. The rise of munitions output in Great Britain towards a climax in 1917 and 1918 made reduction in purchases possible just about the time when it became financially necessary. The greater part of the heavy ammunition programme shifted to Great Britain. Largely as a result of financial pressure, almost all orders in the United States for finished munitions, except motor transport and machinery, were cut off early in 1918. They were replaced by orders for munitions material. These were less wasteful of foreign exchange if more demanding on shipping space.

There was still a financial problem, but from April 1917 it was borne by the United States. Her Government opened its credit to the Government of Great Britain and through her to the other countries of the European alliance. The debts of Russia, France, Italy and other countries to Britain represented a large proportion of her own debt to the United States when the war was over.[1] They had seemed a risk worth shouldering, when she feared for her own survival.

14

When the war was over British society had in its grasp the victory for which men had sacrificed so much. Many, and it is to their credit, were not much interested. They could remember only a generation which had seen the whole of life reduced to the sad philosophy of 'Somebody's got to be the first to hang on the wire' and examples of courage, good faith and fellowship, endurance and resignation which brought some

[1] *History of the Ministry of Munitions*, vol. II, Part III (1921), pp. 81–2.

touch of grace and dignity to the conditions of an inhuman age. But the work of restoring peace could not be evaded. It became the task of a bewildered and war-weary nation to relate if they could victory to the ends for which the war had been fought and to decide what the results ought to be.

If war is the continuation of policy by other means, then its aim is political. The consequences are not to be discussed in terms of profit and loss. They are the relative success or failure of an intention, that intent being to subdue or to change another's will. What the aims of the war were had become the subject of much public debate in Britain since 1917, a year which marked a great change in British attitudes towards the war. American observers whose duties took them to the island have left some extremely interesting descriptions of the state of public opinion at that time.[1] Different groups conceived the aims of the war in different ways and individuals differently within groups. Men were agreed only in what they were against, not in what they stood for. Had they fought to save Britain from invasion? To prevent German hegemony in Europe? To defend the rights of small nations, a Belgium or a Serbia? To preserve the Empire? To establish a League of Nations? To capture colonies and markets? To make the world safe for democracy? To end war? To win a lasting peace? Most men obeyed a medley of conscious private and public motives and unconscious or half-conscious emotions more profound than intentions, as confused as the shouting of a crowd. Every proposition was disputable except one. Men feared the military power of Germany and German domination.

Meanwhile, economic decisions had been taken during the war, in order to win it, which profoundly affected the after-war situation. Much had been done that was of dubious assistance towards the war's main aim, if this included any aspiration towards the ultimate stability and peace of Europe.

The war left two immediate problems for Britain internal to her economy. One was the new distribution of resources. The other was the change in the value of what had been the chief instrument in bringing that new distribution about, money.

The easier of the two to deal with was money. The extraordinary military expenditure came to an end with the armistice and the peace

---

[1] The correspondence of Ray Stannard Baker in the library of Princeton University is especially instructive on the gap between Government and important labour groups. Baker, who later was a biographer of Woodrow Wilson, was special envoy of the State Department in Britain in 1918.

settlement of 1918 and 1919. The full force of inflated money incomes was, it is true, let loose in the economy by mismanagement after the war, in 1919–20. But even this phase came to an end when the boom was succeeded by the depression of 1920–23. There was a mechanical solution for monetary instability available. Money's value could be tied to the market price of gold. Whether the way in which this was done in 1925 was wise, we need not for the moment discuss. There is much to be said for the view that it was an action less important in itself than as a symptom of something larger and in the long run more significant, the attitude and state of mind of official and Government circles in the years just after the war.

Resources were more difficult. The great mass of those which had been transferred to the war sector of the economy mainly between 1914 and 1917 had now to be redistributed to peacetime occupations. Many people supposed that this might take a long time and that the serious scarcities of goods and services caused by the war could not easily be got rid of. But the recovery was in some respects astonishingly rapid. The main European industrial nations, Britain included, got their production going again on peacetime lines in the fierce re-equipment and restocking activity of 1919–20. There was, it is true, another side to this effort. The stronger industrial states were buying in those years against the weaker in the world's raw material markets. The balance of payments deficits of the countries which were short of foreign exchange proved to be one of the breeding-grounds of currency disequilibrium. For large parts of Europe economic recovery came too late to prevent violent inflation. This was one of the failures of postwar economic policy.

But the industrial society of Britain had climbed out of the pit of the man-made dearths of the war. Substantial losses of capital and income were made up. Two years after the armistice the stock of fixed industrial and commercial capital was more or less the same as in 1914, although the rate of capital accumulation was no longer as high as before the war. Incomes took longer to recover, but they were by 1924 back at approximately their prewar volume.[1] More important, their distribution was found to have altered. The famine of manpower in the war had driven up the value of labour, much as industrialization did in an earlier age. The poorest had gained most. It appeared in the industrial towns of 1924 that there were only one-half as many families living in dire want

[1] A. L. Bowley and Sir J. Stamp, *The National Income, 1924, a comparative study of the income of the United Kingdom in 1911 and 1924* (1927), p. 56.

as in 1913.[1] This, together with the perpetuation of heavier taxation for the rich, amounted to a better distribution of incomes.

Economists before 1914 were agreed that a pound in the hands of a poor man had a higher marginal value than for a rich man. Therefore, some measure of redistribution of wealth would be justified. The war had carried much further the redistribution process which was only just beginning in the last years of peace. But prewar thinkers[2] had chosen three, not one, measurements of desirable change in economic welfare. They thought that incomes ought to be more equitably distributed, more stable, and larger, if the widespread and deep meanness of life of Edwardian town and countryside were to be overcome.

Incomes might be a little better distributed after the war. They could hardly be said to be more stable in postwar boom and depression. The slump of 1920–3 was the beginning of an unemployment problem which outlasted the twenties. The numbers unemployed in that decade were seldom less than a tenth of the occupied population, sometimes much more. In important industries, such as coal-mining, the tendency was towards a high concentration of unemployed men in particular regions and a relative stagnation of wages. This want of employment deepened with the world economic depression of 1929–32.

The lack of British economic growth in the interwar period can be exaggerated.[3] Perhaps what needs to be explained is how so much in the way of idle resources could have been consistent, as we see it to have been, with much new development in the way of production and incomes. The increase of real wages of the late nineteenth century was resumed side by side with heavy unemployment. The new growth of the economy was achieved, however, under severe handicaps. Some of these were directly due to the war. They were perceptible in the slow sorting out of patterns of investment and occupation in the twenties. These had outlasted the time of their maximum usefulness early in the century, as the low rate of industrial investment and the check to national income in the early nineteen-hundreds showed. But they had enjoyed a new lease of life in the war, as part of the war-production effort, just when they should have been passing away.

[1] One-fifth, if one makes the rather unreal assumption that all earning members of families were fully employed (A. L. Bowley and Margaret H. Hogg, *Has Poverty Diminished?* (1925), p. 21).
[2] These were the views of A. C. Pigou, *Wealth and Welfare* (1912).
[3] D. H. Aldcroft, Economic Growth in Britain in the Interwar Years; a Re-Assessment, *Economic History Review*, 2nd series, vol. xx (August 1967), pp. 311–26, and H. W. Richardson, *Economic Recovery in Britain, 1932–9* (1967).

The after-war search for a new structure of industry was not helped by the refusal to admit that there was anything the State could do about industrial fluctuations and the level of investment. Nor was it assisted by the restoration of prewar monetary arrangements in 1925 with more regard for finance and the City of London than for industry.

Slow industrial growth reacted upon the state of industrial relations. Great Britain's handling of the most important of all her resources, labour, had never been happy. Relations between employer and employee had been strained before the war in some industries, such as coal, which were to be at the centre of the technical changes of the next generation. The system of industrial relations which grew with astonishing rapidity in the 1905–13 boom could not be regarded, at the best, as anything more than a half-way house.

After 1918 the conditions of 1914 in this field seemed to return. But they could not be wholly restored. What came out of the war was a much strengthened system of collective bargaining, in which employer and employee faced one another on a basis of more equal power than ever before. This might have been an almost undiluted national gain, if they had operated in an industrial world marked by small economic change. Even then, the question which had puzzled the prewar Liberal administration, whether it was not the duty of the State to elicit from both sides in the industrial bargain or even to impose upon them, a wider conception of the general interest than they were of their own wills prepared to concede, would presumably have come back with the next trade boom.

But in the decade after the war collective negotiation had to be carried through in an economy subject to rapid change. Industry was sharply divided, as never before the war, into expanding and contracting trades. The State, which had enforced general rules in 1914–18 of its own in accordance with prevailing views of what was economically and socially desirable in wartime, pulled out of industrial relations. It returned not only to its prewar neutrality between the contending parties, but also to a fundamental avoidance of economic policies. This situation threw an enormous strain on the rules of industry and the rule-making process within it. Some industries saw little change, others a change for the good, from better bargaining machinery. Still other industries, including large and important ones, were exposed to the risk of deep and persistent trouble.

The failure to maintain a high and steady level of employment in the twenties, for which the governments of the day carried a responsibility which grew with time, did much to falsify hopes that had been widely shared in industry in the later years of the war. Men expected a better state of industrial relations, even a different system of industry, once the war was over. These hopes had been aimed, not merely at strengthening arbitration and conciliation machinery, but also at introducing joint consultation on a wide scale between managements and men, both in the public service and private industry. They received an official blessing and formulation in the reports of a Cabinet subcommittee, known as the Whitley Committee, after J. H. Whitley, the Liberal politician who was its chairman in 1917 and 1918. These attracted much attention at home and abroad.[1]

Any such conception of industrial relations would have had formidable difficulties to face in any case. The element of authority in British industry had always been immensely stronger than the element of consultation. The existing organizations of employers and employed were content in many ways that it should be. Both saw a possible challenge to their own power in the idea of joint consultation. As it was, early in the twenties a more primitive form of industrial discipline, backed by heavy unemployment such as had not been known since 1879 and 1886 and persistent as never before, returned. The results did much to justify George Unwin's bitter comment:[2] 'War leads through tribal solidarity to class conflict.' This took place at a time when on the lowest considerations of expediency it was particularly necessary to get resources moving and incomes rising, between the end of the war and the General Strike of 1926.

The idleness of part of her resources did not assist postwar Britain in dealing with the heaviest of the problems which she had on hand. For the restoration of personal incomes and of personal consumption and investment was not the whole economic need of the twenties by any means. Income has no meaning apart from the personal and social purposes for which it can be used. Britain's postwar economic reconstruction needed to provide her with the resources, not only to set private consumption and investment on a satisfactory upward course, so as to satisfy the needs which can only be met with private goods, but also to supply the means, in terms of public goods, for growing social commitments. These were both domestic and international.

[1] See, for example, the two papers from 1919 and 1921 by Elie Halévy, the French historian, in his translated essays, edited by R. K. Webb, *The Era of Tyrannies* (1965), pp. 105–82.

[2] G. Unwin, *Studies in Economic History* (1927), p. 17. Unwin was writing in 1924.

One of the two great public tasks with which she was faced was the abolition of primary poverty with all its attendant evils in her great towns and cities. It became clearer with every day that this problem was far larger than either the prewar reformers or the wartime plans for peace had ever contemplated. A whole collection of programmes in housing, education and public health, of the most extensive kind, were necessary. What was needed was nothing less than to cause or to assist a new society to grow inside an old. This enterprise had to be taken in hand after the loss of a decade to the war. It was a serious matter that it had also to be developed in an economy which was not fully functioning, in the sense of employing all the resources that it possessed, at any time in the interwar years.

Poverty was not only a matter of income. Questions of social status and political power, which in the course of the social development of the country had become tangled with income, were equally important, sometimes more so. The slow transformation of British industrial structure, for which the war was partly responsible, prolonged and exaggerated the poverty which existed. It also threw a heavy strain on industrial relations which in many industries they were ill fitted to bear. The consequent worsening of relations between managements and men was a condition of the General Strike of 1926, although the events of that year cannot be ascribed wholly or even mainly to the war.

The other great task which faced British opinion was the unsolved problem of European peace. Out of Europe's lack of political and social unity the war had come. The lesson of the Russian Revolution of 1917 and of the revolutionary socialism of the years after 1918, it is clear now, although it was seldom seen at the time, had been that the future stability of European civilization must depend among other things, on some reasonable solution of the class conflict generated by the industrial development of the nineteenth century. The extent of Britain's unemployed resources and the deep mutual suspicion which marked industrial relations in some of her largest industries after the war were not a helpful contribution towards this end. Some of her statesmen were uneasily aware of it. But their attention was also distracted by the sheer complexity and enormousness of the European problem. The stability of Europe both in the short and in the long run depended on more conditions than one. Not least, it required a restoration of links with parts of the world economy which had been badly broken by the war.

This was a point where British self-interest and the interests of

Europe appeared to coincide. Much of the economic policy of British governments in the nineteen-twenties was aimed at the revival of that pattern of world trade into which prewar Britain had fitted so well before 1914, partly because as the world's first industrial country she had done much to create it. Multilateral trade and the gold standard system were the means towards this aim. The cost of international restoration, as it turned out, imposed exceptional burdens upon Great Britain at considerable loss to her domestic economic and social policies.

Was this devotion to the slow, hard work of international economic reconstruction rooted in hard practical sense or in an illusion?[1] Was it based upon an abstraction from the economic experience of that wholly exceptional age,[2] the nineteenth century? Later experience, from 1929 on, seems to suggest that to some extent it was. The men responsible for these decisions took too little account of Britain's changed international economic position. They overrated her diminished and still declining power to control events. After all, vast changes in world markets and supplies, industrial techniques and communications, money centres and financial policy, had occurred since 1914, whether due to the war or not.

Did these men also abstract from international, not least European, politics? Was it ever fully grasped that without a firm international order based in political organization, good custom and law, no world market could possibly survive, any more than it had in 1914–18? Was there or could there be any meaning at all in economic interdependence without political security? Only a close examination of the records of the economic and social policies of the British Government in the twenties, now becoming available to historians, can answer these questions. It may one day be possible to say what were the mistakes and failures of those years and whether and where they could have been avoided. Did they arise out of the professional habit of mind of administrators who even in approaching a dilemma treat problems in isolation, each expert taking as given the contested proposition of another? Was there some more widely diffused and fundamental lack of vision in the nation at large, some new hesitation and uncertainty in its sense of direction? Who was refusing to look at the truth, the leaders or the led?

Whatever and whoever's the fault, time was not on Britain's side

---

[1] I take this to be the drift of the criticism of J. H. Williams, *Economic Stability in a Changing World* (1953).
[2] Ragnar Nurkse, *Patterns of Trade and Development* (1962), p. 13.

in framing a new conception of her role in the world, least of all perhaps when private and public men supposed that it was. The two sharpest experiences of the interwar period were the force of technical and social change and the pervading sense of political insecurity. Both interacted more closely as time went on. Early in the thirties the parties to the quarrel of 1914–18 began to rearm against one another. The economic development of Europe had done much to condition the origins and the course of the first war. Now it became bent to the service of a second.

3 Two Economic Historians

R. H. TAWNEY

Why concern oneself now with Richard Henry Tawney? He died in 1962 and the world to which he belonged is already half forgotten where it is not unknown to a younger generation. The practical issues of politics have moved a long way from the questions on which he was brought up and which turned him into a historian and social reformer. We live in a civilization which is threatened by the conflict of haves and have-nots among the world's increasing population and by the risks of nuclear war. These giant problems bear an obvious relation to the social tensions and the strategic calculations of Europe sixty and seventy years ago, when Tawney was a young man, even to the interests of his mature years. But as political questions they are so vast in scale as to be new in kind. With the new problems have arrived new men and new methods.

But simply because late Victorian and Edwardian England, in which he was formed, have almost faded from living memory, this is perhaps a suitable moment to look back at him. In a few more years the mere passage of time will have denied us direct access. He will be known only at second and third hand, with the indirectness of the knowledge increasing as the years go by. There is another reason also besides the personal for thinking of him. This man was a public figure of distinction in his day. He was described by a writer in the *Times Literary Supplement* some years ago as one of the two best British historians of the interwar period, the other being Lewis Namier. It is worth asking how he came to hold that position in the public esteem and what it was that made him a historian of a particular kind, special to his time and place.

A historian is by definition one who thinks about history. A leading historian is presumably a man who has helped to change our beliefs about history. Tawney was certainly a historian of this kind. If we ask, however, what his view of British history was and how he came to hold it, we are faced with a great lack of knowledge about his thoughts and feelings in his early years, which will not be supplied until a proper life of him has been written. One powerful element in the growth of his personality and thinking seems, however, clear. Our knowledge of history is usually spoken of as if it were the consequence entirely of accessions of information, the work of quiet men in universities, a kind of coral reef rising majestically above the sea of human ignorance as one little fact is silently added to another. This view underrates the influence of public events upon men in universities. The tides of social change and his keen sense of altering scales of value in England had much to do with making Tawney as a young man seek new information about the society he lived in. For him, this meant taking a long, hard look at its origins. The events of history, as he studied them, became the material for his thinking about it.

By birth and education, Tawney was an upper middle-class British boy of the end of the nineteenth century. He was born in 1880 at Calcutta, where his father was Principal of the Presidency College. He went to school at Rugby, where he seems to have been a handsome and healthy boy, with a proper addiction to outdoor activities and games. Then he went to Oxford, to Balliol, and failed to get the First which had been expected of him, at least by his father, who wanted to know how he proposed to wipe out this disgrace. The failure is said to have been ascribed by the Master of his College, Edward Caird, to the chaotic state of Tawney's mind. Chaos is not a word which one would naturally apply to the later Tawney. In the absence of a biography, it is not possible to explain what happened. This may have had personal or accidental causes. But it suggests a personality and a mind temporarily divided, confused perhaps by the growth of new loyalties and interests which conflicted with old.

Tawney belonged to a generation which was rather conspicuously at odds with its parents and with established arrangements. Boys and girls of the eighteen-eighties and nineties had heard a great deal about the successes of the Victorian era. The steady growth throughout the century of Britain's population and strength produced among many people of all classes a kind of intoxication. This was a strong element in the imperialism of the last years of the century, as expressed in the two Jubilees of Queen Victoria. Englishmen, like Germans of the same era, came to overrate their position in the world, the enduringness of their power and their ability to control events. Individuals could share this national mood of exaltation or they could react against it. They could argue in criticism that the national record showed defeats as well as victories, not of the military sort alone. They could say that exactly what the nation was most proud of, its growing population, its big cities, its dominating industries, were liabilities rather than assets, at least so long as men accepted them so naïvely and uncritically. They could conclude that, however good the intentions of Queen Victoria's loving subjects, the Victorians had advanced the cause of civilization only in a most ambiguous way. Thanks to the activities of one's parents and grandparents, one had been left with a great mess to clear up in 1900.

These, or something like these, were the emotions of many of the younger generation at the end of the century, as they read William Morris or the Fabian Essays. Tawney shared them. But it would be a great mistake to classify him with the Marxists, the Fabians, the Merry Englanders and the many other critics of the established order, who began to abound in British society about the turn of the century. The sources of his beliefs were alien from theirs and made him in some ways a curiously solitary figure. In an England which was increasingly agnostic he remained a firm Christian and a staunch member of the Church of England.

Tawney's affinities lay with the Christian Socialists of the middle years of the nineteenth century, with the men grouped around F. D. Maurice, who campaigned so hard for industrial and social reform in English society in the late forties and early fifties. He worked with people who in his own day were trying to define what the position of Christianity and of their church ought to be in an advanced industrial society, such as England had come to be. Some of his closest friends at Rugby and Oxford, as in later life, were Charles Gore, William Temple and Henry Scott Holland. These men were clerics and theologians. Scott Holland created the Christian Social Union, the powerful Oxford branch of which Tawney joined. If anyone wishes to know what Tawney and his friends talked about in the early years of the present century, they can hardly do better than consult the files of the *Economic Review*, which was the Christian Social Union's journal until it ceased publication in 1914. This discussed all the leading economic and social issues of the day with a range and scholarly vigour which gives it a strong resemblance to its contemporary the *Economic Journal*, except that the inspiration of the one seems to have been Oxford and religious, and of the other Cambridge and scientific.

Tawney was making up his mind in these early days. Where the personal concern came from which he brought to these debates is not now clear. But when he had chosen and rejected on matters of first principle he never changed his mind. Indeed, the best statement of his innermost personal beliefs in relation to society comes from a much later date in his life, from a paper which he composed, characteristically enough, for discussion at a church conference in 1937. In this account of his views on Christianity and the social order, he raises three questions. First, was there a specific Christian way of life for which Christians were bound to stand? Second, if there was such a way of life, was it in conflict with what he called capitalist civilization or in agreement with it? Third, if a conflict existed between the two, was it the duty of a Christian to condemn the offending social institutions openly and without reservation?

Without expecting the majority of Christians to agree with him, his own replies to these questions were direct and unhesitating. He believed that there was a specifically Christian code of conduct and way of life and that the capitalist civilization he lived in was at war with it. There were, he thought, certain institutions and ruling conditions of contemporary society which were to be condemned by Christians. The first of these was the nation's treatment of its children and young people. Existing institutions ought to promote their health, education and welfare. Instead, they neglected and exploited youth, as the state of the labour market showed. He condemned also the Englishman's worship of class, and opposed to the general admiration of wealth, place and power, the equal value from a religious point of view of all men. He condemned further irresponsible power. By this, he meant such situations of power without responsibility as are created by an industrial society. Finally, he condemned in strong terms the institutions surrounding the ownership and inheritance of property. These were, he held, the chief cause in his day alike of economic and political inequalities, irresponsible power and the neglect of youth.

One may think what one chooses of these beliefs of his. They were certainly part of the man, from first to last. Equally certainly, they were widely different from the convictions of most of his contemporaries, including many radicals.

In the light of these religious and social propositions, British history in the eighteenth and nineteenth centuries appeared to Tawney an age of industrial feudalism. It ought, he believed, to be succeeded by a time when strong government would make the common purpose prevail against the anarchy of individual wills. In his readiness to invoke the

State for the sake of the order and freedom of the whole community, he joined hands with the Fabians and the Webbs, men and women who were otherwise distant from him in the origins of their fundamental beliefs. This was at the same time the point where he parted company with some of his friends of the Christian Social Union. They were not prepared to go so far, and as the movement for social reform gathered force became suspicious of the State's power.

Tawney's convictions strongly influenced his choice of problems to work on as a historian. At the outset of his career, when he went down from Oxford with his second-class degree to face life in Edwardian England, they also made it difficult for him to find a suitable job. He was not prepared to follow the usual paths. He was always polite and often humorous, but his opinions as a young man must have had something of the directness of a well-aimed stone. Fortunately for him, he was not alone in his disapproval of existing society. He found himself in the midst of the sudden upsurge of argument and political debate about economic and social questions which followed the South African War. This grew more and more intense after the Liberals were returned to power in 1906. It was in the Britain of Asquith, Lloyd George and the People's Budget that the youthful Tawney first found his feet as a teacher, a social reformer and a writer. As a lecturer and a tutor to industrial workers, he helped to establish the Workers' Educational Association. When Churchill introduced the Trades Board Act in 1909, making it possible to set statutory minimum wages for certain groups of workers, Tawney accepted the directorship of a research unit to study the working of the Act.

He also wrote and published in 1912 his first book, *The Agrarian Problem in the Sixteenth Century*. This was a youthful but remarkable piece of work. A study in the distribution of landed property in Tudor England, when land was the chief form of wealth, it was intended to throw some light on the remote origins of the unequal British society of his own day. This book marked the beginnings in Tawney of a long partnership between the social reformer and the historian. It was also his first essay in a field to which he returned again and again, that is, the problem of the correct interpretation of the history of Tudor and Stuart England.

Tawney was a man in his thirties when the European war broke out. For him, the years between 1914 and 1918 represented a change of activities rather than of convictions. In one of his rare writings on the war he refers to himself as 'a man of the months August to November

1914'. For him as for many others at that time the political idealism of the years just before the war fused easily and naturally with the idealism which was still very real even in the vast mixed horde of Kitchener's European-sized army, the new citizen volunteers. Britain's war, for those who thought as he did, was the British democracy at war. Going to war meant joining up and fighting. Fighting as a sergeant in France, Tawney was badly wounded in the violent battles of 1916. It is clear from what he says that he shared in common with many other men that strong sense of the solidarity of all front-line fighters which was one of the most remarkable features of the war. When he returned from France he did not hesitate to say that the men at the front felt themselves to have more in common with the Germans in the trenches opposite than they did with civilians at home who lived in a different world. He suggested that the civilians' world was false, created for them by the Press and their own desires.

Tawney's generation had seen much change in England. Many of them came back to civil life when the war was done, determined that it should change farther and faster. They wished to honour promises which they believed had been made to the dead. But death terminates the political contract, as they were soon to discover. The national unity created and enforced by the war and by the sense of common danger had temporarily wiped away the memory of bitter class and industrial struggles in the year immediately before 1914. This solidarity melted when the practical difficulties of living together in peacetime proved themselves to be as intractable as ever. Many men returned to civilian employment who found that civilian employment did not return to them. After 1919 the country was entering upon a long and difficult transition in its economic as well as in its political life. 'The spirit of August-November 1914' was dead.

But not in Tawney and not in some of those he addressed. The twenties and thirties marked the peak of his influence as a public man. He was extremely active in the sphere of politics and industrial life in the years both before and after the General Strike. He was one of the makers of the Labour Party between the wars, not as a practical politician, which he never was at any time, but as a writer, publicist and educator.

The Acquisitive Society (1921) and *Equality* (1931) were essentially works of this political educational character. Their titles describe their themes. They analysed from a general historical point of view what he regarded as the leading characteristics of British society, its concentration on private income and its inequality. They were not works of profoundly original political thought, but perhaps all the more influential for that fact with the public of their time. Tawney at his worst could argue as if there were only two sorts of Englishmen, the many who wished to lead the good life and the few who prevented them from doing so. At his best, he was the wisest and keenest critic British society had had since Matthew Arnold died. He controlled as Arnold did the weapon of a rational persuasive prose, sometimes marred by rhetoric, especially in his earlier writings. He had furnished himself with a knowledge of economic and social affairs which Arnold never possessed or claimed to have.

As a writer upon public questions, Tawney belonged to an age which had both a beginning and an end. His political life was passed between the election of 1906 and the finish of the Attlee administration in 1951. These forty-five years brought two great wars and countless revolutions in Europe. They also, as the result of a transformation in Britain itself, gave Tawney some of the social changes which he had wanted. At the end of the period the nation's youth was no longer so neglected as it had been; it was better fed, better schooled, better doctored. Tawney had been a hard fighter, down to and including the Education Act of 1944, for a genuine system of national education. Something like it had begun to emerge, partly owing to his work. Some inroads had been made upon the harsh and unrelieved inequalities of property and income which were taken for granted when Tawney was a boy. Common services had been provided out of taxation even before the 1914 war in the form of pensions, health and unemployment insurance, and so forth. The inequalities of private income had not greatly changed, but the society in which they existed had changed in some important respects. The Britain of Charles Booth had become that of William Beveridge. Tawney married Beveridge's sister and he was an admirer of his brother-in-law's achievements. That he was satisfied by the reforms he had seen in his own lifetime is unlikely. Given his view of human affairs, which was uncompromisingly religious, he could not much admire any form of society. But the changes which had taken place had to a large extent thrown his purely political writings out of date.

One of his political books at least deserves a longer life. His interests and writings were not confined to Britain. In 1931 he visited China and later wrote out his impressions of the social and economic state of that vast society. These appeared in 1932 under the title *Land and Labour in*

China. They were in a sense no more than the comments of an extremely well-informed traveller, but few of Tawney's writings give a clearer view of the exceptional qualities of his mind. He was both philosophic and practical. The sight of China and his contemplation of her problems roused him to a series of penetrating and closely argued observations, not only as a traveller but as a student of history, society and institutions. They are among the most remarkable of his works, not only for the content but also for their terse and clear expression. Unlike many Western writings about China of that date, they show genuine insight into the structure and limitations of what nowadays would be called an underdeveloped economy. Within the context of events at the time, his advice was sensible and shrewd. He appears to have possessed by nature what Charles Anthony Johnson Brooke,[1] the ruler of Sarawak, an Englishman who had spent a lifetime east of Singapore, once said was the rarest quality among Europeans in all Asia, a respect for the individuality of Asian peoples.

It was as a student of human nature and society also that Tawney approached the history of Tudor and Stuart England. His historical investigations continued to widen and deepen in the twenties and thirties. He had become a notable teacher of economic and social history at the London School of Economics between the wars. The tendency of his work during these years was not only to engage in great empirical inquiries but also to link them with the speculation and analysis of the social sciences, with economics, to an even greater extent with political science and the new and, at that time, unpopular science of sociology.

Tawney's main historical problem remained what it had been when he wrote the *Agrarian Problem*. He sought the origins of his own age. How had one society succeeded another, more powerfully and permanently than by war or conquest? What were the sources of commercial and industrial Britain, which had superseded over the centuries feudal and agricultural Britain? To find these, he went back to the Britain of the Tudor and Stuart monarchy. The three volumes of *Tudor Economic Documents*, published by Tawney and his collaborator Eileen Power in 1928, shifted the study of Tudor economic and social history on to new foundations, so far as the knowledge of primary sources was concerned. But while Tawney was a formidable researcher, he was too

---

[1] The English ruler of Sarawak, in the island of Borneo, 1868–1917. In his *Queries: past, present, future* (1907) a keen and prophetic critic of European colonial policies in Asia as he had known them.

shrewd to regard an inquiry into sources of evidence as the whole duty of an historian. He was well aware of the philosophic and the practical problems which beset the relations of the knower and the known in a subject like history. It was in the effort to solve them that he turned to sociology and the theories of Max Weber, and wrote as a result *Religion and the Rise of Capitalism*, a book first published in 1926, but thought out and delivered in lecture form some years before.

In discussing the economic life of Tudor and Stuart England, Tawney was dealing as a historian with something allied to what would now be called the sociology of economic development. Max Weber was the greatest German sociologist since Karl Marx. It was, however, a comparatively small although significant part of his system of thought that interested Tawney. Tawney, like Weber, but from a very different point of view, was concerned with the relations between religion and economic development. He wanted to know what effect religion had had upon that kind of social change and social change upon religion. Everyone had heard about market forces and their transforming effect. But how exactly did they operate in society and how did they interact with other institutions and functions, political and religious?

For Tawney, as an Englishman and an Anglican, it was natural to ask whether there had not been in this country some connection between the religious changes of the sixteenth century and the economic and social innovations of the seventeenth century? But he was too well informed a historian to attempt to give a simple answer to the question how the middle class had acquired its modern character or to base the economic development of Europe upon the Reformation. He assigned full credit to Max Weber for his perception of the importance of Calvinist doctrine in justifying acts which the medieval Church had often condemned. At the same time he was aware that this argument assumed the existence of economic enterprises which needed, in contemporary eyes, to be defended. His book did not cover the whole ground. He admitted later that the omission of any consideration of the Roman Catholic church and Catholic business communities in sixteenth- and seventeenth-century Europe left a serious gap. Those who today are interested in the general theme of secularization and social change will regard his book as limited.

Partly for this reason, *Religion and the Rise of Capitalism* became a centre of controversy. It was the first of the debates among historians to which Tawney's work was to give rise. Discussions arose then as it did later on questions of evidence and material. It grew even more intense because he insisted on facing the problem of values in history and going straight for it in his own way. This he could hardly do without importing into the argument something of his own values. The personal aspect of his work was not acceptable to everybody, and it was certainly a cause of weakness as well as of strength in his interpretation of history. The risk was, however, one which he was prepared to take.

The willingness to link history with the social sciences was characteristic of Tawney's work, especially in the middle years of his life. If *Religion and the Rise of Capitalism* (1926) shows him going to sociology for illumination in dealing with European history, so, too, did his introduction to the book of his colleague Raymond Firth on *The Primitive Economics of the New Zealand Maori* (1929) indicate his interest or his readiness to be interested in social anthropology. But again he was thinking of Europe and his own times. He expressed the hope that Firth's study of the Maori might provoke some Maori student to write a comparable study of the economic arrangements of Englishmen. He clearly suspected that they might turn out to be on close examination little more civilized, perhaps rather less so, than those of the primitive Maori. One has to remember that he was living in a country which at that moment was wasting a substantial amount of its resources in unemployment and did not know how to bring that absurd and tragic waste to an end. It was Tawney's contemporary, the economist and businessman, Josiah Stamp, who commented that England did not seem to possess a civilized technique of social change.

Sociology and anthropology were highly relevant to the problems which most interested Tawney, being those of how one state of society arises out of another. So did economics refer. But it so happened that the main advances in economic thought of his time, which was in economic theory the age of Keynes and Schumpeter, were made in the effort to explain what happens in developed industrial economies. They were of little help in throwing light upon the course of events in Tudor and Stuart England, before the great transition to an industrialized economy had taken place. In the thirties it was upon an economic and social history of seventeenth-century England that Tawney was understood to be working.

The book was never written, perhaps because of the outbreak of the second European war in 1939, more probably because Tawney did not in the long run see his way clear to write it. It is from Tawney's published papers that one has to guess the lines on which his mind was working. Here again the link between his work and the social sciences became important. This time it was with political science and what would now be called political sociology. Tawney had far too acute a sense of politics and of the struggle for political power not to be curious about the relation between the social changes he was describing in Stuart England and the Civil War. In 1941 he gave a lecture on *James Harrington and the Interpretation of his Age*. Harrington was a political theorist of the Commonwealth who held that forms of government depended on the distribution of property. In the England of his day this meant, for the most part, landed property. Tawney was too experienced and wary a thinker to adopt the simple proposition that the Civil War came because of a change in property relations. But he did suggest that Harrington's doctrine supplied a clue as to what had actually happened in that most confused and confusing of centuries, the seventeenth.

This seems to have been one of the origins of an article which Tawney published in the same year, on *The Rise of the Gentry, 1558–1640*. In this, he argued with great force for the thesis that a change precisely of this nature, transferring property in land from the territorial nobility to the gentry, a wealthy rural middle class, had been one of the leading features of English economic history in the hundred years before the Civil War. He stated his reasons for believing that the conditions of the time had taken away from the economic advantages of the one group, while promoting those of the second. He left his readers with the clear impression that the collapse of the English state in the seventeenth century would not be understood without reference to the loss of a social equilibrium which had existed under the Tudors.

Like his book on *Religion and the Rise of Capitalism*, although on very different grounds, his essay upon the gentry became the subject of a prolonged controversy. Much of this turned, and still does, upon the details of the historical evidence for social change which can only come from the increasing monographic work upon the social history of the seventeenth century. Only an expert in this would be competent to pass judgement upon such matters. Tawney himself admitted, in his metaphorical way, that history needs the microscope as well as the telescope. One who is not a specialist in the seventeenth century can only allow himself a very general observation. The strength of the analysis Tawney employed lies in its concentration upon one great cause or line of causation. This appeared to Tawney sufficient to account in a general way for the cataclysm of the Civil War. But even granted its premises it remains an explanation of a conflict which might have arisen in the seventeenth century rather than of the actual struggle, extending over twenty years, which we call the Civil War. Tawney, to do him justice, never insisted that his argument in and of itself explained the war.

One wonders how he would have got over the problem had he written a full treatment of the war. The strength of the analysis which seeks the single great departure from equilibrium adequate to explain subsequent change is also its own weakness. Of its nature, it isolates for study a particular class of events in history, in this case the economic. It abstracts from the whole society. But society even in seventeenth-century England was a complicated affair, discharging many functions. The better to analyse what happened, the historian deliberately and properly averts his gaze from the simultaneity and interaction of events. To explain a war, however, it may be necessary to consider changes arising not only in one area but in several areas of the functioning of society, even in different areas at different times. These may have come together to force on and create a situation entirely different from that which would have existed if any one cause of change, however strong, had acted in isolation. In combination, and precisely because they were a combination, they may have been far more dangerous to social stability. Would Tawney, one wonders, have had to switch the style of his analysis in order to grapple with the complexity of events? There seem to be some signs in recent writing on the seventeenth century that the move to a more complicated analysis has come with a later generation.

Tawney never did write the history of the Civil War and we remain without his full thinking on the matter. His last book, *Business and Politics under James I* (1958), a study of Lionel Cranfield, merchant and servant of the Crown, was of all his books the nearest to the conventional historical monograph. There are many good things in it, but it does, on the whole, little to advance our understanding of Tawney's interpretation of the history of Stuart England. If further observations and reflections on the subject occurred to him in those last years, they remain unpublished, probably unwritten.

The work of the historian is a kind of prediction of the past. It is a detailed description of what the historian believes to have been the true nature and order of events at some given point of time. It is a forecast, as accurate as information and analysis can make it and as the personal values of the historian will allow, of what we would find actually happening, if by some miracle we could find our way back in time. Tawney was a man who, beginning as we have seen from a highly personal point of view, altered the character of the guesses which his generation became accustomed to make about modern British history.

He helped powerfully to destroy the hold which an interpretation of the seventeenth century, cast mainly in terms of Parliamentary politics and constitutional law and devised in the first instance by the great aristocratic houses in order to explain to themselves and the country their actions at a time when they played a leading role in the politics of the nation, still had upon the public mind down to about sixty or seventy years ago. There had been a tendency in English historical thinking, ever since the eighteenth century, to explain the changes of modern English society in terms of the constitutional revolution of 1688 and the political events which led up to it. Tawney did not believe that the growth of wealth and the transformation of society were a consequence of the constitutional solution adopted to bring to an end the struggle of Crown and Parliament. Nor was he able to accept an explanation of the political contest framed wholly in political terms. He thought that if politics sometimes accounted for social changes, it would be equally if not more reasonable to expect political change to follow movements in society from time to time. This mode of reasoning left the field open for wide differences of opinion about the nature of the society which was being observed. But coming when it did, it was a great advance upon older habits of thought. No man did more to promote it in the field of seventeenth-century studies than Tawney. In his way, this most English of men was responsible for a great change in the Englishman's notion of his own history. His conclusions will not stand indefinitely and they have indeed already been substantially modified, not only by additional information but also by new ways of thinking.

The England of his day, just because it was in process of rapid change, was perhaps likely to produce a great transitional historical thinker and also to leave him soon behind as it moved farther and farther away from old interests and traditions. His own work was deeply influenced by his position in time, by the circumstance that he was a historian living in an age of social crisis, before and after the First World War. It was this that turned him, given his mind and temperament, into a social historian and critic of accepted stories.

A civilization faced with immense transformations and the dangers which arise from them will not abandon—it will certainly carry further —the study of social change which for Tawney was history. At the same time, it will do this by methods consonant with the intellectual spirit and the academic organization of its day. Tawney faced a generation ago a personal problem, of the preservation in his own mind of a balance between history and social science, between both and social philosophy. Western society faces in our time a struggle to maintain its scientific and philosophical balance and to control events in a world where change threatens to outrun human management. English history itself looks smaller and different than it did in Tawney's time. Perhaps on a cool consideration it is no less important than it was. Its significance for us depends upon the values we assign to it. But it will not soon be served again by a mind and an imagination equal to his.

Many stories were told about Tawney during his lifetime, based upon his unusual personality. Nothing has been said here of his physical appearance, which was tall and well built, with a look at once homely and dignified. No mention has been made of the man whose old black hat was famous, making him look, as someone said, thinking of the holes in it, like a street musician caught by gunfire; or of the man who walked his dog on the Cotswolds and threw it sticks to fetch; or of the man who lit the gas under the kettle, but forgot to fill the kettle. Tawney was a great conference-goer. The man has not been referred to here who from the chair of one learned conference observed flames bursting from the matches in the handbag of a woman historian and remarked to her, 'What! Are you prematurely burning?' Or who at another conference told the gathered agrarian historians that what they needed was not more documents but stronger boots. Nor has the historian been described who could be trusted to abandon the room, history and everything else if there were children about. He thrilled and mystified them with postcards sent from abroad signed with imaginary names.

All these Tawneys existed inside one man. Everyone who met him carried away his own story of the Tawney he had met. Tawney's humour and eccentricity were inseparable from his personality. What has been attempted here is no portrait of the whole man. It is rather to try to define the characteristics of Tawney as a historian. Much of his working life was spent in thinking about history and the writing of history. He did not attach undue importance to his own views and methods of study. But he did believe that to cultivate and achieve an insight into the past of the society to which he belonged was part of a rational and responsible existence, as he understood and tried to live it.

JOHN H. CLAPHAM

History became a subject of academic investigation in Great Britain in the second half of the nineteenth century. But its economic aspects did not come to be widely accepted as fit for study in the universities until between the two world wars. When this recognition was granted, it was largely the result of the work of three men: of George Unwin at Manchester, R. H. Tawney at London and J. H. Clapham at Cambridge.

The Man and his Work

Clapham's life was associated with Cambridge from early days.[1] He was born in Lancashire in 1873, the son of a prosperous Manchester jeweller, a Yorkshireman by birth, who had married the daughter of a Manchester smallware manufacturer. Clapham was north country by origin and proud of it, particularly of his descent from Yorkshire farming stock. He retained through life some of the qualities associated by tradition, sometimes quite wrongly, with that part of the country; especially a ruggedness of character and directness of approach which made him some enemies but was also the secret of much of his success, both in academic and practical affairs. He was sent at fourteen to the Leys School in Cambridge and entered King's College in 1892. He studied in the History School during the memorable period of William Cunningham, who taught him economic history, F. W. Maitland and Lord Acton. Clapham was therefore a historian both by training and by taste. As a Fellow of King's he became known to, however, and approved of by the economist, Alfred Marshall. Marshall's influence over him was enduring, as it was with so many men.

Clapham had earlier believed that he might become an ecclesiastical historian, but it was as a Professor of Economics that he went in 1902 to Leeds. There he was active in the new university and wrote a book on 'The Woollen and Worsted Industries' which was regarded in its day as a model industrial monograph. He returned to lecturing and college administration at Cambridge in 1908, but left it for Government service in London during the First World War. This was the second and last break in his connection with Cambridge. He became the first Professor

---

[1] Clapham's Cambridge personality has been described in 'John Harold Clapham, 1873–1946'; a memoir prepared by direction of the Council of King's College, Cambridge (1949).

of Economic History in the University in 1928 and retired from the chair ten years later. He remained active, however, in both administration and scholarship until the time of his death in 1946.

During a long and highly successful teaching and administrative career Clapham managed to find the time he needed for research and had written much. *The Economic Development of France and Germany*, a detailed sketch of European economic history suggested by the war which broke out in 1914, was published in 1921. His major work, *The Economic History of Modern Britain*, covering the century since 1825, came out in three volumes between 1926 and 1938, when he was in later middle age. Then he was invited by the Directors of the Bank of England to commemorate the 250th birthday of the Bank by writing its history from the original records. He began to work in 1938 upon a *History of the Bank of England* in three volumes. Two of these were published in 1944, the third volume covering the period after 1914 remains unpublished. Clapham also initiated and planned, with Eileen Power, the first volumes of the *Cambridge Economic History of Europe*, still in course of publication. He left behind him a brief economic history of Britain down to 1750, and this was published posthumously in 1949.

A tall, powerful man, an athlete and mountaineer, with an excellent general judgement, uniting energy with good sense behind an almost aggressively normal manner, Clapham might have made a success of almost any professional or business career. He could have left Cambridge and college life if he had wished, and he is said not to have been without offers. As it was, his public work, especially in the later years of his life, brought him a knighthood and many other honours. But he did not elect to move from Cambridge or from the life which he had chosen; he wished to be a historian and to be judged as such.

The Nature of Clapham's Empiricism

Of the three founders of academic economic history in Great Britain, Unwin and Tawney were both more philosophic historians than Clapham. It is worth noting that they held a conception of the subject broader and more unusual than his. Economic history with them—and in this they were perhaps prophetic—took a marked sociological turn. It became a study of what is often spoken of as the 'impersonal' aspect of history. The word impersonal, however, is not quite satisfactory, because the guiding thought of both men was precisely the recognition of the significance of personality in quarters where it is not usually looked for, in economic and social life. Economic history became for them all that side of historical study which grows by contact not only with economics but also with anthropology, sociology and social psychology. The point is perhaps best illustrated from Tawney's writings. His *Religion and the Rise of Capitalism* (1926) was an inquiry into the profound shift of social values which both caused and was the result of large-scale economic changes in the sixteenth and seventeenth centuries.[1]

Clapham could understand the meaning and bearing of such investigations. He did not wish to imitate or extend them himself. His bent lay elsewhere and economic history in Britain and North America has tended in the last twenty years to follow his example, with some loss as well as certain gains. The strength of his work lay in his unflinching allegiance to the traditional disciplines of economics and history. While carefully eschewing sociological interests he made two remarkable attempts, in the *Economic History of Modern Britain* and the *History of the Bank of England*, to write the analytical narrative of modern economic history on a scale which in the past had been reserved for the history of the state.

Clapham was a historian who turned toward economics. He was not, like his teacher Marshall, a mathematician and economist who had acquired an interest in and knowledge of history. He turned naturally towards the materials of history: the individuality of the person, the nation and the country; the passage of time; the ceaseless movement of events which never return. He has described this temper of mind very well himself. The historian, he says,

> is proud because, by definition, he is one to whom the tangled variety of human life is attraction in itself; one who will study alterations in the tangle for the love of it; even when his information is such that he can never hope to pick out with assurance the forces at work or measure exactly the change brought about by the aggregate of them between dates X and Y. He cares for the beginnings of things as such. He likes to trace the growth of institutions which have been moulded by man's need to keep alive and man's desire for comfort and prosperity—village communities, trading companies, Christmas goose clubs—although he may not be able to number the

[1] Tawney's introduction to Raymond Firth's *Primitive Economics of the New Zealand Maori* (1929) concluded characteristically with the hope that a gifted Maori anthropologist might some day write an equally faithful account of the people of Great Britain.

community, read the balance sheet of the company, or find the slate of the goose club.[1]

A relish for the practical interests of the world was combined, owing to his training at Cambridge, with the intellectual interests of the economist and the statistician. The tradition of Marshall's Cambridge gave Clapham an important advantage over some Continental scholars of his day. An admirer of Gustav Schmoller and of Sombart, he was never tempted to fall into the errors of the German historical economists or to suppose that the study of history might somehow be made to do duty for the development of economic theory. Marshall's revival of theoretical interests at Cambridge after 1885 and the mathematical turn which he had given to economic reasoning barred the road to any such confusion of aim. Marshall had a significant effect upon Clapham's view of the historian's function. He ceased to be content to describe or narrate; he wanted also to explain and to analyse, to show with precision the form and the movement of things. This he could only do with the help of theory and of statistics.

One of Clapham's grumbles was that theory, which was intended to explain events, gave him as a historian too little assistance. This may appear strange, considering that he lived at Cambridge when the economic theorists there, under Keynes's leadership, were making more important advances than any since the days of Ricardo. But this movement, it must be remembered, came comparatively late. When Keynes's *General Theory* was published in 1936, Clapham was already sixty-three. He never mastered, or troubled to master, the new approach to economics. He belonged to the school of Marshall and Pigou and it was against economic theory as handled by them that his resounding criticisms were directed. His paper of 1922, *On Empty Economic Boxes*,[2] was an attack on what he regarded as the useless abstractness of contemporary theory. It is said to have helped to stimulate the discussions which led to the development of the analysis of imperfect competition at Cambridge in the nineteen-thirties. But the weighty theoretical controversies of the years between the wars and indeed theory of any sort were markedly absent from the books Clapham was writing about that time.

Clapham's interest in economic theory was limited, probably too limited. He said himself that the historian in him was much bulkier than

[1] J. H. Clapham, 'The Study of Economic History; an Inaugural Lecture' (1929), pp. 34–5.
[2] *Economic Journal*, vol. XXXII (1922), pp. 305–14.

the economist. He was less theoretical by nature, for example, than Heckscher. Heckscher, whose place in Swedish historiography is comparable with Clapham's in British, published a memorable *Plea for Theory in Economic History*[1] only a year or two after Clapham's attack upon current theory. Clapham could not have given his books the logical form and sequence apparent in those of Heckscher's works which are available in English. He almost certainly doubted whether history is logical; or rather, whether its logic can be confined within the drastically simplified assumptions of the economist.

This cautious and empirical temper apart, Clapham's limited use of theory certainly had something to do with the type of theory available in his day. Towards the end of his life, the economists were turning from static equilibrium analysis to economic dynamics. Clapham, brought up under the old dispensation, directed his interest towards problems of economic organization rather than those of economic development. His *Economic History of Modern Britain* is strong in the description and analysis of markets and in its explanation of the state of the national economy at particular times. It is far less successful in portraying convincingly the motion from one state to another and in showing us the causes of development, whether these take the form of movements over a long period or the more rapid fluctuations of the trade cycle.

In his own way Clapham discharged the duty laid upon the economic historian by Marshall: to bring economic reasoning to the explanation of the past. In the analysis which he employed and in his choice of his problems, indeed, his conservatism had an unfortunate effect on what was intended to be the greatest of his works. The *Economic History of Modern Britain* spends little time over some questions which have since become of the greatest interest to economists and historians. Still the questions which he asked were broadly economic. He wanted to know what the disposable resources of the nation were; what changes occurred from time to time; how resources were organized; how the markets worked and what incomes for private persons and for the State came of all this. Economic policy and the social results of industrialization came within his scope, but he refused to follow his old teacher Cunningham in using political concepts such as 'mercantilism' or 'laissez-faire' to explain economic developments; nor did he regard the history of the Industrial Revolution as identifiable with social history.

Economic history forms a difficult country to attack, and in his

[1] In a paper read in 1928, reprinted in F. C. Lane and J. C. Riemersma, *Enterprise and Secular Change* (1953).

efforts, Clapham had two valuable advantages: a sense of quantities and a curiosity about technology. He had learned from the mathematically trained Marshall that economics is the study of mutually interacting quantities; he had also an evident natural taste for measurement. '. . . Stories assumed to be familiar,' he remarked in the preface to the *Economic History of Modern Britain*,

> are apt to become good nesting places for legend. Until very recently, historians' accounts of the dominant event of the nineteenth century, the great and rapid growth of population, were nearly all semilegendary; sometimes they still are. Statisticians had always known the approximate truth; but historians had too often followed a familiar literary tradition. Again, the legend that everything was getting worse for the working man, down to some unspecified date between the drafting of the People's Charter and the Great Exhibition, dies hard. The fact that, after the price fall of 1820–21, the purchasing power of wages in general—not, of course, of everyone's wages—was definitely greater than it had been just before the revolutionary and Napoleonic wars, fits so ill with the tradition that it is very seldom mentioned, the work of statisticians on wages and prices being constantly ignored by social historians. It is symbolic of the divorce of much social and economic history from figures that, in a recent inquiry into the fortunes of one group of trades, the tradition of decline appears in the text, some corrective wage figures in an appendix, and the correlation nowhere.

By asking the simple question 'How much?' Clapham worked a revolution in the handling of modern British economic history in the eighteenth and nineteenth centuries.[1] Of course the methods of assembling and sifting statistical evidence have been carried much further since. Nor did Clapham himself invariably handle statistics in the most illuminating way. The empiricism which led him to distrust theory made him reluctant to discuss aggregates at all. This put a whole world of discussion out of his reach. Clapham's work is rich in arithmetical instances; but the set of general relationships on which the analysis of a whole economy turns makes a far more rare appearance. The breaking down of aggregates—an equally necessary if less exciting task—was more to Clapham's critical taste. Farming with him, for example, soon

---

[1] Clapham and some of his critics were aware of the novelty of his application of measurement. See A. P. Usher, 'The Application of the Quantitative Method to Economic History', *Journal of Political Economy*, vol. XL (1932), pp. 186–209.

becomes a collection of systems of cultivation concerned with different products; an industry is reduced to firms of the most varied size and efficiency. In the critical use of figures he was unexcelled.

Clapham's curiosity about technical matters is conspicuous in all his works. He once wrote:[1] 'A patch of earth dug level, a right stroke with a felling axe, a neat bit of welding, a locomotive brought smoothly to rest, even a tidy balance sheet or a quick calculation in forward exchange, all yield the craftsman's, not to say the artist's satisfaction.' The craftsman, not to say the artist in Clapham, was of great assistance to the economist and the statistician in criticizing generalities and bringing argument down to earth.

Clapham's empirical cast of mind was an asset in another direction. It prevented him from falling into the temptation of supposing that a figure or even a well-defined set of quantitative relations can indicate a cause. He sought causes in human motives. This was a sphere where his knowledge of the world, his respect for facts (even where the facts were the moonshine of other men's minds), and his interest in men, stood him in good stead as a historian of Great Britain. There were groups and sections of the nation, including large classes, whom he knew by no means well, but in a broad way the whole mental world of the industrial and commercial middle classes was familiar to him. He thoroughly understood their place and role in Victorian history. He had a particular sympathy with two sorts of men who played a great part in that age; the administrative mind in Government and the select circle of men who held key positions in the City of London. He knew how political decisions are arrived at. Clapman's knowledge of the Cabinet Office in the First World War can be seen peeping out of his handling, for example, of the movements of Sir Robert Peel and Sir James Graham in the eighteen-forties, at the time of the repeal of the Corn Laws. He was one of the first historians to find a place for, among other things, what one might call 'administrative fatigue'.

Clapham's understanding of the habits of mind of the managing and directing classes among his countrymen and of industrial society in the north of England meant that he approached with confidence a vital part of the economic historian's task. For if his first duty is to bring economic reasoning to the interpretation of the past—almost as difficult, Marshall pointed out, as the prediction of the future—his second is to put economic events back into the setting of the society from which the

---

[1] In his introduction to the *Concise Economic History of Britain to 1750* (1949).

economist abstracts them. He must realize the society he is describing in the round and in the concrete.

Clapham was not prepared to follow the lead of those who regard the study of social values and institutions as being no part of economic history. He was aware that, without a knowledge of the unmeasurables which go to make the measured things,[1] any hope of understanding historical events in the true sense must be given up and the work of the theorist and the econometrician is to that extent thrown away. To put the matter in a way which would probably have been more congenial to him, he regarded events as needing both to be explained in terms of causes, linking them with other events, and also understood in terms of the motives of the actors. In pursuit of this work of explanation and understanding he was always prepared to go outside the given facts of the market.

Clapham's relations with some of his forerunners may confuse the issue here. He was a severe critic of some social historians, notably Mr. and Mrs. Hammond, because he thought they were demonstrably wrong in their facts. It is no secret that he did not greatly approve of the kind of social history which they wrote. But he did include the social roots and consequences of economic change as an essential part of his conception of economic history and he wrote at length about them. He wrote about them, however, largely in so far as they might be expected to interest economists or had interested economists in the past. The social questions he handles in the *Economic History of Modern Britain* are, for example, mainly those which had at one time or another been relevant to the discussions of the classical economists: population growth and the evolution of the large family; the development of towns and their urban problems; public health, housing, education, poor law and the social services; social politics, Corn Law, Factory Acts, handloom weavers, Chartism.

The conventionality of the list suggests that Clapham's handling of the social side of economic history lacked novelty. I believe this to be true. He borrowed his problems; he did not formulate new ones. Upon those which he handles, he has almost always something fresh and new to say; but they are clearly less the questions which he has come to pose as a result of his own contemplation than those around which Victorian thought had itself revolved. They are great traditional questions. Clapham would never have felt with that born sociologist George

---

[1] The phrase is not mine. It was used by Edwin F. Gay in a lecture at Harvard many years ago.

Unwin—for whom, however, he had a great respect—that the attraction of economic history lies in its imperfection; because every generalization we can make about it drives us sooner or later to refer to processes of social growth and decay about which in truth we know very little. Clapham's work was without this kind of developed social sense. In this, he contrasts strongly not only with Unwin and Tawney, but also with his French contemporary, Marc Bloch. Bloch was acutely aware that we cannot write economic history without writing social history. And he trained a whole generation of French scholars in that belief. Clapham was interested in people and human groups; he had no theories about them.

In his handling of society, as so often in his discussion of economic events, Clapham was content to observe without generalization. One result of this is that in the *Economic History of Modern Britain* his description of the multitude of social groups who go to make up the nation lacks clear outlines and the nation itself lacks social character. The want of unity and definition in his picture of British society accounts, together with other causes, for the failure of the *Economic History of Modern Britain* to have the effect one might have expected upon historians and the reading public, considering the extremely high standard of the scholarship which went to the making of it.

This criticism must not be carried too far. The task of the historian is different in its nature from that of the social scientist. His business is always with the given situation, whether it is that of a firm or a nation or a civilization. He needs economic and social theory to help him to explain events, but only for that purpose. He is so little wedded to the development of theory of its own sake that as Schumann is reported to have said of the composer, he reaches maturity when he knows the right moment to throw away the theory in which he has been brought up.

A historical situation involves many elements which we cannot explain, as well as those which we can. The historian's business is with the unresolved elements as well as with those which are susceptible of rational explanation. This is because his final aim is nothing less than the recreation of the entire situation, including what puzzles him and may, so far as he knows, for ever puzzle men. The recovery of the past, which would, of course, have little meaning for us if it was not associated with rational explanation, is the ultimate aim of his endeavour. This is the real test of the historian. Can he pull off the miracle and make present to us people and happenings which time has carried away and which might seem to be lost for ever? Historical imagination, the power to take a mortal leap, perhaps into situations and personalities remote from any he has ever met, is his means of vision; but he needs to match it with words, if the vision is ever to become alive. Without this kind of imaginative flair, whatever his theoretical and technical equipment, he may find himself in the position of the sculptor who compared his horse with that of the other sculptor and concluded: 'My horse has all the excellences which a model horse ought to have. But alas! his horse lives and mine does not.'

Clapham's powers of historical imagination and writings, guided by his professional training as economist and historian, were deployed at their full stretch in the *Economic History of Modern Britain* and with even more success, I would say, in the *History of the Bank of England*. He had there been asked to write not a theoretical treatise on central banking but the history of the greatest of British banks; he was dealing not with a whole society but with an institution and a group of men he knew and understood well. The result was a wonderfully good book, which with all its imperfections throws a flood of light not only on the Bank but also on the general history of Britain and the world. That book owes its success not merely to the absence of some of Clapham's characteristic defects, but also to the presence of his full powers as a historian. Those powers included an ability, developed when Clapham was nearer seventy than sixty, to marshal and conduct a narrative adequate to convey a vast and varied mass of material. They justify us in regarding him with all his faults and limitations as the greatest of English economic historians.

4 What is Economic History?

I

Economic history is a study which may be discussed in its relation to either economics or history, for it has grown up to assist both economist and historian. Many of the most important contributions of recent years towards the understanding of modern economic history have been made by men who would regard themselves as economists first and foremost. In this part of the field the interchange of knowledge between economists and historians is continuous. But while economic history is necessary to the economist, it is also studied by those whose prime concern is not the advancement of economics but the writing and explanation of history. Economic history has been well defined as that part of history which requires a knowledge of economics for its full understanding. What economics can and what it cannot do for the explanation of history are of course vexed questions, which lie close to the heart of the intellectual debate of our age. Without pretending to settle them here, economic history will be discussed in this essay from the standpoint of the historian and his concerns.[1]

[1] I have tried to refrain in this essay from over-much reference or quotation and to concentrate on the nature of economic history and of the economic historian's work, rather than upon what economic historians have written or are writing now. Ample bibliographies of the subject can be found elsewhere and are regularly published in journals such as the *Economic History Review* and the (American) *Journal of Economic History*, to say nothing of many others.

In discussing economic history as a part of the historian's work (there is, of course, much admirable inquiry into the past by men whose main interests are in economics or sociology), I should like, if it can be done without ostentation and without imputing to them mistakes which are mine, to acknowledge my debt, extending over many years, to the writings of two Continental scholars, Friedrich Meinecke and Benedetto Croce. These men, the one a Prussian conservative, the other an Italian liberal, maintained in the course of their long lives social and political attitudes and opinions which are not mine and which could indeed hardly be those of an Englishman. They were largely indifferent to the economic side of history and they paid little attention to the social sciences, except political science. But each in his own way seems, for various reasons, to have penetrated deeper

The general purpose of the economic historian is that common to all historians. The purpose is to recreate historical situations—a reliving and recreation of the past which is not only an exercise of the intellect but also an experience of the whole personality, as well as involving an act of communication with the reader which is not the least important of the historian's tasks. The method of the historian distinguishes him sharply from the social scientist. For the historian, describing and analysing historical situations, concentrates naturally upon the uniqueness, concreteness, and particularity of the events he is describing and uses every help of analogy and contrast to bring out and illustrate those qualities in them. The social scientist, on the other hand, considering the same events, is concerned rather with the uniformities they display, with the common qualities of apparently disparate situations. He in his turn uses every technical weapon which may assist him to lay bare and to emphasize such uniformities. The social scientist abstracts from society the particular type of relation which interests him; the historian must use his concreting faculty to recover a past society and the situations which arose in the course of its development.

Does this mean that the social scientist cannot help the historian or the historian the social scientist? By no means. The same piece of knowledge in the hands of either serves different purposes and each has to adapt to his own purpose the discoveries of the other. But each also plays into the other's hands. History and the social sciences stand or fall together, to the extent that their great periods of growth have tended to coincide. It was no accident that the revival of political history writing in Europe in the sixteenth century came at the hands of Macchiavelli and Guicciardini, men who were passionate political analysts and students of the theory of politics; no accident either, that economic history arrived late on the scene. Perhaps the first great piece of economic history writing in English was the third chapter of Adam Smith's *Wealth of Nations*, published in 1776. Economic history had to await the development of the capacity for economic analysis in the seventeenth and the eighteenth centuries.

To say all this does not perhaps make the exact nature of the work of the economic historian much clearer, except that the kind of reasoned

---

than any Englishman of their time known to me into the nature and structure of historical truth. It is significant that both men lived in an honourable state of disgrace with the governments which ruled their countries in the nineteen-thirties and which were, as is well known, committed to very different philosophies of history of their own.

narrative which he hopes to write depends, among other things, on economic analysis. What are the relations and the processes in history which specially concern the economic historian and which make economic analysis necessary if they are to be understood?

It seems desirable to begin by clearing out of the way a number of misunderstandings which have arisen largely out of phrases. Economic history is often said to deal with the 'economic factors' in history, with 'economic motives', or with the 'economic foundation' as contrasted with the 'superstructure' of society. These are words which have strayed from mathematics, or psychology, or even architecture. They may well have a use in history, but they are often so applied as to be largely meaningless, where they are not seriously misleading. The misleadingness consists in their being very generally employed in the conviction that there must be in history a certain range of motives or a certain kind of institution which is specifically economic and which thus defines the province of the economic historian. There is good reason to doubt this belief.

The business of the economic historian is with a certain kind of historical problem. But these problems may arise in connection with motives the most diverse and institutions the most varied. Like economics itself, economic history rests upon an observation so general as to be more or less applicable to man everywhere: that he cannot satisfy all his desires fully or at once and must therefore make what appears to him the best use of his resources, allotting them as best he can among competing ends. Such ends or purposes are, of course, both personal and social. This necessity, shared by men of every society and of every age, to bring their ends and their means into some kind of relation, to adapt ends to means and means to ends, is the true economic necessity. It is also the beginning of economic history, for it imposes economic choice. The act of choice lies between one use of resources and another, and men being social, their choices work themselves out through social institutions. Economic choice includes those important, even fateful, choices which decide whether the resources of an individual or a people or a world shall grow or diminish in relation to the wants to be satisfied. It covers all the processes of economic growth and decay.

Economic choice forms the centre of economic history.[1] This might

---

[1] It may be said, what becomes of choice in a society dominated by custom? Alfred Marshall's comment seems apposite here, although it does not cover the whole ground. 'To say that any arrangement is due to custom is really little more than to say that we do not know its cause. I believe that very many customs could

almost be defined as the record of the economic choices which appear to the historian to have been the most interesting and important that men have made; how and why they came to make them; what the execution was, and the economic consequences, so far as we can tell.

If this is true, it follows that there are no specific economic motives, or rather, there is only one. This is the economizing motive itself, the desire to overcome relative scarcities, to make the best use of any resources that one has, in a given situation, in relation to what one wants. For the rest, the motives at work in economic history are as varied as human nature. They are, however, looked at by the economic historian from a special point of view, in so far as they lead to economic decisions.

When it is said, as it so often is, that money-making motives form the material of economic history, it is the economizing motive which is meant, working itself out as it does in our Western world through the institutions of a money-using, market-organized society. But it would be too narrow a definition of economic history to confine it to societies which know the use of money and the market. Economic changes and choices may be made by men and societies too primitive to have knowledge of either. Nor is it true, even where the market and money are known, that the prime economic decisions are always market-made. In modern Europe and North America many of the major economic decisions have been and are taken by governments. This is still more true of the centrally planned economies of eastern Europe.

There are then no specific economic motives. Men make economic choices under the pressure of different motives at different times. Furthermore, living as they do in different societies, they make their decisions according to different schemes of values and according to the habits and structure of the society they find themselves living in. Economic doing involves social being. Similarly, there are no specific institutions which act as the sole vehicles and makers of economic decisions, constant and recognizable throughout history. Over long periods the major economic decisions in society may be taken over the camp fires of primitive hunters; over other long ages, in the village communities of

---

be traced, if we only had knowledge enough, to the slow equilibration of measurable motives: that even in such a country as India no custom retains its hold long after the relative positions of the motives of demand and supply have so changed, that the values which would bring them into stable equilibrium are far removed from those which the custom sanctions.'—*The Present Position of Economics* (1885), p. 48. Custom, that is to say, is the medium of economic decisions for some societies. In other societies they are made through the State and the market. Whether the motives at work are measurable or not in any precise sense is another matter.

peasant cultivators; over others, in the recognized markets for money and commodities of industrial and commercial cities. Organized churches have their own economic history; organized states have theirs. Whoever has the disposition of resources is the maker of economic decisions, and those decisions are made through whatever institutions seem appropriate to the doer at the time.

2

If economic history is the record of economic choices, it might appear that men are free to do as they please in the distribution of their resources. But it is of the nature of economic decisions, being choices to overcome scarcities, that men are not so free; or rather they are free only in the sense that they must choose. They must adapt themselves to limits, whether these are set for them by physical nature, by their own want of knowledge and ignorance of alternatives, or by the other circumstances of the situation in which they find themselves, whether that is primitive and simple, or civilized and complicated.

The great phases of Western economic history seem to have arisen in this way, out of the dilemmas created for men by the scarcity of means to satisfy their wants, the penalty for failing to do so being sometimes no less than extinction. The processes, for example, by which in remote times agriculture, even of the most simple forest-burning, extensive variety, came to be adopted by the hunters and food-gatherers of prehistoric Europe are lost to our view.[1] But they presumably had something to do with the gradual multiplication in the number of hunters and the relative scarcity of game, in some regions always, in all regions at some seasons.

Agriculture once established, it made possible a world of cultivators and of town-living craftsmen and merchants. The requirements of agriculture prepared the way for the agricultural ages and for some of the major problems of later history. Agriculture needed land, and land, it seemed, could never be enough. How or why, in the half-settled Europe of late Roman times, land-hunger became acute among the German tribes, is not wholly clear.[2] But it was so, and out of the decisions of the

[1] Much careful work has been done on the chronology and other aspects of this change. See, to mention only one book, J. G. D. Clark, *Primitive Europe; the economic basis* (London, 1952).
[2] The late Professor Koebner has considered the point in *The Cambridge Economic History of Europe*, 1 (Cambridge, 1941), pp. 19-20.

tribes to seek new land with increasing frequency beyond the Roman border sprang much of the settlement of western Europe and the fall of the Empire.

Under the far different circumstances of the nineteenth century the lack of opportunities on the land in Europe, arising out of a variety of conditions, decided many families to move to the United States and other countries overseas. Of course, land shortage was far from being the only cause of emigration, but in countries like Ireland and western Germany in the first half of the century it was a strong reason, given the opening up of land at that time for settlement elsewhere.[1]

Land scarcity in the literal sense has been and still is one of the great formative powers of economic history. Translated into terms of the need at particular times of particular sorts of land for particular purposes, and made the object of the observation and ingenuity of many men now forgotten, it has been the source of the farming systems of the world, as well as of dearths and famines. It has also been a cause of conflict. Every schoolboy knows of the clash between agriculturalist and cattleman in the American West of the last century. But that was only one of numberless disputes in history about the use of land, often additionally complicated by differences of race and culture and religion.

Physical scarcities of an easily understandable type also played their part in that Industrial Revolution of the eighteenth century in England which was as decisive a turning-point in European history as the adoption of tillage had been thousands of years before. It has been remarked with much truth that Britain's industrial success in the eighteenth and nineteenth centuries depended on her richness in the two great new raw materials, coal and iron.[2] But the wealth of her resources in coal and the successful use of coal for smelting would not have been discovered but for the gradual encroachment upon the woodlands over centuries by agriculturists and others, the growing relative scarcity of wood fuel in particular districts, and its role in the iron producer's costs.

Crude physical scarcity therefore plays and has played a great part in economic history. It has also influenced men's views of that history.

[1] There were important complications of 'push' and 'pull' behind the European emigrations of last century. Were people pushed overseas by 'pressure of population' or were they 'pulled' there by new opportunities? On the American emigration, Brinley Thomas, *Migration and Economic Growth* (1954), and M. L. Hansen, *The Atlantic Migration, 1607–1860* (Cambridge, Mass., 1940), are instructive.

[2] Charles Singer and others, editors, *History of Technology* (Oxford, 1957), vol. III, p. 712.

Much of the impression created among Englishmen over a hundred years ago by Malthus and his *Essay on Population* (1798) arose from the telling effect with which a complete view of history was derived from the observable relations between population and the land available for food. In a country such as Malthus's England, where primary poverty, in the sense of not enough to eat, was common, that view seemed to fit well with what people could see for themselves.

It would be an unduly simplified vision of economic history, however, which described it as a record of choices arising out of the conflict between physical needs, constant and overwhelmingly powerful though they are. Even where human needs have an obvious physical basis, they have become so adjusted and are so closely tied with custom and habit as to be properly described as social or cultural needs. Other needs, such as those of art and religion, seem to possess no clear physical basis whatever, although they have an obvious physical expression.

This social pattern of human wants has an important bearing upon the work of the economic historian. If economic history is the study of how men have chosen to use their resources to satisfy their wants, we have to recognize that there is a fundamental mobility about men's ideas of their wants which lends a certain elusiveness to the conception of a resource. This is not only or even primarily a question of changing techniques, although a change in technique can revolutionize our ideas both of our wants and our resources. It is a question of economic logic. For what is economically logical, in the sense of a rational distribution of resources in one state of society, may not be so at all in another.

An illustration may make this clear. When Englishmen went to Australasia in the nineteenth century they found, among the Maoris of New Zealand and the Australian aborigines, a conception of what was a good use of land which was, not unsurprisingly, entirely different from their own. To hunting and food-gathering peoples it seemed natural that they should collect their subsistence according to an established annual routine over hundreds and even thousands of square miles of virgin country. To the incoming grazier or stockman, with his head full of the knowledge of money and European markets, this was economic madness. He proceeded to take over the land, in the name of a higher civilization. In the conviction that he stood for a higher civilization he may possibly have been correct, but he was hardly superior in economic logic. It would be very difficult indeed to argue that the land was not rationally used, from the standpoint of the Maori and the aborigine, given the state of the culture of each at the beginning of the nineteenth century.[1]

This matter is of some importance in understanding the economic history of countries and people outside the Western circle and the European impact upon them. It also bears upon economic history nearer home. One could not, for example, relate the economic history of Britain over the past half-century without reference to the arrangements and the values of European society as a whole. European economic arrangements have had their own special logic, which cannot be explained apart from Europe's history, including two great wars. If, for instance, a Maori or an Australian aborigine of the early nineteenth century had been able to return to contemplate the economic affairs of Europe in the nineteen-thirties, he might perhaps have felt that his own efforts at economic rationality needed rather less defence than had at one time been supposed to be necessary.

To study his chosen subject, therefore, the economic historian needs to abstract from the web of events in historical time those situations which involve acts of economic choice. But it is hardly likely that he will make much of them unless he either knows already or takes the trouble to get to know a great deal about the society from which he abstracts. Particular economic decisions and situations mean very little, detached from the context of the society in which they take place. This may not be obvious to the student of contemporary problems. In the shorthand of day-to-day economic discussion it is possible to take for granted a knowledge of the society the economic arrangements of which are under debate. When we move, however, out of our own parish in time and place the extent to which economic choices depend upon the existing structure of society and its accepted values becomes apparent. The economic historian must, by the nature of the problems upon which he works, be prepared to employ economic analysis of the kind and to the degree which is necessary to explain the situation he is rebuilding and, so to speak, reliving. But he should also be, if not by training, at least by inclination and experience, something of a sociologist, too—an observer and re-creator of the codes, loyalties, and organizations which men create and which are just as real to them as physical conditions. Of the processes of this social world, we know, to

---

[1] R. H. Tawney made this point of the relative rationality of economic systems in his own unforgettable way in an introduction to Raymond Firth's book, *Primitive Economics of the New Zealand Maori* (London, 1929).

be sure, very little.[1] The deliberate study of social structure and values and of the transformations which come over them is still something of a novelty among historians, while the nature of the relations between economic and social change is a fundamental problem not to be discussed here. But whoever observes and reflects upon the one is likely to find himself observing and reflecting upon the other and will be led to consider those hidden springs of social growth out of which all history comes.

3

Economic change is, one might say, the first great theme of the economic historian. It covers all the transformations in the distribution of their resources which men think it necessary to make, whether privately or publicly, whether in peace or war, whether in time of the rise or the fall of civilizations. This accounts for some of the importance of the study of economic history for us living in an age of great economic developments, when thinking men in almost all countries are concerned with problems of practical economic dynamics that can hardly be solved without reference to history.

Perhaps one of the first things to be said about economic change is that to write its history, especially in modern times and when attempted on a large scale, covering it may be the economic life of a nation, requires the help of the economist and the statistician. This may sound a little intimidating—despite the analogous connection which has long existed between the political historian and the political scientist—but the reasons are clear enough. The great complexity of economic situations, in which the elements at work are rarely few or simple and where what has to be traced is often an elaborate series of calculations and actions, each conditioning and in turn conditioned by the other, makes it necessary to analyse or, in other words, pick out the significant relations. This is necessary even to describe a given state of affairs; still more, if one is going to understand the elaborate dynamics of the change from one state to another.

---

[1] It seems unfair to write this without mentioning the name of George Unwin. Of all the English economic historians of an earlier generation, he perhaps most successfully communicated the sense of the fundamental relation between the economic and the social. See, for example, his (posthumous) *Studies in Economic History* (1927). There was, however, in his work no direct relating of history to sociology.

The work of the economist lies with such analysis. His interest in economic relations is different from the historian's, since he uses them to build theoretical or abstract models of the economic world. But it is only with the help of such models, however simple,[1] that the historian can get forward with his own work of reconstructing historical situations. It is not, of course, the business of the historian to 'prove' the validity of economic theorems or indeed to prove anything. He approaches the economist for certain intellectual tools, concepts and categories which are necessary to his own work. To the economist familiar with the full range of theoretical work, the use of theory by the historian must always seem very elementary and imperfect, if not positively misapplied. But elementary or not, it is indispensable.

If he is to be a judge of theoretical tools, the historian must keep an eye on the economist's work-bench. Indeed, it is probable that the connection between the state of economic theory and the writing of economic history is a good deal closer than many people would suppose who have not closely considered the matter. It might be correct to say that every great departure in theory, as under Adam Smith and Ricardo, and thirty years ago under Keynes, makes possible a new kind of economic history. Marxian theory certainly occasioned a new kind of history. But this is too large a matter to be pursued here.

The statistician comes in because economic decisions about what to do with resources turn naturally upon questions of quantity. They involve the allocation of amounts. How much income shall be saved, how much spent? How much land shall be given over to crops, how much to stock? How much shall be allowed in the factory for wages, how much for raw materials? How much money can be earned in one job, how much in another? If he is dealing with a society accustomed to numbers and accounts, the historian often finds that the men whose actions he is studying have begun his statistical work for him. They have already counted the sheep on the manor and the amount of wool sold in the year; the number of ships at sea and the value of the cargoes; the number of the workpeople and the amount of raw material. The contemporary figure is often highly important; it may have settled opinion and determined policy at the time. But it is rarely enough by itself. Any historian studying these transactions in a later age almost

[1] Professor D. Walker, 'Economics in East Africa', *Makerere Journal*, No. 2 (1959), pp. 14–26, points out that a certain amount of model-building is necessary to understand the working even of a wholly unindustrial economy. One might add that it is still more necessary when tracing the transition from agriculture to industry or from one type of industrial economy to another.

always wants to analyse them in a slightly different fashion, from an angle which is often suggested to him by the interests of the world he lives in. He also requires to look at relations and interactions which the contemporaries of historical events were unaware of or felt no need to consider. In a word, he feels the need to cross-examine the evidence for himself. The historian's interest is not the same as that of the men he is studying. This becomes particularly evident if he is following events over a long period, beyond the life of one generation.

The provision of national historical statistics is becoming professional work. The time has already arrived when it seems worth while to publish such collections.[1] But many quantitative answers to his own questions the historian must ferret out for himself. Such work is at a low level of *expertise* compared with what mathematicians are used to, being nothing more than the simple arithmetic and accounting of history, but it has to conform to sound standards. Sometimes it needs the statistician's advice.

A figure, a table, or a graph can be critical in economic history, for it may bring to the final test our view of how or why things happened. At the same time, it must be allowed that much statistical work is in the nature of description rather than explanation. Emphasis and degree are, however, important matters in history. Quantities may assist to define the limits of a problem, even if they do not serve to solve it.

It can therefore truthfully be said that important parts of the study of history are becoming mathematical. There are, however, important limits to the helpfulness of statistics. The systematic quantification of history, without an equally careful observation of qualities, may be more than unhelpful. It can be definitely misleading. The economic historian, to put things shortly, has to learn to live both with the quantities and the qualities, and above all, to cultivate that kind of judgement 'at the back of the head' which acts as a guide towards what is important both in quantitative and qualitative things.

One way of avoiding sad mistakes is to vary the point of view. In the observation of economic change, it may be instructive to turn from the history of the economic system as a whole and from the study of aggregate figures and general statements, which often obscure the varieties of individual and group behaviour, to the study of individuals and small groups. This is to come in many ways nearer to the sources

---

[1] See, for example, the extremely useful volume published by the United States Bureau of the Census, *Historical Statistics of the United States, 1789–1945* (Washington, D.C., 1949), since revised.

of change and certainly to avoid some of the mistakes of generalization. The record of what has actually happened in and on farms and estates, towns and manors, cities and factories, railways and banks, industries and markets, is a part of economic history so immensely important that it might almost be said that the worth of our general histories depends on the value of the regional and local and industrial studies behind them.

The men who have produced economic changes, sometimes radical and far-reaching, more often limited and imitative, have arisen in many different classes and lived in different walks of life. But whether noblemen or plantation-owners or farmers, merchants or bankers, shipowners, railwaymen, industrialists, auctioneers, or shopkeepers, they have left records behind them, sometimes of great historical interest. The practice of conserving, out of family and historical interest, the records of landed estates is ancient. The preservation of business records, in the sense of the papers of industrial, commercial, and financial houses, is relatively new. It has become increasingly common as it has come to be recognized that the past decisions of businessmen form much of the fabric of modern Western economic history.

Studies which may be conveniently described as business history, because they are written with the help of business records, are becoming steadily more important. Their relation to general economic history has been admirably described by Professor Ashton. 'The contribution that business history has to make to the parent study is by no means small. For it is in the individual firm . . . that we can observe the operation of economic forces at first hand . . . Decisions reached in the counting house or the board room may affect the course of events quite as much as those made in public assemblies.'[1]

It is important to know the minds of the businessmen because they, far more than governments, have settled the course of investment, the rate of technical development, the methods of management, and the other determinants of economic change. But to understand that change perfectly, we also need to know the mind of labour. This is hard to do, for want of written evidence. The worker's search for work, whether it has taken the form of a move from Welsh farm-land to the coal valleys of Glamorganshire or from Italy to the Argentine or from Ireland to the United States, has altered the face of the world. His shift from occupation to occupation in the last century and a half has refashioned

[1] Professor T. S. Ashton in *Business History*, Liverpool University Press and the Business Archives Council, 1, No. 1 (December 1958), p. 2.

the centuries-old society of Europe. But direct evidence of what was in his mind at the time he moved is as often as not impossible to come by. There was a man, for example, in the sixties of last century, an apprenticed currier, who after marriage in Gloucestershire migrated to London to find work among the tanneries and leatherworks on the south side of the Thames. When the boom of the early seventies broke, he moved to other tanneries and leatherworks at Woodbridge in Suffolk, only to return after a short interval to the west of England, where he took up employment in his wife's trade of tailoring in the same small textile town from which he had first set out. Every step in this man's movements must have been the subject of much pondering and much discussion in the home, yet nothing survives of it but oral tradition. It is an example of what is well known to anthropologists but is sometimes oddly minimized by historians, that conduct in itself as deliberate and rational as any other may leave no documentary evidence behind it.[1] Mainly for this reason, that most important branch of economic history, the history of labour as a factor in production, is extraordinarily difficult to write. It succeeds best at the point where the working man came into contact with institutions and persons—Poor Law officers, trade-union secretaries—concerned with his search for work and his conditions of employment and where they have kept records. But his own voice is too often missing, to the grave discomfort of any historian with a sense of evidence.

4

Economic change is one of the great permanent themes of economic history. Economic welfare, to use the clumsy conventional phrase, is another. They are closely related, but separate. The one is the history of the wealth of nations, of the creation of incomes and production. The other is the record of the influence of the wealth of nations upon their well-being. What good, if any, came to society from all this? The two themes are intertwined. Most men would find it hard to discuss economic change without raising sooner or later questions of welfare;

---

[1] Compare the interesting discussion on the difficulties of writing African history in Professor Gluckman's foreword to Gann, *The Birth of a Plural Society: the Development of Northern Rhodesia under the British South Africa Company* (Manchester, 1958), p. ix. The problem is far from being limited to Africa or to labour. Consider how much is decided nowadays over the telephone, without record.

almost equally puzzling to consider welfare without coming up at some point against questions of change.

The weight of emphasis tends to shift from time to time. The theme which has been in the ascendant among economists and economic historians has varied with circumstances. David Ricardo discussed, nearly a century and a half ago, the distribution of wealth. But he treated it very much as a condition of the wealth of nations, that is, as a cause of the differences between stationary, progressive, and declining economies. Forty and fifty years ago, on the crest of the great wave of prosperity in Victorian and Edwardian England, there was a certain tendency to take economic change for granted and to concentrate upon problems of economic welfare. The late Professor Pigou introduced that term before the First World War to describe what was then a new branch of economics, and what might be described as the Hammond-Webb approach to economic history matured in the same age. Very different conditions in the last thirty years have restored the dynamics of economic progress to first place in economic discussion and among economic historians too. But economic progress divorced from economic welfare makes no sense. A balanced view of economic history requires that justice be done to both themes, as well as to one other yet to be mentioned.

The good which men may derive from economic change is usually thought of in terms of their command over goods and services. In proportion as that command is increased or diminished, they tend to regard themselves as benefited or injured. But when this kind of judgement is applied to historical situations, considerable difficulties arise. Substantial changes in the economic life of a nation may take place over a long period. Within that time, not only does one generation give way to another, but the whole style and way of life may change. Imprecise answers only are possible to questions about changes in the standard of life.[1]

[1] Professor T. S. Ashton has put the point practically. 'The truth is that it is not possible to compare the welfare of two groups of people separated widely in time and space. We cannot compare the satisfaction derived from a diet that includes bread, potatoes, tea, sugar, and meat with that derived from a diet consisting mainly of oatmeal, milk, cheese, and beer' ('The Standard of Life of the Workers in England, 1790–1830', *Journal of Economic History*, IX (1949), p. 33). The commodity standard is not, of course, the only possible one. One might compare Sir John Clapham's use of mortality and expectation of life as a test of economic welfare; for many purposes, a very good one. Dr. D. E. C. Eversley has pointed out to me how closely the two things, standard of living, so far as we can measure it, and expectation of life, tend to march together, to the extent that they can be used as checks upon one another.

The concept of a standard of living has itself something impalpable about it. Some kind of answer is required, however, from the historian, and it has to be as definite as possible. It is an important part of his work therefore to try to give some clear meaning to the effect of historical changes in production and in money incomes upon nations and social groups. He has to consider whether their riches or their poverty afforded them an adequate living by the standards to which they were accustomed. The changes which have taken place from time to time in social or national income; its division between groups, classes, and individuals; the fluctuation of incomes, whether due to harvests or to the state of investment and trade, and its effect upon the well-being of particular people—these are the problems involved in the concepts of economic good and economic welfare. One has only to enumerate them to see that these questions include some which have deeply agitated societies from time to time. They have mixed themselves with, although they are far from having been the sole cause of, wars and revolutions.

What has already been said of the necessary association of the economic historian with the economist and the statistician in the piecing out of the complicated process of the creation of incomes and production, holds good here, too. Without the help of analysis and measurement, it would be difficult to decide what can be known and how far it can be known. But other knowledge may be just as valuable. The economic historian must be prepared to pick up bits and pieces of other people's techniques as he goes along. If a knowledge of metallurgy or soil chemistry might not come amiss to the historian of agricultural and industrial production, a student of welfare among large industrial populations may profit by the experience of the doctor, the magistrate, or the professional social worker.

There is, however, more to be said about economic welfare than can be contained in statements about income. For most men, what they earn in the way of income is of no greater importance than the conditions under which they earn it. Hours and conditions of labour may be as good a sign of the effect of economic change upon the well-being of a people as the quantity of goods and services which they consume. The impact of economic events can in this respect be very great indeed. If all possible changes are taken into account, for example, in the move from agriculture to industry, what comes out may be nothing less than a transformation of industrial relations and of the organization of society. Most men would hold that a new system of social relations in industry or a new way of living, in cities and towns perhaps instead of villages, represents for them a change in every respect as important as any income which they may get, or fail to get, out of the new arrangements.

The history of industrial relations is therefore a most important part of economic history. The attention paid to it fifty years ago by some of the founders of economic history in Great Britain, by people so different in their general outlook as the Webbs and W. J. Ashley, was a recognition of the hugeness of the changes brought about by the industrialization of the nineteenth century. Like other types of history it depends upon documents. Many of these are to be found among the records of trade unions and industrial firms. The kind of problems which arise go, however, far beyond bargaining about wages, hours, and conditions. Industrial relations raise the whole perplexing question of the incentives to labour and of why people live and act as they do. They require us to bring into focus the individuals and the groups in industry, if we are to understand the human relations which social institutions and law merely form and modify. The historian may need to be something of a psychologist and sociologist, as well as a lawyer, if he is to understand the thoughts and emotions which lie behind those relations.

If human relations in industry are complex and difficult to grasp, the sort of alterations in the life of society which tend to go with major economic change are even more difficult to expound. They are difficult to capture in words. Qualities and changes of quality are the things to be expressed. Nevertheless, they cannot be put aside in favour of more manageable things which have been christened economic goods because these carry money values and are consequently roughly measurable. It could be said with much truth that the chief function of economic change in history has been not so much to alter the standard of living, in any ordinary sense, as to bring new varieties of human and social life into being.

It may be objected that the historian of welfare cannot be impartial or objective. When he deals with the results of economic change in terms of comfort and happiness, freedom and justice, good and evil, he is moving out of the field of economic analysis into that of ethics and social philosophy. What he is watching and describing are changes in social values, and he cannot but take up an attitude towards them. His subject becomes involved in value judgements. This is, of course, true. But it does not appear that his difficulties in this respect are greater than those of, say, the historian of politics or religion who endeavours to set Church and State in some relation to the life and movement of society. History free of all values cannot be written. Indeed, it is a concept almost impossible to understand, for men will scarcely take the trouble to inquire laboriously into something which they set no value upon. But if the historian cannot escape judgements of value and the clash of judgement, he can at least know his own order of values, acquaint himself with his sources of bias, and strive to put himself in the shoes of the people he is dealing with. Here it is a victory to understand those one disapproves of and to write with sympathy and insight of states of society far removed from one's own.

The struggle for historical understanding is not the same thing as a willingness to vote all economic arrangements equally sensible or all states of society equally good. A good state of society may be ill served by its economic arrangements; a particular society may direct its economic arrangements with intense and driving rationality towards evil ends. But the historian resembles the society which he describes in at least one respect. He does not pick up a knowledge of what is rational or good by the light of nature, but by a lengthy and imperfect process of experience. The more he is aware of this, the less likely he is ever to be satisfied with what he writes in this difficult field.

5

Between economic welfare and politics there is an obvious link. Welfare concerns the ends of human and social life. It easily becomes a matter of public concern and draws the attention of the State. Government, as the supreme law-making body, invested historically with the care of the interests of the whole, is interested in decisions which involve the alternative use of resources, because they affect the welfare both of those making the decisions and of other people. But government also concerns itself with those decisions to serve its own purposes. Not only does the machinery of the State become involved in the ceaseless competition between social groups for economic advantage and monopoly power. The State has an interest of its own to preserve. What is from one point of view private wealth is from another public revenue and war potential. Without these two, the State cannot survive, if only because it is itself involved in a struggle for power in a world without law.

These have been the commonplaces of public life in Europe for centuries. We cannot then get away from the State in economic history, however much we try, and least of all today, when the State becomes constantly more powerful and effective. But what is meant by welfare and what is understood under the heading of economic development have, of course, meant different things at different times, and different things to different people.[1] The history of public policy in the sphere of economic growth and welfare is an impure subject in the eyes of those who prefer their economics pure, for it is considerably mixed with other things than economics. But pure or impure, and ceaselessly reminding us as it does how much politics there must always be in political economy, it is an important topic. With economic welfare and change, it forms the third great theme of the economic historian.

The history of modern economic policies in Europe began with the rise of nation states, three centuries or more before the French Revolution. What those states did in the way of trying to mobilize resources and to promote the economic welfare of their subjects in peace and war is still matter of controversy among historians. The effects of their policies and the nature of the influences and interests which lay behind them are still being unravelled. But the general relation between public authority and economic activities extends, of course, far back behind the nation state and far outside the limits of Europe.

Only in the eighteenth and nineteenth centuries did a type of economic policy and thinking arise in Europe which seemed to break with the age-old connection between public authority and economic life. This was chiefly the result of the teachings of the English classical economists and the acceptance of *laissez-faire* doctrines. Whatever the effects of such views on public policy, there were certainly great gains to be had from them in the field of social thought. They made possible, for instance, the recognition of economics and sociology as studies independent of political science. The insistence on the 'spontaneous forces of social development' as those which are chiefly important for the understanding of economic history is one to which historical studies owe a great debt. It led to the observation of a vast range of activities by individuals and social groups which a State-bound conception of history had neglected. The *laissez-faire* view was not, by the way, that the State had no obligations or interests in the economic field. It was that public authority need only act when individuals and groups could not take decisions or make contracts for themselves, or when the public interest required that something be done which would not otherwise

---

[1] Some idea of the changes which in this country have taken place over the centuries in the public sense of what is and what is not desirable and allowable in the economic field may be gained by turning over the pages of Sir William Holdsworth's great *History of English Law*.

be done at all. The *laissez-faire* philosophy was itself a philosophy of the public purpose, for behind it lay a clear-cut and well-defined view, the validity of which will not be discussed here, of how the public interest in economic development could best be achieved and economic welfare promoted, given certain states of society.

Since then the wheel of public policy has come full circle. Even in the West, let alone those countries which run centrally planned economies, the State has become an active guardian of economic welfare in a manner undreamed of in the nineteenth century, and an industrial investor and innovator on the great scale. This turn of events makes it more rather than less important that the history of economic policy should be well, thoroughly, and independently written.

There is perhaps a special reason why economic history studies should always have been closely connected with public policy. This lies in the potentially explosive nature of the relation between economic and social change. Social change of a kind dangerous to the stability of society may arise, of course, on any of the many sides of the life of man, and economic change is not the only source of social transformation. But it remains true that economic changes of a major sort have been and are a standing invitation to social conflict. One might almost say that the only question has been, not whether conflict would follow change, but how it should be dealt with. Some must gain and others lose, both in economic and social ways, by almost any economic change, and some in any case will gain more than others. Both gain and loss may occur to the same man and to the same society. Conflict may arise between groups, between nations, or within individuals. The last-named variety of conflict may be the most important of all. It menaces the integrity of human personality, and unstable personalities threaten the stability of society, as unstable societies in their turn threaten personality through the instability of their relationships.

The resolution of conflict must be regarded as a necessary means by which individuals and societies grow. It is in this way that they acquire the character which we see them to have. Solution has to be achieved, however, if it is at all, by different ways and means. The majority of changes and conflicts individuals and groups can somehow cope with and reconcile for themselves. In a more profound sense and in the long run, the task of reconciling human nature to itself and the world it lives in seems to fall to religion and the arts. They can provide a fundamental resolution of tensions. They have historically made possible the summoning up and release of new energy, capable of building up new social forms of power and beauty even out of the ruins of past societies. The significance of the State for economic history is that, in the short run, much of the business of resolving social conflicts falls to it.

The final position of the State and of public policy in the history of economic development and welfare is and must always be hard to judge. It is so, partly because economic policy is clearly open to grave mistakes of calculation in determining the correct quantitative relations of things, and partly because of the values involved in the situations to be handled. Problems of public economic policy, like all questions of the distribution of resources, are matters of more or less. The determination of quantities may be critical in the development of a nation's economy. These problems are also at bottom questions of the public interest. Conflicts have to be reconciled within a larger whole, and the price of reconciling and resolving them has at some time or other to be paid. The typical question of public economic policy is in the double form: how much of the available resources shall be distributed to this purpose or that, and for what social ends? What values and whose values are being served by a given distribution of resources?

The answer to such questions obviously cannot be wholly quantitative and scientific. They raise issues of political expediency and of social philosophy. Economic policy has to be looked at by the economic historian primarily as a means to given ends, to be judged in terms of its economic effectiveness in distributing means between ends. But the historian cannot altogether neglect the fact that not only other means but other ends may well have been possible.

The history of economic policy, being a part of public policy, encounters questions which are as old and as difficult as the concept of public interest itself. However statistical and technical the form in which these questions are asked and settled, they run at bottom in the shape of the question which meets us in the works of Macchiavelli, the first great modern student of the public interest. He asked in effect: How much public evil is to be tolerated for the sake of how much good? (In this world the one is not to be found without the other.) Macchiavelli could answer that question in the confident tone of a man who knew passionately what he wanted and in whom the historical sense was weak. The historian cannot reply so easily. He sees new goods and new evils arising at different times in history. He knows both that they are evil and good in some fundamental sense, and also that they are relative to the circumstances of the time.

This question of public values is raised in an acute form by economic change and by public policy in relation to it. New means may radically affect the accepted ends of society, and great transformations of accepted ends may revolutionize the distribution of resources. Much of the interest of economic history in the nineteenth century, when under the impact of industrialism and the revolution of expectations new conceptions of the public interest began to emerge, arises out of problems in this class. It may easily be seen that the most minute research into details cannot clear up all the problems which arise in the course of investigating the history of economic policy.

The historian of policy is a student both of the quantities of the historical situation and of other men's values, which are also historical facts. He is not without values and views of his own, and he is addressing himself to an audience, whether learned or lay, which has its own views and values. Nevertheless, the difficult and inconclusive kind of history that he writes is indispensable. Few things can be more necessary to society than the historical self-analysis which asks where one's economic ideas and social values came from, and which considers whether events have proved them to be true or false. The importance of such history does not lie in its certainty, for it is always uncertain, but in the need which the historian shares with other men to re-examine from time to time the basis of his assumptions.

6

What has been said so far may briefly indicate the strange fusion of direct description and narrative, explanation and evaluation, which forms the work of the economic historian. It is a mixture shared no doubt with other forms of history-writing. The effect is possibly more paradoxical in the economic sphere. The economic historian, dealing with the economizing principle in human nature, is on the face of things in touch with one of the most constant and rational and intelligible forces in history. In fact, he may well find himself, as in writing the economic history of war, dealing with the mathematics of pure passion. But such as his subject is, so must his methods of inquiry be. They are only partly to be compared with those of the scientist measuring and explaining indifferent nature. Yet they are not ill-adapted to the study of beings of intention and will, such as men are.

An interesting question which arises out of those methods concerns the writing of economic history. The writing of history is not simply, as might perhaps be supposed, a question of communicating dead information in a suitably dead manner. It is part of the task of interpreting and of bringing to life historical situations. Strictly speaking, the economic historian's work is not done until he has selected the form of words in which he proposes to do this and to communicate his own view of the past to other men. Those men will, of course, also have their view, which the historian will seek to change, if what was his personal interpretation is to become a part of the public mind. In this context, what is the relation between the form of communication to be adopted by the economic historian and the classical type of historical narrative? Is there any room for narrative in economic history at all? Ought the economic historian to regard himself as carrying out a kind of structural analysis of historical situations? If so, what is the model of such an analysis? Or is he writing one kind of analytical narrative, as the political historian writes another? The literary problems of writing economic history deserve far more attention than they have ever received. They are bound up with the character of the discipline, that is, with the purposes of the historian and of the historian's readers. But they can only be alluded to here before passing on to another question.

No systematic consideration of the relation between economic history and general history will be expected at the end of a short essay. It would be fair, however, that any reader should ask what that relation is, and a few remarks may be attempted on the subject. They may amount to little more than drawing out some implications of what has been said already.

Perhaps it would be useful at this point to draw a distinction between general and universal history, so as to avoid confusion. For the two concepts are distinct. General history or integral history, as it could better be called, deals with the whole society of which it is the record. Universal or world history is, one assumes, the record of all societies, of the whole human world.

If universal history is to be written in a perfect form, certain difficult conditions have to be fulfilled. The idea assumes that the histories of the various peoples make, in some sort, a whole or a universe. But the histories of separate peoples can only become a whole by virtue of experiences and values which are common to them all and which outweigh differences that may be profound. Ranke, the great German historian, felt able in the last century to write the histories of the nations which have made up the circle of European civilization and to regard what he wrote as being universal history, something more than the sum of national histories. Such history-writing is obviously far removed from the confusion of our time. It represents the end-product of a long process, both in history and in the historian's mind. Value and fact are both necessary for it. The most we can hope for in our age is that, since history begins in the struggle of men to understand the life of the society to which they belong, and since that effort starts so often in the encounter with men who are the bearers of different traditions and standards, then perhaps out of our divisions and conflicts universal history in the true, Ranke-like, sense may one day rise again.

Meanwhile, the economic historian needs, for his own purposes and in a kind which is a good deal less than perfect, universal history. The encounter of men with men which makes world history has been to no small extent economic. The history of the economic development of one nation almost always requires the economic history of other peoples to make it fully intelligible. This is not only a matter of the spread of economic institutions, as they come to be copied in lands remote from the place of their origin. The vital processes of growth or decay in the economy of a people may be connected with the intimacy or remoteness of its economic relations with other countries. The economic theorist may for his own purposes and from time to time feel the need to consider a closed economy, without foreign trade, migration, or international credit. The economic historian is seldom able to contemplate such a singular state of society. If he is considering men who know, even in the most primitive way, how to exchange things, how to augment their resources or to satisfy their wants by doing so, or who possess the natural human habit of wandering, their economy is likely to be linked with that of others. The tread of the caravan and the winds that blow upon the sea have united the economic destinies of many peoples who grew up in isolation from one another. In more modern times, when the interchange of ideas and goods and tastes is incessant, the relation between economic developments in one part of the world and another may be so close as to be extremely hard to disentangle. Without going back for an example to the Italian or German cities of the Middle Ages, or to the trade of seventeenth-century Holland, the correct interpretation of what actually happened in England in the eighteenth century, when she took the first long and irrevocable steps towards an industrial economy, depends to no small extent upon what we think of the developments which took place at the same time in other countries known to have been in close touch with her. Why the Industrial Revolution took place in Britain and not in some other land,

and whether British industrial developments can be understood without reference to the whole trading area of which Britain formed so active a part, may be questions which it is impossible to answer. But they are well worth asking.[1] Much of the study of modern economic history consists in putting to the historian's materials just such questions, not only about Britain, but also about Australia, the United States, tropical Africa, and the many other countries which in the eighteenth and nineteenth centuries became tied together for the first time into something which could be called, with fair accuracy, a world economy.

Questions concerning the relations between economies affect not only long-term development as world conditions alter over long ages, but also the changes and chances of much shorter periods. No one could go far, for instance, in the economic understanding of Victorian England, its perpetual transformation of expectations, its many changes of mood, the uncertain and uneven movement of production, consumption, and money-incomes, and the other details of the day-to-day economic history of the time, without paying the closest attention to the many links which bound England to other economies in every quarter of the world and the responsiveness of her balance of payments and her credit institutions, consequently of her whole economic system, to the succession of events abroad.

The economic historian needs universal history in order to grasp the broad trend and the flux of the events which he is describing. He needs it not only in its breadth, because he is studying one society among others, but also in depth, because the relationships he is studying go back in time and some of them go very far back. A student of English economic history is, almost by definition, a student of the economic history of Europe and of more than Europe, over periods of time which deepen with his purposes.

General history, or integral history, is something different from this. Seen from the standpoint of the economic historian, universal history is the study of economic relationships in their full extension in space and time. General history is the examination of economic relationships in their connection with the other sides of the life of society. It may be useful at this point to repeat something that has already been said. Economic history, it has been suggested, is the study of a particular class of historical events. These are the events which arise out of economic choice, where men find themselves faced, as they daily do, with the

[1] For a discussion of this sort, see, for example, K. Berrill, 'International Trade and the Rate of Economic Growth', *Economic History Review* (April 1960).

need to make their resources go round among the ends which they set themselves. Their decisions and the outcome of those decisions may be studied at many different levels. But they are all events and decisions of an economic kind, requiring from the historian some degree of economic knowledge. The kind of judgement demanded is, it is true, rather that of political economy, which has to take account of other things besides economics, than the strict and formal analysis of the economic schools, necessary though that is.[1]

Economic choices, it has also been argued, just because they are imposed by the scarcity of material means compared with ends, are unintelligible without reference to the other activities and qualities of the men concerned. The historian needs especially to be familiar with the social values of the people he is watching. For their economic decisions were taken in the service of those values, and without a knowledge of them the historian can hardly imagine how they thought they could be advantaged by the steps they took, or judge the results, whether by his standard or by theirs. He is likely also to find both their ends and their resources powerfully affected by a particular institution, the state.

On the view so far set out, two particular activities of a non-economic kind, the search for what men regard as a good life—easily identified by most of us with the life we lead—and the political struggle for power and for law, appear as permanent fixed parts of the historical scene. They are as inescapable for men as economic choice itself.

Granted this conception of history, economic activity becomes one of a number of social activities, and the economic function one of a number of functions, which any society must discharge if it is to live and cohere at all. The making the best of resources is for the sake of those other functions and for the sake of that social coherence, rather than for its own sake. Economic action is for the sake of living, and the economic world carries a social meaning derived from activities beyond its own boundaries. This seems to be the conclusion to be drawn not only from European experience but also from the history of society in many other parts of the world at many levels of culture.

All this may seem obvious enough. But when we face the question, what determines the relation of these various social activities and the movement of society under their impulse, we leave certainty behind

[1] The difference between economic science and political economy has been best drawn perhaps by an American scholar, O. H. Taylor, in his *Economics and Liberalism: Collected Papers* (Harvard University Press, 1955). See particularly p. 225, where he insists upon the part which value judgements must necessarily play in judgements upon economic policy.

and find ourselves handling problems both important and puzzling. What are the relations between the ends of society and its means? How far do the means determine the ends or the ends the means? To what extent do social institutions, which embody in themselves certain relationships between ends and means, acquire an independent existence of their own, which makes them the potential master as well as the agents of the society they are supposed to serve?

General questions of this direct and difficult sort have given rise to great philosophies of history, usually achieved under the pressure of unusual circumstances by a kind of heroic simplification from the flow of events. Macchiavelli in one century, Marx in another, have given us supreme examples of such abstracts of history and society. It is not possible to read the one man, without becoming possessed as he was by the primacy in history of political power and of the struggles which surround it, or the other, without becoming convinced that economic change is the independent variable upon which all other things hinge. So compelling is genius, that it takes a conscious effort of mind to remind oneself that these are mighty abstracts of experience, that they are far from exhausting reality, and that perhaps what is being left out is as important as what is being included. Renaissance Italy was a land of many activities besides politics, and in nineteenth-century England, where Marx lived and wrote, there were working men and women who would not only have denied his premises but maintained with calmness and fortitude throughout their lives views almost precisely opposite to his. Their views on a matter touching their own experience have to be respected.

Economic history studies in England have owed a great deal over the last forty years to general discussions of this nature, much of it arising indirectly out of the existence of the Marxian system. One might instance Max Weber's well-known writings published in Germany before the First World War, which argued, not, as has sometimes been supposed, that Protestantism gave rise to capitalism, but that there was a distinct element in European capitalism which could only be accounted for by the presence of an ethic which was Protestant in origin. At the hands of R. H. Tawney, whose *Religion and the Rise of Capitalism* was published in 1926, this thesis became the centre of one of the major historical controversies in this country of the interwar decades.[1]

[1] Max Weber's articles, originally published in the *Archiv für Sozialwissenschaft und Sozialpolitik*, XX, XXI, were translated into English by Talcott Parsons under the title *The Protestant Ethic and the Spirit of Capitalism* (London, 1930).

Abstracts of human experience there must be. At the same time, it may be suspected that the spirit of our time is, by contrast with the nineteenth century, which produced both the idealistic philosophy of history of Hegel and the materialistic theory of Marx, averse from general constructions and total explanations in history. This scepticism is not merely the result of a refusal by historians to consider general ideas. On the particular point which interests us, the relation between economic activities and the other functions of society, the historian often thinks, and with reason, that he has ground to suspect unitary explanations of general history. His observations suggest that the operative causes at work in different periods have often been different in their intensity and in the system of their relations, and that the smoothing away of these differences by philosophers of history does not help but hinders historical understanding. The historian tends therefore to favour explanations of historical situations which are, so to speak, tailor-made to the events to be described. This sense that the life and truth of each historical situation is to be found in the situation itself, and that general explanations lead us away from them as often as they lead us to them, is one of the most valuable parts of the historian's training. For this reason, historians will always tend, not so much to deny the possibility of general explanations of history, as to be highly critical of their effectiveness.

European experience in the last half-century has tended to undermine the faith in general explanations which seem to achieve unity and system at the expense of truth, and has reinforced the caution of historians. Wherever men have been free to reflect upon that experience, they have found it disillusioning and perplexing in the extreme. They have seen much blood shed and atrocious deeds committed on behalf of philosophies of history for which the most final claims had been made. They have perceived or they have seemed to perceive that while many mistakes are possible in this life, perhaps the worst is to substitute theory for life, to take the abstract for historical reality, and to act accordingly. In this mood, all kinds of scepticism and cynicism, natural and unnatural, flourish, the inescapable reaction against the falsities of a violent confessional age. One great philosophy of history of the nineteenth century—the Marxian—continues to propagate itself in the void left in the world by the death of conventional beliefs and traditional forms of society. In western Europe we live, it seems, in an interim between two ages in thought, marked by the features of such a time.

What can be said, in these circumstances, about the relation between the economic historian and general history? His study of economic choices needs to be, from one aspect, universal, and from another, related to society as a whole. At the same time, the general explanation, the philosophy of all history, is rightly suspect. It may even be surmised that a great change is coming over the meaning of words, and that what is understood by the 'meaning' of history and its 'explanation' are increasingly something different from what was meant by those phrases in the nineteenth century, which saw the heyday both of the natural sciences and of the great philosophies of history. Should the economic historian then eschew speculation, refrain from looking for the causes of things, and be content with a measure of understanding of history shallower than exacting standards would demand?

The argument by analogy is always dangerous. But it may be that some clue to the proper course can be found in what appears to be happening elsewhere, in a field which in Adam Smith's day was closely related to economics and economic history, in moral philosophy. There, too, one reads, the general system is out of fashion, although it may be conceded that there is 'no reason why we should not still look at human beings in general in their context in the world'. Moral philosophers, it appears, have been 'too much concerned with moral theories to pay very much attention to how people actually decide, or what moral decisions are really like'. An improved moral philosophy would include 'both description of the complexities of actual choices and actual decisions, and also discussion of what would count as reasons for making this or that decision'. One is told that such descriptions would need to be 'long, complicated, and realistic', and that moral philosophy, in the result, would be 'much more difficult, perhaps much more embarrassing to write than it has been recently . . .'[1]

Whether this is what moral philosophers now agree upon and are doing, whether the systems of the past are regarded as strictly meaningless without far more careful study of the actual processes and structure of the moral world which they were supposed to explain, only a moral philosopher could say. But the position reads curiously like that in the relation between our ideas of general history and the study of actual historical situations. Indeed, the resemblance between the programme for moral philosophers so sketched out and the work of the economic historian, among other historians, is close, even to the ultimate difficulty

[1] The quotations are from Mary Warnock, *Ethics since 1900* (Home University Library, 1960), pp. 205–7. The use of the analogy with historical studies, which may be most misleading, is, of course, mine, not Mrs. Warnock's.

and embarrassment of any explanation of actual human conduct.

Perhaps it is just in this way, by treating economic choices as what in fact they are, acts of the whole man, and by studying them in their full range and complexity, that the economic historian can best assist the cause of general historical understanding. The sense of universal history and a comprehension of the structure and development of the social world in which the individual has to live, move, and act, and which in turn he helps to make—these were the aims of the great European philosophers of history of the last century. They were fine and proper aims; but they were realized with a success which now seems to us limited, and because inadequate, dangerous. A pursuit of the concrete and analytical truths of history, persevered in with a consciousness of the narrow limits of the historian's vision and the obscure pattern of cause and event, must appear laborious and unsatisfying compared with the great speculative systems. But it may turn out to be in the long run no less philosophic, and a more secure guide to action in a world which is and must always remain doubtfully known to us.

5 The Communist Doctrines of Empire

The Communist literature upon imperialism is enormous. So, too, is the literature of criticism and counter-comment upon it. I shall therefore be forced to confine myself to stating, as clearly as is possible within a brief space, the nature of the doctrines concerned and some of the questions to be solved, if we are to reach a settled opinion upon them.

Certainly no judgement on such a topic can be final. The Communist interpretation of empire is in essence a view of political human nature and of the motives which govern it. It follows that such a theory can neither be wholly proved nor wholly disproved by resort to historical or statistical arguments, or shortly, by the appeal to experience. When it is the interpretation of experience itself which is the problem, it is clear, an accurate determination of the facts of experience can form only a part of the process by which the truth is reached. To become intelligible, these facts must be related according to some principles of economic or political theory; and into our choice of such principles there will enter assumptions about human nature which depend on the experience, conscious and unconscious, of each one of us. A true understanding of history must consequently always be far more limited and subjective than either the political or economic theorist, or the historian, usually cares to believe.

Yet the matters concerned are so important that discussion upon them cannot be wasted, even if we believe that the correctness of any opinion that can be reached must be to no small extent dependent on a sort of general balance of considerations, which everyone is free to strike for himself or herself and to re-strike from time to time.

I

Present-day Communist views about the economic origins of empire may be said to be a systematization of certain general ideas which were already alive in the minds of educated men a century or more ago. It is their association with Communist politics and with the materialist philosophy of history which has cut them off so to speak from their origins and given them their modern eminence.[1]

In the economic discussions of the early nineteenth century there was much debate among the writers of the day, first as to possible future checks to the undoubted material progress which Western society was already making, and second, as to the true causes of the profound poverty in which the rest of the world continued to live. These were questions whose importance and difficulty were about equal to one another.

Adam Smith in the eighteenth century had pointed out with force that the prime cause of economic progress was division of labour, and that the most efficient cause of the improvement of the division of labour was the employment of capital. Therefore, the foundation of present and future improvement seemed to lie in the constant accumulation of capital.

These abstract propositions appeared to be established upon a reference to the living world, where the societies employing the most capital were also the wealthiest and those using the least were the poorest. They confirmed the faith of the business classes in the importance of capital and the virtue of thrift. Yet they had been criticized, very early in the century, and that from the standpoint of plain common sense.

If this teaching were true, then capital created its own uses. Yet did

[1] H. Grossmann, *Das Akkumulations- und Zusammenbruchsgesetz des kapitalistischen Systems* (Leipzig, 1929), examines the relations between communist and classical economists from the Communist point of view. My treatment owes a good deal to his diligence and insight, although I have read the literature for myself and happen to disagree with his main beliefs. Richard Pares, 'The Economic Factors in the History of the Empire', *Economic History Review* (May 1937), was helpful. There are some penetrating discussions of the Communist theories in German; for example, Arthur Salz, *Das Wesen des Imperialismus* (Leipzig and Berlin, 1931), and, better still, Walter Sulzbach, *Nationales Gemeinschaftsgefühl und wirtschaftliches Interesse* (Leipzig, 1929). I have not attempted to cover again ground which they have often tilled thoroughly. The English literature is generally inferior to the German, although Maurice Dobb's *Political Economy and Capitalism* (1937) includes a clear little essay written from the Marxian point of view. Those who relish bibliography will find a valuable list in W. L. Langer, *The Diplomacy of Imperialism* (New York, 1935), vol. i, ch. iii.

not the accumulation and whole working of the means of production depend upon consumption and was it not perfectly clear that a fall in society's consumption, if sufficiently acute, would slow up or stop altogether the accumulation of capital, by rendering it unprofitable?

Such arguments had been raised by Malthus, against his friend Ricardo, with a vigour equal to Adam Smith's own, in the year 1820.[1] He, indeed, would have made it the main business of political economy to determine the point where, 'taking into consideration both the power to produce and the will to consume, the encouragement to the increase of wealth is the greatest'.

This was a fruitful beginning in the analysis of the complex forces which determine the volume of output, income, and employment throughout society as a whole. But it was no more than a suggestion, and the attention of Malthus's contemporaries soon fastened upon other and, on the face of them, more pressing and practical problems.

Taking the accumulation of capital for granted, as a 'natural process', other writers put such questions as these. As capital increases and the competition for profitable investment grows, must not the rate of profit fall, over the long period of time? If the rate of profit falls, must not the accumulation of capital cease and economic progress come to a stop?

Although it was conceived differently by different writers, the 'natural tendency of profits to fall' hung like a nightmare over the speculations of the classical school of economists, from whom, in those days, the majority of educated men took their opinions on such subjects.

Ricardo had predicted in 1815 that, as the world's population began to press upon its food supply, profits would be ground between a rising cost of living and rising rents.[2] Mill, the leader of the next generation in economic thought, held that the opportunities for investment must be limited by a country's physical resources and by the demand of other countries for its exports. He believed that a limit existed which must sooner or later bring about an oversupply of capital and fall of profits, unless broken by new inventions, or investment in countries or colonies abroad.

[1] T. R. Malthus, *The Principles of Political Economy* (London, 1836, 2nd edition), reprinted at Tokio (1936); see especially the Introduction and Book Two. The whole controversy between Malthus and Ricardo has been reopened in modern times by Mr. J. M. Keynes, *The General Theory of Employment, Interest and Money* (1936), and *Essays in Biography* (1933).

[2] Ricardo's essay on *The Influence of a Low Price of Corn on the Profits of Stock* (2nd edition, 1815, in Gonner, *Ricardo's Economic Essays*, 225–53) indicates the drift of his thought. Mill's influence dates from *The Principles of Political Economy* (1848), Bk. IV, ch. iv, sec. 2.

Here the varied and uncomfortable speculations of the economists felt the influence of one of the great practical forces of that age. England after Waterloo, from having been a borrower, was becoming a lender, It is, therefore, perhaps hardly surprising that it became fashionable to defend foreign investment, not merely as profitable business or a stimulus to international trade, but also on the highly abstract ground that it acted as a brake upon the 'natural tendency of profits to fall'. Mill had laid it down in 1848 that 'up to a certain point, the more capital we send away, the more we shall possess', owing to the beneficial effects of investment abroad upon accumulation at home.[1] Here he was only following a contemporary writer, the colonialist, Gibbon Wakefield. For Wakefield had boldly argued that the economic difficulties of England in the thirties and forties arose out of overpopulation and oversupply of capital.[2] He proposed to remedy both evils by sending men and capital to the colonies.

It was therefore the actual belief of many intelligent men, following the classical school of political economy, that the natural workings of the economic system led to overaccumulation of capital and that foreign investment and colonization were the natural and beneficial consequences. This train of thought is most clearly and interestingly expressed in the lectures delivered at Oxford between 1839 and 1841 by Herman Merivale, who is the better witness because he was an intelligent and well-informed man, a staunch Liberal, and from 1859 for many years Permanent Under-secretary for India.[3]

Accepting the natural tendency of capital to accumulate and of profits to fall, Merivale admitted a 'most important practical consequence', that 'the abstraction of capital from productive industry may, under certain circumstances and for a certain time, be the most effectual mode of preventing a reduction of profit and stimulating further accumulation'. He therefore ranged himself with equal caution and clearness with the 'young and sanguine sect of colonial reformers' who contemplated 'a reconstruction and great extension of the British dominion beyond the seas, on principles of internal self-government and commercial freedom'. The old colonial system he would not

[1] Mill, *Principles*, Bk. IV, ch. iv, sec. 8.
[2] Wakefield's opinions were set out in *England and America* (2 vols., 1833), and *The Art of Colonization* (1849). He is quoted by name by Mill.
[3] Merivale was Drummond Professor of Political Economy in Oxford and his lectures made an impression as an able and discriminating criticism of the Wakefield schemes; they have been recently published (1928) under the title *Lectures on Colonization and Colonies delivered before the University of Oxford 1839–1841*.

defend; yet colonies, he urged, are of definite advantage to the mother country, since they increase international trade; all nations gain, but the mother country not the least. Great Britain ought therefore to be among the first to shoulder the risks of trade and settlement in new lands.

In this way the new colonial school of the early nineteenth century actually accepted—the economic arguments they employed were not of course necessarily sound—the later Communist thesis that empires are a form of investment, serving to keep up the rate of profit on capital at home.

At the same time, they accepted it, as will later be seen, on terms that ill agree with the rest of the Communist argument. The empire they conceived could not by any stretch of imagination be termed a result of monopoly-capitalism, for it was to be the Free-Trade empire of a Free-Trade and *laissez-faire* Great Britain.

Nevertheless, the correspondence of ideas with the later Marxian schools clearly indicates the origin of the economic conceptions which today form the staple of the Communist analysis of empire.

In Mills' own time (he died in 1873) the theory of accumulation was already sending out new variants. Mill had believed that the fall of profits and slowing-down of accumulation would be the necessary phase before society entered an age of stationariness, where the pursuit of wealth would be at a discount compared with other and more valuable forms of human activity. Other men had different views of what was best for society and were as ready as Mill to use the theory of accumulation to show that what they desired was necessary and indeed an inevitable law of the society in which they lived.

2

Like the classical economists with whom his resemblances are close, Karl Marx, the first volume of whose *Capital* appeared in 1867, the last in 1894, sought a scientific explanation of economic phenomena. Like them, he found the causes of things in the motives at work among men and the explanation of future things in the predictable consequences of present motives.[1]

[1] The volume of *Capital* most relevant to the argument which follows is the third, translated by Untermann (Chicago, 1909), especially part iii, on 'The Law of the Falling Tendency of the Rate of Profit', which gives Marx's view very clearly. For Marx's general theory, E. Roll, *A History of Economic Thought* (1938), ch. vi.

Surplus value, wrung out of the worker to whom no more than a subsistence wage is paid, formed in Marx's view the obvious incentive to capitalist production and its constant driving force. To replace existing capital as it wears out and to increase its quantity so as to augment the mass of surplus value is the prime need of the capitalist. The accumulation of capital therefore becomes the 'law of motion of capitalist society'.

Accumulation is hastened in modern societies by division of labour and especially through the use of plant and machinery. Fixed capital, therefore, comes to play a more and more important part in production. Here Marx's argument abuts on the later contentions of Lenin. For he was confident that the competition of large and expensive plant must sooner or later give rise to monopoly, as a self-protective device to keep the rate of profit up. The device was a palliative and would fail to maintain the profit on capital, capitalists would be forced to introduce still more machinery, displacing more workers, and finally would be compelled to attack the living standards of the workers themselves. 'The natural tendency of profits to fall' would end in social revolution. How different from Mill's stationary state!

Upon this general argument, Lenin's explanation of empire was built. He wrote in 1916, in the shadow of the crisis of Western civilization created by the war of 1914.

It had been Marx's view that the fall of profits might from time to time be checked by temporary forces; by more rigorous exploitation of labour, lowering of wages, or increase of foreign trade. Lenin now added, by the forcible seizure of foreign markets, too. There was little in his argument that was essentially new, except the assertion that imperialism must prove the last stage of capitalism, before the law of capitalist collapse became fully operative.

An economic explanation of modern English imperialism had already been given by Mr. J. A. Hobson, in a book which arose out of the South African War.[1] He had refused to argue that all imperialism, even modern, is economic at bottom. Admitting the three P's—Pride, Prestige, and Pugnacity—he contended that the chief influence was the search for markets, arising from the inability of the home market under capitalism to absorb either the goods produced or the accumulated capital. The gains of empire were not illusory, although they went to the few, to the planter and the mine manager and the colonial official,

[1] J. A. Hobson, *Imperialism* (1902), republished with an interesting preface in 1938.

above all, to the speculator and investor. This was an able and interesting book and it was used with approval by Lenin. The other half of Lenin's argument was largely supplied by the work of Rudolf Hilferding, a young Austrian physician, who was always a little rueful over the conclusions which Lenin later drew from his work.[1]

It was the growth of monopoly which interested Hilferding and, especially, credit monopolies. He had little difficulty in showing how greatly monopoly had grown in Continental industry and banking since Marx's time, and how the banks had extended their power over industry. This growth of what he called finance-capital he linked up with other forms of current monopoly—with the trust and the cartel, the tariff and the protected colonial empire.

These were the ideas which were fused by Lenin, writing in Zürich in 1916, into what is today the official doctrine of Communism upon empires.[2]

So far as the argument can be summarized, it might perhaps be stated thus. The economic essence of modern imperialism is monopoly-capitalism. Monopoly arose out of free competition, in accordance with the Marxian laws. Production has become concentrated in cartels, syndicates, and trusts of all kinds. At the same time, equally important monopolies have arisen in credit; and the extension of the influence of the banks over industry has tended to form great national financial monopolies. Concentration of control, however, has only postponed the fall of profits, and consequently opportunities for investment abroad have become vitally important. Imperialism therefore is nothing but monopoly-capitalism. It is, however, the last stage of capitalism. Competing economic empires bring war, war brings revolution, and revolution will finally overthrow capital and imperialism together.

Lenin wrote during the world war; so, too, did Bukharin, who set forth similar ideas.[3] Both men express the hopes and convictions of practical revolutionaries, who were certain that the war was about to bring the movement they represented to victory.

Lenin's book was a practical politician's pamphlet, not a scientific treatise. The author's success in the political sphere has given it such a reputation, however, that it stands to other Communist theories concerning empire as orthodoxy to heterodoxy in the early ages of the

[1] Hilferding, *Das Finanz-Kapital* (Wien, 1910); I have used an edition of 1923.
[2] V. I. Lenin, *Imperialism the Highest Stage of Capitalism* (2nd English edition, London, 1934).
[3] N. Bukharin, *Imperialism and World Economy*. (American translation. The original was written, according to the preface, in 1915.)

Christian Church. Nevertheless, a consideration of Lenin's theory is bound to suggest several limitations springing partly from the materials at his disposal, partly from the nature of the theory itself.

The history of the hundred years before 1914—the greatest lending age in the world's history—certainly has shown over and over again that loans may be fatal to borrowing people and states. The British occupation of Egypt and the French conquest of Morocco are familiar instances of financial assistance first entangling and finally destroying weak governments. Just as in the Indian village the money-lender, that indispensable member of Eastern society, profits from the cultivator both when he is prosperous and when he starves, and is well hated for doing so (not only as a usurer but often also as a man of alien faith and race) so in the nineteenth-century world the money-lender of Western blood conducts his operations often in a tangle of intrigue and conflicting interests which has materially contributed to inflame international relations. Many of his transactions were innocuous, but the influence of investors did from time to time deflect the policy of states, and the chanceries have often converted international finance into a sinister interest.

The most distinct, not to say glaring, example of the impact of finance upon politics in British experience is to be found in the history of the South African War, when leaders in the investment of British capital in South Africa exerted a real personal influence over both South Africa and British politics. There is another instance from those times which deserves to be better known, or known in its proportions, for it has been often quoted by those unfamiliar with all the circumstances.

About the year 1894, when affairs in the Transvaal were drifting to a crisis, the London *Saturday Review* changed hands, being bought by Alfred Ochs, Beit, and others intimate with Cecil Rhodes. At a slightly later date, by a further arrangement of shares and a change in the position of Frank Harris, the editor, the paper was brought fully into line with the politics of that group. Fearing German intervention in South Africa, its foreign policy was moulded accordingly. A discourse on 'the biological conception of foreign policy', of 1st February 1896, arrived at the remarkably scientific conclusion, *Germania est delenda*; and on 11th September 1897 the *Review* published an article in the same strain which became famous. It is true that at the time of the Fashoda crisis the *Review* was advocating German friendship and the crushing of French pretensions in Africa; but its earlier articles against Germany, which represented nothing more than the views of a small group with financial and political interests in South Africa, are still quoted in Germany today as a serious description of British foreign policy before 1914.[1]

There is, therefore, forceful proof in the history of the nineteenth century for Lenin's thesis. Investment helped to make the empires, and investors often cultivated political interests. It will be remembered, however, that Lenin's book professed to be much more than the exhibition of empiric facts. It set forth a body of economic and social theory of extremely comprehensive character and described capitalist accumulation and collapse as general laws of society.

Lenin's book was written largely out of Continental experience. Great Britain, however, as the largest foreign investor known, is the best test of his theory. He takes no account of the very large investments of the first half of the nineteenth century in an age when the economic organization of England was intensely competitive and colonial expansion much out of fashion with its people. Capital flowed abroad in vastest volume when active development was proceeding at home and slowed down with the onset of internal depressions; so that 'saturation' was clearly a highly relative thing; nothing more than a relation between two expectations—of future yield on investments at home and abroad—strongly influenced by the slowness with which a once peasant people accustomed itself to the idea of a rising standard of life.

Neither does his thesis ride more firmly to the facts of the great age of colonial expansion, in the last quarter of the century. The houses handling foreign investment remained independent of the rest of the London money market and the money market remained divorced from manufacturing industry, which financed itself in the provinces, down to and after the war of 1914–18. During the same period vast masses of our investment continued to go, as before, to countries outside the British empire and largely beyond the control of British policy.[2]

The issues are certainly more complicated than Marxian writers have been willing to suppose. Experience shows that the wealthy countries of the West have lent money throughout the world. It does not

[1] Dr. Angelika Banze, *Die Deutsch-englische Wirtschaftsrivalität* (Berlin, 1935), pp. 42–9, has gone into this discreditable episode in a sober and unexaggerating spirit.
[2] On the course of British investment, now pretty thoroughly known, L. H. Jenks, *Migration of British Capital to 1875* (New York, 1927); H. Feis, *Europe the World's Banker 1870–1914* (New Haven, 1930); and C. K. Hobson, *Export of Capital* (1914). 'The Report of the Committee on Finance and Industry', 1931 (Cmd. 3897), and Feis make clear the different organization of the London and Continental money markets.

follow that such capital would have continued accumulating in those countries, if it had never been lent. Foreign lendings were not born necessarily of monopoly or of accumulation which would in any case have gone on. Great Britain in the last century lent enormously, long before her industry or her credit system showed the least tendency in the world towards monopoly; but had there been no openings abroad for her capital, much of that capital would never have been saved at all. She had so much to lend, because she lent indefatigably; only the economic developments abroad made possible by her loans brought about the further increases in her wealth out of which new loans were raised. And she lent chiefly when she was herself making full calls upon her capital for home development, not—as some may suppose—when development at home drooped unprofitably. These well-known things are not perhaps inconsistent with the Communist case, if it is contended simply that investment abroad was necessary for such an accumulation of capital as Victorian England had come to regard as 'natural', and that such investments often brought political consequences; but they are seriously inconsistent with that case as it is usually stated, among others by Lenin.

3

There was already a Communist theory of empire in the field when Lenin wrote. This was Rosa Luxemburg's, published in 1912. It, too, was a variant of the law of accumulation, based upon Karl Marx.[1]

How is capitalist accumulation practically possible? This was the question that Rosa Luxembourg posed. She sought the answer to it throughout economic literature. Her own solution was based upon classical economics and Marx. It also represented an attempt to correct errors in Marx's reasonings, as she conceived, and this earned her the stern disapprobation of more orthodox Marxians, among them Lenin.

Rosa Luxemburg discovered the secret of accumulation and of empire in the demand of non-capitalist peoples for goods capitalistically produced. She satisfied herself that the accumulation of capital was impossible, if the goods turned out by the capitalist machine could find a market only among the capitalists and their workers. The money

[1] Rosa Luxemburg, *Die Akkumulation des Kapitals* (Leipzig, 1921; preface dated 1912). One volume has been translated into French, under the title, *L'Accumulation du Capital*, tome i (Paris, 1935). Fritz Sternberg, *Der Imperialismus* (Berlin, 1926), appears to owe a good deal to Rosa Luxemburg.

turned into fresh investments of capital by the capitalists could only be realized by the sale of goods to those who stood outside of capitalist organization—to the peasant populations of Europe and, above all, to the colonial worlds outside Europe. Empire was consequently essential to the continuance of capitalism; and again, it was a curse to the capitalist countries that possessed it. The area of the globe is limited. Empires consequently mean imperialist wars and war threatens the very foundations of capitalism.

The great similarity between the ideas of Lenin and Rosa Luxemburg arises out of their common preoccupation with the problem of the accumulation of capital. The division is a difference of emphasis, since no hard and fast line can be drawn between export of capital and export of consumable goods. Lenin stresses the element of monopoly and the search for additional profit by investing capitalists; Luxemburg, rather, the competitiveness of capitalists and the necessity of markets. Both have had a wide influence and have opened important questions of economic theory and history.

Memory will suggest numerous examples of the influence which traders in primitive countries have exerted in modern times upon the overseas expansion of the states of Europe. In this connection it is worth recollecting that the trade incentive to colonial empire remained operative throughout the period described by Lenin as the period of financial capitalism.

To take a single instance—few imperial moves of modern times have been more clearly instigated by the trader than Bismarck's annexation in 1885 of the Cameroons—a part of the world where there was no white capital whatever beyond the floating capital of traders of various nationalities.

> Ich bin ein Bub von Kamerun,
> Der deutschen Kolonie;
> Fürst Bismarck hatte viel zu tun,
> Bis er erworben sie!

He might not have carried through the task without the assistance of the two Hamburg firms, Woermann and Jantzen & Thormählen. Bismarck appears to have regarded the first German colony as a natural extension of the German tariff of 1879—as a *Schutzgebiet* for German trade abroad. It was the Hamburg traders who in 1883 asked for a colony in that part of West Africa to take Germany's surplus goods and supply her with raw materials. Nachtigal, the imperial German

Commissioner who made the annexation, carried, as a rider to his official and general instructions, the specific orders of the two largest German traders on the coast, to claim for Germany whatever land those firms had already acquired or intended by treaty to acquire in certain named places. When the Cameroons had been annexed Bismarck proposed to hand over its government to the traders; they modestly declined, contenting themselves with a couple of trading monopolies, while the Chancellor was forced to set up what he hated—an official administration. Despite the avowed economic aims of the German Government, it is fair to add that they did not exclude justice and conscience—better deeds might not have followed finer words.[1]

Similar instances might be drawn from French and British history of about the same period; but without pursuing the matter further, one must grant the truth of empirical observation behind Rosa Luxemburg's work. It will be recollected, however, that that book claimed the truth of a comprehensive theoretical system, not merely that of historical observation. Nevertheless, the economic theory employed is probably far more limited in its scope than the author supposed.

The relation between accumulation and lack of purchasing power, which we all are tempted to treat as simple, is pretty certainly complex. Experience shows that shortages of purchasing power do from time to time occur throughout the highly industrialized communities of the Western world, although the causes are still unsettled, notwithstanding a century of discussion of the trade cycle. In any case, it appears that a persistently low level of consumption in society is far more likely to slow up or check altogether the accumulation of capital than to bring about an oversupply of it. An oversupply of capital does appear from time to time in particular industries, but this is a different matter, and merely represents the error of investors.

All of this, once more, is possibly not inconsistent with the Communist explanation of imperial expansion; yet it fits ill with the fundamental causes of expansion as they are often conceived in simple terms of underconsumption and oversaving.

4

The theories outlined above deal at length with problems of international relations; but the original question which they set themselves

[1] H. R. Rudin, *The Germans in the Cameroons, 1884–1914* (London, 1938).

to answer was very different—in what way and at what point will capitalism destroy itself, so as to show itself subject to the Marxian conception of social development?

It was for this purpose that there was evolved the law of capitalist accumulation and the variations of it created by Rosa Luxemburg and Lenin.

In these discussions the heirs of Marxian thought showed themselves fully aware of difficulties which orthodox political economy skated over or altogether avoided. There is much that is penetrating and true in their views of history, in their handling of the trade cycle and other major questions of economic theory.

That the 'laws of motion of capitalist society', however, have been conclusively established and verified either by Marxian or by orthodox economics cannot be admitted, notwithstanding a century of debate. The existence of at least two Communist theories proves that the Marxians are not agreed and orthodox economics is not more united. Many important things have been established and differences no doubt are less than they seem, but the existence of a large body of instructive thought is very different from the one great logical and inductive law which Marxian thought set out to find, which was to predict the course of Western civilization.

The original quest of such a law was perhaps a mistake. The development of economics first among the social sciences and its early and natural entanglement with political positions of opposing kinds, has called out everywhere a spirit of dogmatism over its findings. The natural presumption is that the explanation of society requires many social sciences, not one, even if that one numbered among its founders men as able as Adam Smith and Karl Marx.

Over a century ago a new social law was described, which was comparable in its domination over educated men with the influence of the 'law of capitalist accumulation' today. The Malthusian law was thoroughly scientific in its origins; it was logically argued, laboriously verified, publicly detested, and ardently believed. For two generations the law governed English social theory and even English politics, so far as an idea can rule men. Yet no one today imagines that Malthus, fine scientist as he was, so fathomed society that its problems can be understood and controlled by a simple recital of his formulae.

The theories which we have been discussing already show some of their limits and may be supposed to be in process of being reduced from the level of dogma to the more tolerable standing of fertile thought.

Cast wholly in economic terms they omit the political elements which are essential to war and colonial empire. It is reasonable to believe that man is a political as well as an economic animal. The war of 1914-18 was perhaps, as Croce says, a war of historical materialism, but this materialism was political as well as economic; State and business community together schooled the world to put wealth and power above peace. The European state system, as a quasi-independent and self-perpetuating force, is excluded from the Marxian picture. Yet the State shook itself free of law and authority a century and a half before public thinkers were prepared to give the same sanction to economic competition, and one of the earliest uses of its modern freedom was for overseas dominion.[1]

Politics and economics are not yet wholly annexed to the kingdom of rational behaviour; yet for the utilitarian psychology which unites Marxian with the classical political economy, the broad instinctive life of man remains like a river underground, not so much unheard as unexplored. In the daily life of societies it constantly bursts to the surface and leaves little in history of the simple patterns of our theories. Where is the ground for supposing that war and domination are always the consequence of economic or political calculation?

The domination of one society over another is a social and not an economic phenomenon, although it is often in large part the result of superior economic organization. Imperialism is the result of the exploitation of advantages of every kind, in a world where races and peoples seem no more equal in resources or civilization or ability than are individuals.

In some of the remote parts of China adjoining Tibet the thoroughly medieval society of Tibet exercises a kind of imperialism over the mountain valleys, where it steadily expands as against the primitive mountain tribes. It is carried forward by wealth, for it is usurer to the poor peasants; by population, for it settles; by the victories of its religion and clearer intellectual life over the confused superstitions and ignorance of the mountaineers. Exactly similar forces have given Western society control of modern Africa. But if this is so, then, however great the influence of the Western trader and investor in the modern world, imperialism is likely to continue long after capitalism has been forgotten; for differences of national income and resources, culture, and

---

[1] Much that the Marxians omit is to be found in R. G. Hawtrey's subtle and realistic *Economic Aspects of Sovereignty* (1930); still more, in Friedrich Meinecke's *Die Idee der Staatsräson* (Berlin, 1924; 3rd edition, 1929).

social organization will survive the private capitalism of the West. Societies unequal in strength in many ways will still meet and out of their conflicts of interest imperialism of new kinds will arise.

Yet some old temptations to domination can perhaps be removed. The most important source of strength through which one society can come to dominate another lies in political organization and leadership. Hardly less potent however, is developed wealth. Here the Communists have at least assisted to raise by implication problems of perennial importance in a modern way. How far the grave economic inequalities of the world are natural; how far they may be due to an inadequate private enterprise, or an ill-founded reluctance to employ organization and authority to overcome them, are questions that cut deep into present-day colonial and commercial policies.

6 Problems of the British Coal Industry between the Wars[1]

I

To talk of the problem of this or that industry is common enough, as we all know. This kind of language is usually employed when the question is political; what is to be done by the Government of the day about this or that industry? The phrase is no doubt useful and sensible in this context, and in this sense we can properly talk about the coal problem. Yet if we wish to understand the recent history of the coal industry the first step towards wisdom lies in seeing that there was not one coal problem only; rather there were several, and to trace the interrelations of all of them would require the utmost help that theory and experience can give.

Many questions in the economics of the coal industry have always been of a highly regional character and will remain so. This is largely owing to the domination which geological circumstances exert, so that the uniformity which exists in many branches of manufacture cannot be reproduced on the coalfields. Within the conditions which generally surround deep mining, there is a great difference between a field which is approaching exhaustion such as the Lancashire and Cheshire, and a great centre of unworked reserves such as the present Midland (Amalgamated) District, which includes south Yorkshire and great part of the Midlands, where much new development went on between the wars in rich seams. Again, there is a fundamental difference of condition between one coal-mining part of Scotland and another; for the Lanarkshire field is in decline and the future development must go east, bearing with it much of Scots industry and national life. Within each coalfield, also,

[1] Published in 1945. A few, but not all, contemporary references have been deleted.

conditions vary indefinitely from pit to pit and from working to working, while every extensive piece of new development meets its own peculiar combination of underground conditions.

The highly specialized markets which the different fields and pits serve have been scarcely less important in creating the characteristic regionalism of this industry than its physical conditions, with which they are intimately connected. For many purposes, although it must sound paradoxical to say so, it is a serious mistake to think of the coal industry as producing simply coal. Those who run the mines think of themselves as supplying their customers with gas-coal or coking coal or household coal or large steam coal or some other variety of coal which is in demand. Some industries can afford to be catholic in their tastes; electrical generating stations, for example, can burn the worst muck that ever came out of a mine. But for many industrial purposes the different sorts of coal are no more interchangeable than are the different kinds of steel. The problems of County Durham, which produces gas and coking coal of high quality for the steel industry of the north and the gas industry of London and the south coast, are different from those of an anthracite region such as the western parts of South Wales. Household coal producers have their own interests and special view of the world. Means of communication between producer and market also produce important divisions. Above all, in this country there has long been a profound, although nowadays less obvious, divergence of interest between the fields supplying the inland market of Great Britain, whether by railway or coasting steamship, and those which used to depend heavily upon overseas exports and the bunkering trade, such as the coal valleys behind Cardiff and the fields which export from the harbours of the north-east coast.

All this is the commonest information of the coal trade. But those of us who stand outside must keep the regional character of the coal industry constantly in mind if we are to understand its history. Not only does this regionalism mean that the economic interests of the different fields and pits are often widely divergent and sometimes as a consequence opposed, but these divergences and clashes have found striking expression throughout the industrial relations and the politics of a highly contentious and most political industry. But for our purpose the regionalism of the industry may be taken as given. It was not one of the specific problems of the industry during the interwar period, for it is as old as coal-mining in Great Britain. The problems of those years were national, in the sense that they affected the volume of employment and the rate of wages, the volume of capital investment and the rate of profit, throughout the coal industry as a whole, although with important regional variations. It will be suggested here that so far as there was anything which could be called a coal problem in those years it lay in the interaction of the many causes at work; a mingling so constant and inveterate that the whole only too often appeared a mass of complexity too great for solution. Yet it was just this emergence of formidable national problems which gave the regionalism of the coal industry extraordinary significance for our period. The industry was singularly unfitted, by its past experience and the ingrained habits of mind and temperament which proceeded from it, to cope with a crisis which demanded general conceptions and concerted measures. The narrow view complicated infinitely the task of dealing with the economic problems referred to and constituted itself a problem of the first magnitude; a political problem of the leadership and working together of the coal industry.

In the paragraphs which follow the economic problems of a national scale which beset the industry between the two world wars and the solutions adopted at the time will be described in roughly chronological order. This is not the only angle from which they might be considered. They might be analysed in their relations and proportions, as those appear today. There would be much value in such an analysis, but it is well to point out that in applying it one would be employing a view of the true nature of the events which itself grew up slowly during those years. The growth of that conception of the history of the industry, the mere fact that opposed views were held by different persons or even by the same persons at different periods and that these had a determining effect from time to time upon events, is a very important part of the story. Chronology brings this out, and it may perhaps help us to avoid, by paying close attention to thoughts and feelings now forgotten, the genial ineptitude of the man at *Othello*, who was overheard to mutter as he watched the action of the play, 'With a little give and take on both sides, all this might have been avoided'.

2

It will be necessary to go back for a moment to the period before the first World War, especially to the years of rapid mining development between 1880 and 1913.¹ The extraordinary success and activity of that time, the high profits, the overflowing royalties, implanted standards of what was normal and natural in the minds of many colliery-owners, managements and royalty owners which were carried over into the postwar period, where they played an important role. Among the mineworkers, the same period saw a swift growth of trade unionism and political consciousness and a marked radicalizing of the social philosophy of most of their leaders. This development belongs to the sphere of social history rather than of economics, but it was to have a decisive effect upon the way in which the economic problems of the interwar age were met.

The coal industry, as is well known, reached in 1913 a peak of aggregate output and of export sales, which had been rapidly expanding for more than half a century. The annual average production of the British mines in the 1850s had been seventy million tons; in the nineties, it was over 200 million tons. The output of the year 1913 was 287 million tons, nearly one-half of the European output of those days, of which ninety-four million tons went out of the country, including coal shipped for steamer use.² Yet the swift upward rise in the British coal output was not without parallel elsewhere. The period between the Franco-German War and the First World War was an age of vast coal developments. Production in the United States was ahead of our own in 1913, while that of the country we were about to fight, Germany, was not only very large but had grown since 1870 far faster than our own.

The truth was that in the industrializing Western lands of the nineteenth century the coal industry enjoyed almost a monopoly as the source of fuel and power. It was not until the latter years of that century that the rapid spread of the use of electricity and oil showed that other forms of energy were available than coal burnt in the raw or coked. Electricity developments helped the dazzling progress of German industry in the early nineteen-hundreds; even conservative Britain, radical where she was most sensitive, began to bunker her battle-

[1] Some of the more important sources for the history of the British coal industry between the wars are quoted below. See also (each written from its own angle) the P.E.P. (Political and Economic Planning) *Report on the Coal Industry* (1936), and two recent books, by no means uncontroversial in character, which throw a backward light: M. Heinemann, *Britain's Coal* (1944), and Harold Wilson, *New Deal for Coal* (1945). See also, among older books, A. M. Neuman, *Economic Organisation of the British Coal Industry* (1934), and (an American view) I. Lublin and H. Everett, *The British Coal Dilemma* (1927).

[2] Ministry of Fuel and Power, *Statistical Digest*, 1944 (Cmd. 6639), Table I.

cruisers with oil. These things foreshadowed a vast change, which was to be accelerated by the ensuring war, in the fundamental business of supplying energy to the world's industries and warmth to those of its populations who live in temperate climates. But the immediate effects did not upset the rate of growth of the demand for coal. World consumption is estimated to have increased on average by about four per cent per annum for many years before 1913.[1]

This swift, reliable increase in demand accounted not only for the forward surge of the coal industries, but particularly for the expansion of British coal exports. The output per man per shift in the mines of this country compared favourably with that of all the major coal-producing countries except the United States, where natural conditions were exceptionally good.[2] Combined with her oceanic position and the relatively cheap rail-haul from mine to port, low production costs enabled Great Britain to dominate the sea-borne coal trade of the world. The grasp upon big export business, much of it essential for the industrial life of other nations, and of bunkering at ports all over the world, was to be a factor of the greatest political and strategic importance during the four years of war which followed.

The output of 1913 was reached in a world where the conditions of coal production and consumption differed in many ways from those of today. It is worth noting that to mining engineers, whose eyes are fixed less upon aggregate output than on output per man per shift worked, this age of the famous peak now appears to have been a pioneering age. The men of the coal industry before 1914, the employers, the mining engineers, the workmen, the machinery makers, were, we read, 'a great race of men . . . whatever their faults . . . fit to rank with the greatest of Britain's industrial pioneers'.[3] This description is undoubtedly just, and draws our attention to the technical aspect of coal-mining.

Broadly speaking, coal winning in Great Britain before the First World War was pick and shovel work. While machinery and power were employed in the shaft for taking down and bringing up the men, for raising coal to the surface, for ventilation, for some of the illumination and other purposes, the actual business of hewing coal at the face, loading it into the tubs and to a small extent of moving these about

[1] *World Coalmining Industry* (International Labour Office, Geneva, 1938), I, 75.
[2] The British output per manshift was higher in those days than that in the Ruhr coalfield, our only important competitor; Ministry of Fuel and Power: *Report of the Technical Advisory Committee on Coalmining*, 1945 (Cmd. 6610), para. 154.
[3] *Ibid.*, para. 19.

underground, was done by hand, at the cost of the maximum physical effort of which men are capable. Much of it was not only hard work; it was also an intensely skilled handicraft of a co-operative nature, created in its traditions and practices largely during the nineteenth century.

The introduction of machine mining had been begun before 1914, but it was no more than a beginning. In 1913 the percentage of the output mechanically cut was only eight per cent of the whole. The number of mechanical conveyors used at the face was still fewer; about 360 conveyors against 2,900 coal-cutters. Other forms of underground transport had scarcely begun to change. Endless rope haulage was general, while at the face hand-tramming and pony-putting persisted by the side of the new conveyors.[1] The roads underground followed the seams and were often undulating and tortuous, as many a visitor to the coalfields has learned to his cost, unsuitable for any but the form of transport already in use.

The organization of the industry was dictated by natural conditions, by the scale of demand and the varied habits of consumers, and by the productive methods of the time. Generally speaking, undertakings were numerous, ownership dispersed and the average output per mine small. But there was a tendency, marked though gradual, for the number of pits to decline and average output to go up. Production became concentrated within larger undertakings in proportion as markets expanded and the capital expenditure required for mining at great depths increased. These tendencies continued during and after the war. By 1924 there were in this country 2,481 mines producing coal as a principal product, belonging to about 1,400 colliery undertakings. But of these, 323 undertakings produced, in the year 1923, over eighty-four per cent of the output.[2] Since so many undertakings were able to survive, it follows that many were very small and the costs of output per ton varied greatly. This industry was at one and the same time the stronghold of an old-fashioned and intensely competitive individualism, and of the most modern and highly integrated concerns, especially at the point where its activities became linked with those of the chemical and heavy metallurgical trades.[3]

[1] *Ibid.*, paras. 20, 21 and 22.
[2] *Report of the Royal Commission on the Coal Industry*, vol. I, Report (Cmd. 2600) (1925), p. 47. For the official meaning of the words undertaking and mine and an explanation of the variations in the official figures, see the Annex to the same *Report*, Section I.
[3] A valuable general description of the industry on the eve of the First World War is to be found in H. Stanley Jevons, *The British Coal Trade* (1915).

The one great unifying factor in the coalfields, where local and regional influences were paramount, was the labour question. An industry so lavish of the effort of muscle and tendon maintained a huge labour force.[1] Much of the growth of the British mining population was as true pioneering settlement as that of the new farming and mining countries abroad. Where expansion was carried on far from the towns the colliery companies supplied the houses; hence the miners' rows of Scotland, the dismal townships of north Derbyshire and Nottinghamshire and much other bad and indifferent housing. This tradition was pursued even during the interwar period on the last new coalfield to be opened up, that in east Kent.[2] Many miners and their families have consequently been segregated, especially in South Wales and the north of England, under conditions which make the worst of their isolation from the rest of the nation. This separation imparts a deep imprint to the mining communities which are subject to it. More than anything else, it has helped to give the character of a social war to the economic disputes over questions of wages, hours and working conditions which grew in number and range as trade unionism developed among the miners. It made the miner one of the best trade unionists and often one of the worst politicians in the island, and it partly accounts for the rough way in which the interests of the nation have been time and again pushed aside by both parties to the big disputes on the coalfields, as well as for the ignorant reaction to those events of a general public which knew, and was content to know, little or nothing of the causes behind them.[3]

If the structure of the coal industry and its industrial relations were still of a nineteenth-century style, so too, it might be added, was the

[1] The peak of employment did not exactly correspond with the peak of output. Even more persons were employed for a few years after the war than the 1,107,000 who were working in the industry in 1913 (Cmd. 6639, Table I). But the immediate after-war years were in some ways exceptional, as will later be seen.

[2] Ministry of Fuel and Power, *Kent Coalfield, Regional Survey Report* (H.M.S.O., 1945), paras. 81–5, contains some interesting comment.

[3] There is a large and growing literature on industrial relations in the coal-mining industry, much of it obviously partial, although usually throwing some light. On the immediate pre-1914 period, see, for example, Mr. Jack Lawson's life of Mr. Herbert Smith, *The Man in the Cap* (1941), and Mr. Ness Edwards's *History of the South Wales Miners' Federation*, vol. I (1938); undocumented and prejudiced, but written with inside knowledge. Of a more academic stamp, there is Mr. W. D. Stewart's discussion of the Minimum Wage Bill of 1912 in his *Mines, Machines and Men* (1935), and Prof. D. H. Robertson's contemporary account of the strike of that year, *Economic Fragments* (1931), pp. 58–86. But the true history of these years, making full use of all sources of information, has yet to be written.

British coal consumer. There is often a heavy price to pay for the excitements and the gains of a pioneering age. Much has been heard of the famous dust-bowl of the United States and elsewhere, created by the heedless exploitation of the last century. Nineteenth-century Britain lived without shame beneath the dust-bowl in the sky created by the coal smoke of its cities. We were most wasteful consumers of coal, judged by the standards of a later time. This situation had altered little by 1914 and coal utilization was not studied seriously in this country until the First World War created shortages of fuel.

3

From this brief description of the pioneering or heroic age it will easily be seen that the incursion of the State into mine-ownership during the 1914–18 war was generally regarded as a move of the most extraordinary kind, since it was judged by the standards of the past. Control was, however, forced on by an accumulation of difficulties in the production and distribution of coal. These led to the taking over first of the South Wales field, which was vital for the fleet and the mercantile marine, in December 1916, and of the entire industry by the second Coalition Government in March 1917. It is not necessary to say much of the history of the control;[1] it was a wartime expedient, and its main problem, how to obtain coal at any cost, was different from that of the interwar period, when the question came increasingly to be how to reduce costs in such a way as to afford a return to capital and labour, even at very low prices. War prices were high, immediate postwar prices even more so. The best work of the control seems to have lain in maintaining the exports which were vital to the conduct of the war, in organizing distribution on the inland market and controlling prices at home and abroad. Few improvements in the methods or organization of production can be recorded as a consequence of its labours. Output per man fell heavily, from causes of which some of the most important were outside the powers of the Coal Controller; for example, no effort had been made to retain labour in the industry, and a quarter of a million men are said to have joined up by August 1915; a heavy blow to an industry

[1] The history of the control has been told by Sir Richard Redmayne, *The British Coalmining Industry during the War* (1923). See also the evidence given by the late Sir Arthur Lowes Dickinson, who had been Financial Adviser to the Coal Controller, before the Royal Commission on the Coal Industry (the 'Sankey' Commission) in 1919, Minutes of Evidence, vol. I (Cmd. 359).

which depended much on the muscles of the young adult man.

The story of the decontrol of the coal industry has been told elsewhere.[1] It was done in a hurry, under the pressure of the world-wide collapse of prices and depression of trade, in March 1921. A heavy loss had been incurred. The bulk of this loss was caused by the bad trade from the end of 1920 onwards and would in the ordinary way have fallen upon the industry. But the fact that any loss at all had been suffered was enough to damn the control in the eyes of many, while the accumulation of the deficit had become rapid enough to alarm the Government. Furthermore, the mines had become the centre of violent controversy. For the miners pressed their demand for public ownership of the mines as soon as the war was over, and in the spring of 1919 a Royal Commission was appointed to examine this and other questions, under the chairmanship of Mr. Justice Sankey.

The Commissioners were united in recommending that the private ownership of unworked coal should cease and private royalty rights be transferred to the State. They were not agreed on the question of public or private ownership of the mines. The Government of the day chose not to act upon either question. In view of the fact that no convincing refutation of the case for public ownership of the unworked coal had been made out and that private royalties were actually abolished some twenty years later, the failure to settle the matter then and there must be judged a serious blunder. The miners, who thought that the mines ought to have been taken over, too, and who in general much overrated the possibilities of the Commission, felt that they had been let down by the rest of the community, not for the first time. The suspicion of Government promises and fair words so engendered had its influence on the course the miners followed in the next few years. Meanwhile, despite their disappointment, they felt their position strong. The Commission's findings resulted in a wage increase, which was followed by another, to meet the constantly rising cost of living, obtained by a three weeks' strike in the autumn of 1920. Most miners valued more than these wage increases the reduction of the working day to seven hours, exclusive of winding times, which had occurred under the Seven Hours Act of 1919.

The Sankey Commission was a major incident in the history of industrial relations in the coalfields. Yet neither the two big parties to the dispute nor the Government discussed the future of the industry in

[1] R. H. Tawney, 'The abolition of economic controls, 1918–21', *Economic History Review*, XIII (1943).

any other terms than those drawn from its highly successful past. In fact, the pioneering age was over; the age of intensive mechanical coal-mining was about to begin. But the ambiguity of events is such that it would have taken a wise head to see great trouble approaching the affairs of this industry in the early twenties. It is true that decontrol was followed immediately by drastic wage reductions, intended to bring labour costs into line with prices as they tumbled down from inflation heights. These were enforced by the owners in the teeth of a desperate strike from April to July 1921. But the stoppage created arrears of orders to be cleared off in the next six months. The next year saw a big coal strike in the United States and a wholly unlooked-for demand for British coal in that country. The French invaded the Ruhr in 1923, and the decline in German output again left a great gap to be filled. By 1925 the influence of these windfall demands was over,[1] and it began to be possible to see the long-term prospects in something like perspective.

Unfortunately, a cool examination of these prospects was out of favour at that time with the colliery-owners, and no less so with the workers, both of whom found themselves facing an immediate crisis. The export trade worsened rapidly towards the end of 1924 and throughout the first half of the next year. The return to the gold standard in 1925 was the last straw for the big exporting districts such as Northumberland and Glamorganshire.[2] The position in the eyes of the owners was comparatively simple. Output per manshift was still below the prewar figure, and output was only maintained by the aid of a swollen labour force;[3] coal prices were high, profits negligible. Labour costs formed seventy-one per cent of the total costs of coal winning; mechanization might reduce these, but it would be a slow process and by itself it was not enough. Wages must come down or hours of work must be increased, probably both. The owners therefore announced, as they were indeed entitled to do, that they would not renew the national

---

[1] Sir (then Mr.) Ernest Gowers, Permanent Under-Secretary for Mines, pointed out the confusion and misleading influence of these events on the expectations of the industry in his evidence before the Royal Commission on the Coal Industry (the 'Samuel' Commission) of 1925 (Report, p. 4). It is interesting to compare with this Prof. J. H. Jones's remark on the attitude of delegates to an international coal conference at London in 1929 towards the impending industrial depression (*The Coalmining Industry* (1939), p. 377, footnote).

[2] Economists hardly need to be reminded that the influence of the return to gold on the coal industry formed the subject of a famous and penetrating chapter in Mr. (now Lord) Keynes's pamphlet, *The Economic Consequences of Mr. Churchill* (1925).

[3] Cmd. 6610, para. 32.

wage agreement which had been reached in 1921 and renewed in 1924.

This announcement carried a double significance; it meant that wages were to come down and that they were to be reduced in competition between the different fields. Every miner, and especially every worker in the export fields, knew what his fate was to be. Before the war, all mining wages had been settled by collective bargaining upon a district basis. Following the flat-rate increases which were granted to meet the war cost of living, national agreements had been instituted. These were highly prized by the miner, who knew the vulnerability of his wages position in an industry where interdistrict competition was always lively and in bad times intense. He valued hardly less the principle of the minimum wage which the two national agreements embodied. For the miner, therefore, everything was at stake; and this accounts for his belligerency and tenacity in the struggle that followed, in the General Strike of May 1926, and the long coal stoppage. It lay behind his adherence to the senseless war-cry (so it seemed to the outsider whose pocket was not affected) of 'Not a penny off, not a minute on', and his heroic loyalty to leaders who led his cause to disaster.

So much requires to be said of the dispute of the middle twenties, the product of great sufferings, great passions and great mistakes. As for the Government of the day, it paid money for time to think, but seems to have thought to little purpose. Wages came down competitively; Northumberland and Durham, for example, maintained a greater proportion of overseas trade than other districts and also captured a considerable proportion of the coastwise coal trade of the country during the remainder of the interwar period, because the reduction of cash wages per shift went further there than in any other coalfield.[1] National negotiation disappeared; it was not until 1936 that the establishment of the Joint Standing Consultative Committee of owners and men, with power to discuss all questions of common interest, not excluding general principles applicable to the determination of wages under district negotiations, appeared to acknowledge that the purely district view was becoming out of date. The question of the minimum did not become practical politics again until the 1939–45 war.

Meanwhile, the hours in the working day were lengthened from seven to eight, exclusive of winding times, by legislation in 1926, and it was not until 1930 that the day was shortened again to seven and a half hours. A Coal Mines Reorganization Act, in 1926, was another result of

---

[1] The figures of wages, costs and proceeds for the period are analysed by J. H. Jones, *op. cit.*, pp. 46–7.

the stoppage; its practical effect was almost nil, and the problem of the structure of the industry had to be taken up again, as will be seen later. The main importance of the dispute of 1925–6, therefore, lies in this, that the solution adopted for the slumping sales and profits of the early twenties was certainly not that of the miners, who had taken up an impractically rigid and long-term position in favour of any other costs being reduced except labour costs; was not even that believed to have been preferred by the Government of the day, who inclined towards the middle way of the Samuel Commission, without nourishing fervour enough to carry it into law; but was entirely that suggested by regional competition within the industry. It took the form of an attack upon labour costs, to the exclusion of other costs, by the most simple and direct way, the alteration of wages and hours. The way in which this was done embittered the relations of managements and men for the rest of the interwar years and made extremely difficult the introduction of those other methods of reducing costs which were essential; for these required for their perfect success the intelligent and willing co-operation of the miners.

4

Looking back, it is impossible to see the events of 1925–6 as anything other than a tragedy, as terrible and heroic as most, produced on the one hand by the peculiar brand of rugged individualism, both nervous and swashbuckling, which was fashionable in the coal industry of the twenties and on the other by remarkable leadership among the miners, combined with a temporary vogue for the Direct Action idea of 1912 and a wonderful absence of political wisdom. The question now is, however, whether the policies which followed and were largely the cause of the great stoppage succeeded in curing the ills of the industry. The whole of the events of 1925–6 had been an attempt to shake free from business depression; but, it soon appeared, without success. The reduction in output continued throughout the interwar years; that for the years 1935–7 was still on average nearly sixteen per cent below that of the three years 1911–13. The fall in the volume of employment was much greater, mainly owing to the increasing efficiency of labour, being twenty-eight per cent for the same period. There were, of course, better and worse years for both production and employment; the general industrial depression made the years 1929–33 very bad indeed, quite nightmarish in the recollection of anyone who visited the stagnant export fields at the time; from then onwards there was a slow recovery. Prices and profits ruled low, improving from 1933. The average profit per ton for the last ten years before the war, from 1929 to 1938, was no more than sevenpence; this was a profit, but low and nothing like, it is said, what was needed for new investment in the industry.[1]

This was a profoundly unsatisfactory position, from the point of view of everyone except the consumer, who gained a temporary advantage from exceptionally low prices at the expense of his own long-term interest in the new capital growth of the industry and of the miner's family. It directed attention towards a circumstance which was known in the twenties but had been too often swept aside in that violent warfare.

At an early date those who knew conditions abroad pointed out that there was an international depression of the coal industry. This was so throughout the twenties and the thirties, and it provides the key to much which would be unintelligible from British experience taken by itself. Both the productive and marketing aspects of the industry were undergoing changes of a very important and widespread sort. On the demand side, the most striking fact was the dying down in the rate of increase of the demand for coal. This did not exclude increases of a local or temporary kind, but the trend was world wide. As a result, the four per cent per annum estimated rate of growth of demand of the years before 1914 contrasts with an increment of only 0·3 per cent per annum over a period of nearly a quarter of a century from 1913 to 1937.[2] The fact was more easily observed than explained, and it cannot be professed that any perfectly satisfactory analysis of it exists. Broadly speaking, the monopoly of coal as a source of fuel and power, which had been crumbling before the First World War, broke up after it. Oil, natural gas and water power were the chief substitutes, but substitution was not always easy and much of the growth of new energy-providing industries was non-competitive or complementary in its effects. It is certain, however, that there was some displacement of coal, although the extent of it would be hard to measure statistically.[3]

The main new influence affecting the position of coal seems, however,

[1] J. H. Jones, *op. cit.*, p. 369, footnote; Cmd. 6610, paras. 65–6 and Appendix I.
[2] *World Coalmining Industry* (International Labour Office, Geneva, 1938), I, 76.
[3] There is a good discussion of the statistical difficulties involved in the International Labour Office's above-mentioned publication, I, 82–94.

to have been fuel economy. The period between the wars was not long, as the life of industries goes, but numerous striking examples of growing effectiveness in the use of coal might be collected for this period from the industries, especially the public utilities and the heavy industries, of the leading industrial states. The inventiveness of the United States, where the average fuel efficiency of industries and railways is reckoned to have increased between 1909 and 1929 by approximately thirty-three per cent,[1] was outstanding; but British electricity and gas undertakings, blast furnaces and railways, and the industries of Japan showed the same clear trend.

This admirable development in the power of the world's industrial system to provide a larger amount of goods and services with the same or a less consumption of coal was not always to the disadvantage of the coal industry. Its general effect was, presumably, to stimulate the total demand for industrial energy, so the coal industry gained benefits, even while it was losing ground. But the adverse effects were sharply felt in a world where the coal industries had, until the First World War, been expanding rapidly and were themselves growing more efficient in turning out more coal for each man employed and for every shift worked.

Already, before 1929, the growth of the coal industry in Europe had been arrested. Output on the Continent increased between 1913 and 1929, but only by approximately the amount representing the fall in British production. In the United States, the coal industry did not grow at all over those same years, judged by the amount of coal won. This lack of development created fierce competition between field and field in the United States, with serious consequences for the American miner's wages. In Europe, where no common political institutions existed and where three big coal-exporting countries were to be found in Great Britain, Germany and Poland, the fight was not only between field and field but also between one sovereign state and another. This was especially clear after 1929, when the onset of the world industrial depression aggravated the situation beyond measure. The fight was the fiercer because from 1925 onwards a remarkable change had been coming over the technique of deep coal-mining, and the Continent had been one of the main centres of innovation. The immediate effect of technical progress was to increase substantially the productivity of the mines, although the bulk and in some countries the whole of the increase in output per manshift due to this cause was obtained after 1929.

Potential overcapacity was no new thing in the coal industries, where

[1] *ibid.*, p. 95, quoting papers of the Second World Power Congress, 1930.

pits do not easily go out of business and where the expensive apparatus of modern deep mining makes it important to continue production so long as there is a hope of earning anything towards overheads. This had been observed in the United States as early as 1900 and noted in Great Britain early in the twenties. Throughout the interwar period, and especially during the period of deep industrial depression between 1929 and 1932, the capacity of the coal industries of the world to produce more coal and lignite than the market could absorb at prices which would cover costs of production was an international problem. Surplus capacity, that is, the difference between the amount which existing mines, without any additional investment of fixed capital, could produce and the amount of current output was reckoned to exist, according to the best calculation that could be made in 1929, to the extent of about one-fourth in Germany, from a fourth to a third in Great Britain and about one-half in Poland.[1] This alone would have been sufficient to account for the marked lowness of coal prices throughout the world, without the crisis of credit and the down-swing of real investment in industry which began internationally in the year these estimates were collected.

The problem was not without its hopeful side; the world's increasing ability to supply its current needs of fuel and power with a smaller expenditure of labour was an indispensable step towards better standards of living, for coal-miners as well as other people. But this could be in the long period only. The short-term effects were very different. The details of the struggle for coal markets which marked the twenties and the thirties are well within recollection, the more so because the governments, especially the European governments, took a hand with the usual apparatus of protective duties, subsidies, export bounties and controlled prices, preferential railway rates and so forth. Mining workers bore most of the burden, by a partial breakdown of labour standards; the domestic consumer played his part, by subsidizing export.

None of these measures removed the general depression among coal industries. Their general effect was to push about the burden of that depression from country to country, from field to field and from pit to pit, under a system of temporary and partial advantages. That international agreements of some kind would sooner or later be necessary was the advice of international bodies such as the Economic Committee of the League of Nations in 1929 and the International Labour Office in

[1] *The Problem of the Coal Industry*, Interim Report on its International Aspects by the Economic Committee of the League of Nations (Geneva, 1929), p. 9.

1938. Hard experience was beginning to bring practical men round to the same way of thinking.

Great Britain, as the largest participator in the international coal trade, stood to lose most by the general depression of coal industries. She endured it, at heavy expense to her social and political life. Perhaps it follows that she had most to gain from international agreements, if they could be obtained; but throughout the twenties the British industry was in a weak position to seek agreements of this sort, because of the numerous managements which had to be consulted. An increasing perception of the international element in the situation and a growing recognition that, for the time being at any rate, an inelastic demand made it idle to hope to expand coal sales even at very low prices, brought about a change of mind in the industry towards the end of the decade which happened to coincide with a change of government. The law which followed, the Coal Mines Act of 1930, represented a turning away from the policy, now bankrupt, of 1925-6. The ideas of the thirties were to prove unfavourable to rugged individualism and ultimately even to regional competition, at least of the old, full-blooded type.

5

It is usual to take up a party attitude towards the origins of the Act of 1930.[1] But economic necessity counted for more than party views, and it is probable that some such law would have been passed about that time, even if the relative strength of parties in Parliament had been different. The fall of British labour costs after 1925-6 had been a formidable shock to foreign competitors, but they were not without resources to meet it, which they had proceeded to apply. Whatever advantage had been gained was by this time pretty well exhausted and some new move was obviously necessary.

A foreshadowing of the Act is to be found in the schemes which were promoted in the immediately preceding years for the restriction of output and control of prices in some of the coalfields. These examples of collective action came from South Wales, Scotland and the Midlands.[2] The Scottish owners tried to restrict output with the aid of a levy on coal sold in the inland market. The South Wales companies

---

[1] 20 & 21 Geo. V, c. 34.
[2] The schemes are described at length by J. H. Jones, *op. cit.*, ch. VI.

were more interested in enforcing minimum prices on the export markets by a similar levy and compensation scheme. Neither plan was of much importance. The Lancashire, Yorkshire, Nottingham and Derbyshire owners proved themselves more effectual. For two years, from 1928 onwards, their Five Counties Scheme restricted output and subsidized export sales with some success, while they handled the Humber Coal Exporters Association with a vigour which reduced the latter from independent buyers and sellers of coal to brokers for the exporting collieries.

From this experience it became clear both that combination to restrict output and maintain prices was possible in practice, and that some element of compulsion would be needed to make such schemes completely successful. The justification for encouraging them seemed to lie in the facts of the situation. Unless a further attempt to force down wages was to be tried and the events of 1925–6 repeated, some other means must be found to restore the finances of the industry. Between 1924 and 1928 there had been a fall of ten per cent in the volume of sales and thirty-three per cent in prices, with a resulting conversion of an average profit of one shilling and twopence per ton into an average loss of elevenpence.[1] The industry was so far from being able to contemplate a further reduction of wages that it had to expect that sooner or later wages must be raised from the very low levels to which they had fallen. Meanwhile the miners' opposition to the eight-hour day continued very strong. It was with the aim of restoring profits and paving the way for an improvement of wages and hours that the Act passed. The reorganization and re-equipment of the industry, which was the main hope of effective competition in the future, also needed to be financed in some way; for without it the future both of profits and wages was precarious.

Bearing all the motives in mind, it is hardly surprising that the Act of 1930 was a law of mixed character. It fell into four parts. Part I set up machinery regulating the production, supply and sale of coal. Part II established a Coal Mines Reorganization Commission. Part III reduced by half an hour the length of the working day, which had gone up to eight hours in 1926. Part IV provided for a Coal Mines National Industrial Board by which, had the Board come to life, wages and conditions of work would have been settled by national negotiation. The fate of the different parts of the Act was as various as their nature. The schemes set up under the first part of the Act lasted in the first

[1] Cmd. 6610, para. 65.

instance for three years; but Parliament renewed the law at the end of that time and the schemes played an important part in the Mines Department control during the early years of the 1939–45 war. The shortening of the working day endured. The other provisions were abortive. The fate of the Reorganization Commission will be noticed later. As for the Industrial Board, this was an attempt to undo what had been done in 1925–6 and restore a national basis for wage bargaining. The owners as a body cold-shouldered it from the start and it soon lapsed. Wages continued to be negotiated by district agreements throughout the interwar years, with the slight modification already referred to introduced by the existence of the Joint Consultative Committee from 1936 onwards.

The real importance of the 1930 Act, therefore, lay in its provisions for the control of output. This proved to be the beginning of a series of developments by which the organization and the spirit of the coal industry were profoundly affected. For the control of output was put into the hands of the industry itself. The scheme was divided into two parts. There was a 'central scheme' for the regulation of the production and sale of coal throughout Great Britain, administered by a central council of colliery-owners; and a district scheme within each district for the regulation of the production, supply and sale of coal within the district, administered by a 'district executive board' of local colliery-owners. The main intention was to raise prices by controlling output, rather than directly to control prices. The part of the central council was consequently important. It had the task of allocating a maximum output to each district, adjusting such allocations from time to time, and inflicting fines for output which exceeded them. The district executive boards divided the allocation among the collieries, assigning to each a standard tonnage in proportion to past output, and imposing penalties for non-compliance. The boards had also the power to fix minimum prices. The colliery quotas, that is, the proportion of the standard tonnage of each undertaking to be produced within a given period, became transferable among the undertakings of the district so long as the allocation for the district was not exceeded.

Extensive powers were conferred in this way upon the colliery companies. Neither the mineworkers nor the consumers of coal were represented upon the central council and the boards.[1] Neglected as the

---

[1] This did not escape the students of cartels, especially of those familiar with the different organization of the German coal industry; see D. H. Macgregor, 'The Coal Bill', *Economic Journal* (1930).

consumer usually was in the early thirties in this and other schemes to assist industrial producers, he could not be passed over in complete silence. Provision was, therefore, made for committees of investigation to be formed; a national committee to investigate complaints by consumers against the operation of the central scheme, and district committees to investigate complaints against the district schemes. These committees consisted half of representatives of owners and miners, half of consumers, with independent chairmen appointed by the Board of Trade. Owners and miners, it may be noted, had a common interest in rising prices, by reason of the ascertainment system by which since 1921 the proceeds of the industry had been divided between them in each district on a recognized proportion. In the ensuing years these committees did not play a distinguished role.

The control of output began to develop, although only after serious teething troubles, for an important minority of the colliery-owners was hostile to the Act. It was soon found that the control of output did not solve the problem of maintaining prices. Some owners found that under the quota allotted to them they had a surplus, which they proceeded to sell at a reduced price. Besides, the general recovery of all prices in the thirties after the world depression was slow and suffered a set-back in 1938. There was a revival of competition then, which brought about a considerable tightening of the schemes. There had already been a move towards the control of sales, sometimes going as far as the establishment in particular districts of central selling organizations. By 1936 every district scheme had been amended to permit such arrangements.[1] The central council had also acquired powers to give directions to the executive boards not only on the quantity of coal to be produced but also on the terms and conditions of sale. These powers it proceeded to apply, with the encouragement of the Government,[2] in 1938. Towards the end of that year it issued directions to all districts governing:

(1) the prices of all coal sold on the inland market outside the immediate neighbourhood of the pits or in any area where two or more districts were in competition;
(2) rail-borne and coastwise prices, mainly in respect of sales to London and the south of England;
(3) prices and supplies of coal for export.

[1] Departmental Committee (The 'Monckton' Committee) on the Distribution of Coal, Coke and Manufactured Fuel; Minutes of Evidence, 28 July 1938, p. 2.
[2] *Eighteenth Report of the Secretary of Mines* (1940), pp. 26–7.

While this great extension of price control was being carried through, central selling was being established with real success in one or two districts, notably Lancashire and Cheshire, where the district executive board traded under the name of the Lancashire Associated Collieries.[1] In other districts the central control of sales became the rule, each colliery continuing to sell its coal and seek its customers, but submitting each contract to the sales committee of the district board. One of the largest producing areas in the country, the Midland (Amalgamated) District, had a system of its own by which groups of collieries sold through selected agencies, subject again to the oversight of the district board.

These were all ways and means to control pit-head prices and sales. But the success with which this was being done, although varying from district to district, had already before the 1939–45 war raised the question of what the future relations were to be between the organized cartel which had been established in the coal industry and the middlemen and retailers. There were no specific powers under the 1930 Act to extend control of the sale of coal to the whole of the distributive trade, but there was an element of control over distribution in the power included in the schemes for the registration of distributors. The matter had not developed, but it was sure to do so sooner or later and it is a great misfortune that the Departmental Committee on the Distribution of Coal, Coke and Manufactured Fuel which, in 1938 and 1939 under the chairmanship of Sir Walter Monckton, had begun to collect a mass of most valuable evidence on this side of the coal trade, was forced to discontinue its sittings owing to the outbreak of war.

The development of an organization controlled by the colliery owners and with the direct encouragement of the Government of the day, to control the output, prices and pit-head sales of coal throughout Great Britain, under the 1930 Act, was clearly a move of the utmost importance. In this country it must be regarded as part of that great movement towards trade association of every kind and that relaxation of English law to permit of organizations in restraint of trade which to an increasing degree marked the latter part of the interwar period. It marked a complete break with the traditions of the coal industry and is the strongest possible proof of the immense change in the economic fortunes of that trade which had taken place since 1914. Yet it would be well, if this were the place, which it is not, to look at the 1930 Act in a

[1] Its practice was very fully described just before the war in evidence before the Monckton Committee, mentioned below.

still broader setting. In order completely to understand the events in the British industry in those years, we must compare them with the price-fixing in the American coal industry, first under the National Recovery Act, later under the Acts of 1935 (the Guffey Act) and 1937; and with the methods by which the German coal industry, accustomed to cartel methods since the nineties of last century, maintained its position in contested markets during those same years.[1]

Some of those in close touch with the British industry at the time regarded the Act of 1930 as important largely because it set up for the first time an organization capable of entering international agreements on behalf of the British collieries as a whole. Negotiations with the Continental coal industries for an international coal arrangement covering the export trade were begun in the thirties. In 1938 the colliery-owners decided, with the agreement of the Mineworkers Federation, that failing such an arrangement coal exports should be subsidized by a levy on other sales. The Government declared at the same time that they would not stand by and see the destruction of the British export trade. An understanding was reached with Germany; an agreement similarly defining relative shares in the export market had already been reached with Poland. The exports of these three countries covered ninety per cent of the European coal export trade, which was the largest in the world. An international coal agreement may, therefore, be said to have been in sight when political events in the spring of 1939 put an end to the negotiations.

6

The mere idea of international negotiations, still more of the heavily subsidized competition between big national coal organizations which was the alternative, raised difficulties in another quarter. No cartel and no government could help the industry, neither could it fight its own battles, if it neglected its competitive efficiency.[2]

[1] The material for a comparative judgement exists in Prof. J. H. Jones's book, published in 1939 and already several times quoted. This is certainly the most thorough analysis of the coal statistics of the interwar period which is available, whether its conclusions are accepted or not.

[2] This is a matter on which a flood of light was thrown by the publication of the *Report* of the Technical Advisory Committee of the Ministry of Fuel and Power during the 1939–45 war, better known as the Reid Report from the name of the chairman of that Committee, Mr. (later Sir) Charles Reid. It appears to be a serious reflection both on the conduct of the industry and upon the governments

Now this was a matter in which the Coal Mines Act of 1930 did not help, largely owing to the fate which overcame Part II, dealing with reorganization. Instead of being translated, as some had hoped, into a scheme of control over prices and sales, aimed at restoring the profitability of the industry so that long-term re-equipment could be financed, the law became a device by which the available business was spread among weak concerns and strong, efficient and inefficient; all enjoyed the benefit of fixed prices and restricted output, while the expensive and systematic technical re-equipment of which the industry was beginning to stand badly in need after the lean twenties was postponed indefinitely, because few were prepared to face the great changes in the structure of the industry which would have been necessary to take full advantage of the latest developments in mining technique. On the face of it, the situation created by the deliberate cartellization of the industry from 1930 onwards directly conflicted with the needs of industrial efficiency. It is worth considering how this came about.

The Coal Mines Reorganization Act of 1926 had been intended to increase the tendency towards the amalgamation of concerns which existed in the industry but was developing very slowly. The initiative was expected to come from the industry; but it was not forthcoming, and, if it had been, the conditions to be satisfied before the Railway and Canal Commission would have been found impossible. The Commission was enjoined not to confirm any scheme unless it was in the national interest to do so, and in the case of an amalgamation scheme unless (i) the scheme would reduce the cost of production or disposal of coal, (ii) it would not be financially injurious to any of the undertakings concerned, (iii) it was so drafted that the terms of the scheme were fair and equitable to all the persons concerned. It is obvious that the air of the twenties was unhealthy for compulsory amalgamations.

The Coal Mines Act of 1930, in its second part, took up the matter again to the extent of creating a Coal Mines Reorganization Commission consisting of five commissioners appointed by the Board of Trade, which could itself draft schemes, although it was supposed to do its main work by promoting and assisting schemes within the industry. The conditions to be satisfied were still the exceedingly difficult ones of 1926. The Mining Association's attitude was sufficiently expressed by its

---

of the interwar period that no such systematic investigation into the state of mining technique at home and abroad had been carried out during those years. The remarks which follow lean heavily on the Reid Report, already quoted above in other connections.

request to the Government of the day, in October 1931, that the Commission be dissolved. This was refused and the Commission took up its work, but among so many difficulties that in 1935 the Government temporarily suspended its activities and reviewed its powers. A new Coal Mines Bill was introduced the next year, which abolished the conditions imposed upon the Commission by the law of 1930. The opposition of the Mining Association and of the Federation of British Industries was extreme; the Bill was withdrawn and the reorganization section of the Coal Act, 1938, took its place. This Act transferred the functions of the Coal Mines Reorganization Commission to the new Coal Commission, which took over royalty rights in the coal at the same time. The powers of compulsory amalgamation which had been granted by the Coal Mines Act, 1930, were slightly increased, but the Commission's work on such schemes was postponed until 1 January 1940. The Commission's activity in this respect lay dormant throughout the war, and it was only in its last few months that the Coalition Government's proposals for the coal industry revived the question of the compulsory formation of larger undertakings.[1]

Such was the history, the unsatisfactory history, of the attempt in the interwar period to revise the structure of the coal industry by law. Reorganization by law had only one achievement to its credit during the whole twenty years between the wars. One major problem was disposed of, after much delay and with no immediate effect. This was the question of the ownership of unworked coal. The Coal Act, 1938, provided for the unification of coal royalties in the hands of the State by the payment of a compensation sum of sixty-six and a half million pounds to private owners. The controlling body became the Coal Commission. This move brought British law into line with that of most countries, but its bearing on the efficiency of the industry was only indirect. The attempt to make the operations of coal-mining conform to the rights and boundaries of private estates on the surface had injuriously affected the layout of pits and stood in the way of necessary developments; but no immediate opening for reform was provided by this Act, since, broadly speaking, coal leases in force at the time of the transfer continued in force unaltered except by the change of lessor. In any case, the transfer was not completed until 1942.[2]

[1] Coal Mines Reorganization Commission Reports to the Secretary for Mines; *Eighteenth Annual Report of the Secretary for Mines* (1940); J. H. Jones, *op. cit.*, pp. 120–7.
[2] *Eighteenth Annual Report of the Secretary for Mines* (1940); *Economist*, 2 May 1942; Cmd. 6610, para. 169.

Meanwhile the structure of the industry was not, of course, wholly immovable. Closing down of pits and amalgamation of concerns was forced on the industry, especially in some parts of the country, by the trend of costs and prices. Thus there were large amalgamations in South Wales and Lancashire in the years of chronic depression from 1929 to 1933.[1] But important as these were locally, they left the general picture of an old industry full of many undertakings and many pits substantially unaltered. Meanwhile the whole question of the proper economic size of the undertaking was assuming a different shape from that which it wore in the twenties, owing to the increasing pace of the technical revolution.

The aim of the mining engineer was coming to be the mechanization of the actual process of coal winning. This meant that he must do three things if the job was to be complete:

(1) Cut coal at the face with machinery, instead of by the hand pick.
(2) Remove the coal from the working place by machinery, i.e. by conveyor, to a place where it could be got away to the shaft by the main haulage system of the mine.
(3) Load the coal cut by the machine on to the conveyor not by hand shovelling but by power machinery.

The coal-cutter, the pneumatic pick and the conveyor were already known and were coming into the pits in numbers in the early interwar years; but the power-loader is essential to complete the process of mechanized coal winning. In all countries the power-loader came late, owing to the technical difficulties involved. Later still came the machine which both cuts and loads—a most remarkable machine, but without practical importance in the period we are considering.

Mechanical coal-cutting and conveying increased rapidly between the wars. Between 1927 and 1939 the tonnage of coal mechanically cut per annum rose from 58·5 to 142·2 million tons. The tonnage mechanically conveyed along the face was increased from twenty-eight (in 1928) to 134 million tons over the same period.[2] These were striking developments. They meant that coal-mining as the nineteenth century had known it was going out and with it the old-fashioned miner, owner and

---

[1] The process of voluntary amalgamation can be studied in the *Industrial Surveys* of South Wales and the North East Coast Area prepared for the Board of Trade by the Universities in those parts in 1932; and in the *Eighteenth Annual Report of the Secretary for Mines* (1940).

[2] Cmd. 6610, paras. 36, 38.

mine official. But those who knew the coalfields abroad, where the mechanization of the coal face and the improvement of roadways were also becoming fashionable, were less satisfied. The position was not so satisfactory as it at first appeared, despite all that had been done.

Productivity was going up, but slowly and unevenly. The 1914 level of output per manshift in British mines was reached again and slightly exceeded in 1927. It continued to advance slowly but steadily, except for a slight set-back in 1930–1, till 1936.[1] In 1927 output per manshift for all persons employed both above and below ground had been 20·61 cwt. By 1936 this was up to 23·54 cwt. There was a falling off in later years, as there was in other countries at the same time, and the figure for 1939 was 22·88 cwt. That is to say, there had been an increase of only eleven per cent in the efficiency of the industry, measured in this way, since 1927. Even so, there were big differences between the various fields, as analysis of the national average shows. Thus in Scotland during that same period output per manshift fell by a fraction, despite a considerable increase of coal-cutting and conveying. Output per manshift at the face, on the other hand, jumped up from fifty-six to seventy-six cwt. Warwickshire and Staffordshire and the Midland (Amalgamated) District, composed of Yorkshire, Derbyshire, Nottinghamshire and Leicestershire, caught up and improved upon the output per manshift in the big 'old-exporting' fields; but those fields, namely, Durham, South Wales, Scotland and Northumberland, 'achieved little or nothing in the way of increased output per manshift during the twelve years under review'.[2] These differences were in part due to natural conditions, in part to the age of the workings; thus the advance of the Midland district, which possesses large reserves of coal and many large modern pits, as against some older ones, had been foreseen in 1925. But some part of them was in the opinion of experts due to an unevenness of technical advance which might have been avoided.

To cut a long story short, the pace was hotter abroad. From 1925 onwards a big gap in relative efficiency, which was not altogether due to differences of natural condition, had grown between Great Britain and some other countries. In 1925 output per manshift in this country, while it had slipped a little behind the German (Ruhr) output, was ahead of the

[1] *ibid.*, para. 44.
[2] Cmd. 6610, paras. 44, 45. By far the best sources of information now on regional matters are the *Regional Survey Reports*, published by the Stationery Office in several volumes for the Ministry of Fuel and Power and for the Scottish Office in 1944 and 1945. They vary in quality, but are quite indispensable, covering as they do all the coalfields in great detail.

Dutch and not far behind the Polish. By 1936 the German output was 1,710 kg.; the British 1,195; the Dutch 1,781; the Polish (in eastern Upper Silesia) 2,073. There had by this test been an increase of productivity between 1913 and 1936, as the International Labour Office Committee pointed out, of at least 117 per cent in Holland; of eighty-one per cent in the Ruhr; of seventy-three per cent in Poland; of fifty to fifty-one per cent in Belgium and Czechoslovakia; of twenty-two to twenty-five per cent in the United States bituminous industry, and in France; and of only ten per cent in Great Britain.[1]

Figures, both absolute and percentage, are notoriously misleading without detailed explanation. Those quoted here are chiefly significant when taken in conjunction with the opinion of the Reid Committee that the idea of intensive mechanized mining, which began to come into the British coal industry in the twenties, never developed as it might and should have done; whereas some coal industries abroad went through a veritable revolution in their methods. The British coal industry was more mechanized than ever before in 1939; but compared with the Continental fields it was more technically obsolescent than it had ever been.

This is a singularly disheartening conclusion, although one has to remember the comparatively high efficiency of the British industry until 1925. It appears to be the ancient story that those who have been successful are tempted to try to go on being successful in the old way until new conditions make this impossible. On the other hand, Continental engineers had difficulties of their own in devising suitable methods of underground haulage; for they often could not take the roads through the coal, as was possible in the flatter seams of Great Britain, until those seams began to be exhausted, but were forced to drive them straight through the solid rock. This may have been the beginning of that advanced system of locomotive haulage below ground which widened the whole conception of mechanized coal-mining and is a logical development of it as well as the means to an outstanding saving of human labour. An underground haulage system which does not use the locomotive tends to be the bottleneck in British pits today,[2] in pits where mechanization at the face is well developed, and especially where power-loading is being brought in.

Complete mechanized coal-mining forces on changes at every point

---

[1] *World Coalmining Industry*, vol. I (International Labour Office, Geneva, 1938), pp. 108–9.

[2] i.e. in 1945.

in the transport serving the mine, both below and above ground and in the shaft. It also creates large new problems in the illumination and ventilation of the pit, in the laying on of power and at almost every other point of the layout and equipment of the mine; problems not always easy to deal with, since the technical adjustments must be made with regard to the safety of the mine and the existing laws which govern it. Nor is this all, in addition to the properly laid down, equipped and maintained pit, mechanized mining requires in effect a new kind of mine worker and official to run it. A start was made in this direction at particular pits between the wars, but the trend of events was making indispensable comprehensive training schemes for the industry such as were worked out in Holland and Germany during that period, together with a complete departure from many practices and old preconceptions on the part both of the workers and the managements.

Finally, it may be added, the thorough overhaul of British mining methods would have required for its success a radical overhaul of the method of wages payment throughout the industry, such as was not attempted until 1944 under the stress of war, as well as a much more forthcoming attitude towards the use of machines on the part of the workers. But here the movement towards technical reform struck upon the miner's memories of long years of unemployment and underemployment and upon his deep-rooted suspicion of the mine managements. The owners, too, were not without their suspicions. They had not always much confidence either in themselves or their industry; the fear that the mines might one day pass to the State made some unwilling to invest, just when investment was most needed and when bold investment might perhaps have averted the object of their fears. In a word, great changes, mental and moral, were necessary prerequisites to the successful use of the new methods and they were not forthcoming, or at least not on the scale which the situation required.[1]

7

We are nearing the end of a story which contains more than its fair share of human ill-fortune, shortcomings and mistakes; it only remains to sum up the argument. The fundamental economic problems of the

[1] On all these matters, the Reid Report (Cmd. 6610) is detailed and illuminating. The *First Report of the Committee on the Recruitment of Juveniles in the Coalmining Industry* (1942) also throws a strong light on the interwar years.

British coal industry between the wars were set by a revolution in the production and consumption of fuel and power of world-wide scope and far-reaching character, which began as far back as the last quarter of the nineteenth century, when oil and electricity began to break coal's temporary monopoly. The issue so posed could not have been avoided, whether or not a world war had taken place between 1914 and 1918; it would still have concerned Great Britain more than any other country, because of her dominating position in the world coal market and because coal is the only abundant raw material in the island. The fuel and power revolution threatened the economic base of Britain's political power and her national existence, and had already done much before 1914 to bring to an end the industrial leadership which had been hers for a time in the nineteenth century. What the First World War contributed was an aggravation and confusion of the evils of what was bound to be a period, perhaps long, of difficult transition.

Whether private ownership, left to itself, would have successfully completed the process of readjustment, not only to its own satisfaction but also in a way to satisfy the best interests of the nation, will now never be known, for the Second World War brought the industry under Government control once more, and the present Labour Government have announced that they intend to take the mines into national ownership. This can, however, be said without hesitation, that the record of the industry between the wars does not afford satisfactory evidence that the change would have been successfully completed under private ownership, while the technical obsolescence of the industry revealed by the Reid Report (a symptom, rather than a cause, of the failure to solve economic problems, although it was rapidly becoming in itself the cause of further trouble) suggests that the position had deteriorated at the end of the period as compared with the beginning. The failure to maintain a reasonably steady flow of youths into the pits year by year was perhaps an even more serious reflection on the policies which had been pursued; for without trained men even the best machines cannot be worked.

What was most notable about the industry was that the loss of its foreign markets, the state of its industrial relations and the increasingly urgent problems of its capital accumulation reacted upon one another in a peculiarly disastrous fashion throughout this period. An industry thus situated could not hope to become attractive to investors, although it was peculiarly in need of capital, and no industry so short of capital could cut the knot of its industrial relations by offering a better standard of living to its workers. Hence the tendency, counteracted no doubt here and there by energetic individuals, for the industry to settle down in the thirties to a regime of modest profits and low wages, secure behind a barrier of fixed prices and restrictive practices, in melancholy contrast to the exuberance of the days of heedless success.

Only leadership of an uncommon quality could have forced a way out. Unfortunately this was not forthcoming, for whatever reasons, although men of first-rate ability were present on both sides of the industry. The leadership became, on the contrary, acutely divided, one half sitting in the board-rooms and managers' offices of the colliery companies, the other half in the union lodges. Big changes in mine management and discipline as well as in the traditional union views of production would have been necessary to overcome this division and the deep conflict of loyalties which it introduced into the life of the coalfields. Nor was the want of effectual leadership compensated for by a corresponding firmness on the part of the governments of the day. A great mistake was made in the disputes of 1925-6, when the colliery owners were allowed to win an unqualified victory which their expressed policy certainly did not deserve, to the detriment of the rest of the nation and the long-term interests of their industry. And a mistake perhaps scarcely less fatal, although this is more contentious, was the failure to put behind the administration of the 1930 Act any well-thought-out conception of public policy, while the Act itself could hardly be described as a well-thought-out measure. The bulk of the electors, it must be confessed, showed themselves as indifferent as the governments which represented them both to the economic troubles of the managements and to the justice of the miners' cause.

Since 1939 the situation has obviously changed in some important respects. For a few years at any rate the shortage of fuel in Europe will create an entirely different situation from the potential overproduction of the years between the wars. In the long run, however, the problem of the substitution of new forms of fuel and power for old will become less avoidable than ever, now that the search has ended with the unlocking of atomic energy. It might properly be said that there is a coal problem no more, only a fuel and power problem. Probably the least important thing that has happened is the decision of the Government to assume the permanent ownership of the mines, for it is clear that while the transference from private ownership will change the setting of the sort of questions which have been here discussed, it cannot of itself solve them, although it may well be more favourable towards their solution than private ownership was or could have been. Meanwhile, until they are solved, an industry which for a hundred years before 1914 was a prime source of the wealth, power and civilization of Great Britain, will remain an actual and potential cause of poverty, weakness and division, offsetting its many past and present services to the nation and the world at large.

7 A Warwickshire Colliery in the Eighteenth Century

A Warwickshire colliery-owner, more deft with pen and ink, possibly a trifle more business-like than some of his fellows, but improbably more literate and self-conscious than they, began to note down particulars of his business in a memorandum book, a few years before the outbreak of the conflict with the American colonies. This book survives; a kind of scrap-book, headed 'Memorandum [sic] of the Colliery'.[1] The entries run from 1st March 1774 down to the year 1794, though they include a note or two of earlier date. Most are strictly business-like; notes of payments on and leasings of coal, numerous records of the progress of canals and turnpikes, comparative costs of running Newcomen and Watt engines at the mine, and so on. But the diary is in part personal, as well as a collection of business memoranda. Under 1785 lies the entry: 'In this year October the Revd. Dr. Edwards was married to Miss Lushington by the Bishop of Llandaff.'[2] It is difficult to say whether business concern or pure curiosity stands behind another comment:[3] 'In February 1777 Mr. Dudley Attorney died— Many Forgeries were discovered after his death.'

There is no title or signature to prove who was the writer of this document: but the internal evidence appears conclusive. We learn on the first page that the other partners in the colliery were named Ferneyhough

---

[1] This document is now in the library of the University of Birmingham, having been purchased by the Faculty of Commerce from a Birmingham bookseller. One or two sheets of the accounts of the Warwickshire Exhall Colliery, of about the same date, were also on sale, but were judged too fragmentary to be worth purchase. Letters and accounts are frequently referred to in the memoranda, which it is to be hoped may one day be recovered.

[2] Fifty pages of the notebook were numbered by its writer. I have usually placed a reference to the page where it possesses a number; where it does not, I have given the year and, if possible, the month of the entry.

[3] Memorandum of the Colliery, p. 17.

and Whieldon, and, in an effort to work out the proportions of shares, the author's share is put down on the opposite leaf: 'F. Parratt's share is $\frac{3}{8}$.' The colliery is recorded as having purchased an engine from the Boulton and Watt firm in Birmingham, in the year 1776. Now the fourth Boulton and Watt engine was erected in that year for Messrs. Parratt, Ferneyhough and Whieldon, of the Hawkesbury Colliery, Bedworth, County Warwick.[1] It appears, therefore, that the writer was F. Parratt and the colliery in which he was concerned owned the Hawkesbury mine.[2]

Parratt was not a partner in a struggling concern. On the contrary, his enterprises yielded a good return. He owned a three-eighths share in the colliery; and some closes known as the Glasshouse closes, which had been purchased many years before, in 1721, for £700 by Stanier Parratt. This latter ground was coal-bearing and he received a royalty or 'Mine rent' of one shilling and sixpence a ton on the coal worked.[3] Though not averse to expanding his business, Parratt was content. He noted happily at the beginning of his diary, that his own and his brother's property 'yielded us a handsome income'. There is little sign here of the boundless monetary ambition which has sometimes been supposed to animate the capitalist of all times and places.

This was in 1774, when the affairs of the colliery seem to have flourished. Parratt came into his share of the business on 1st March, whether by death or on an arrangement, he does not say. Ferneyhough and Whieldon held a quarter share each. Mr. Taylor possessed a share of one-eighth in the colliery, dating from ten years before,[4] and a small share in the Glasshouse property. At this time, we learn: 'Coals were got at eight Pits and two more were sinking or preparing. The Coventry Canal was finished and that to Oxford was navigable as far as Braunston.'[5] The number of pits in work at any one time seems to have varied, but the total output of the company that year was reckoned at 1,800 tons in a fortnight[6] and sometimes 2,000 tons.

[1] Erich Roll, *An Early Experiment in Industrial Organisation* (1930), pp. 38, 39. According to Roll, the Hawkesbury engine was set up in 1777. But it is evident that this postdates events by a year, as will be seen below.

[2] One of the latest entries in the book, in a different hand, recording the sale of the Hawkesbury engine, speaks of it as sold by the Bedworth Colliery. I have sometimes referred under this name to the colliery which combined both the Hawkesbury and the Bedworth pits.

[3] Memorandum, p. 1.

[4] *ibid.* There are several references to Taylor's share, upon which some question had probably arisen.

[5] *ibid.*, p. 3.

[6] *ibid.*, p. 5.

A Warwickshire Colliery

From time to time the affairs of the company took a new turn, as new coal was leased or royalty payments were met. The royalty system brought the partners into touch with an interesting assortment of landowners. The universities appear as taking an unobtrusive but profitable part in the industrial developments of the time. Christ's College, Cambridge, received in 1772 a payment of £210, the fourth instalment on coal in the Astrills.[1] Three years later, it was coal under the land of the Lords Craven and Clifford which was under consideration and arrangements to work it were come to in 1777.[2] The year 1777 seems to have been an expansive one. It saw the Craven and Clifford leases executed and a decision taken to pay £4,800 in instalments to a Mr. John Burton, for other coal rights. Burton's business morality was felt not to be above suspicion; 'a large Erasement in Burton's Deeds gave strong Suspicion' that he had quietly annexed valuable property to himself and owed his rise from ground-bailiff to royalty-receiver to forgery.[3] Leases on the coal seem to have been taken up at various lengths; twenty-one, thirty, fifty, fifty-one years, sometimes longer.

The royalty system, however, worked in this part of Warwickshire much as it worked elsewhere: there is nothing specially worthy of remark in it. The Bedworth Colliery, however, has in the past been properly recollected as one of the very earliest enterprises to install the steam-engine of James Watt. Bedworth was already a steam-power-using colliery before the Watt engine was available to purchasers. In 1774 there were already a couple of engines working at Hawkesbury and a third engine at the Bedworth part of the company's property. The partners were not satisfied with their performance. The consumption of coal was regarded as excessive; at any rate, there are many signs that it was watched and noted. In a fortnight of November 1774 the Hawkesbury machines required sixty-four tons of coal, Bedworth engine sixteen tons.[4] The pits of the company were evidently deep enough to make water a vexatious problem, more so possibly than was usual in the Warwickshire field. A new boiler was installed in one of the engines, called the 'deep Engine', so that 'by having two Boilers we might be safe as to our Water'. This deep engine is spoken of as a new engine, in that year (1775), but new or old, engines of the Newcomen type were not regarded by the partners as fulfilling their requirements.

[1] ibid., p. 4.
[2] ibid., pp. 18, 19.
[3] ibid., p. 18.
[4] ibid., p. 6.

In the very following year, a visit was paid to Bloomfield Colliery in the Staffordshire Black Country and to Willey Forge, near Broseley, Salop. At these two places engines of the Watt type were at work, the first of their kind in the world.[1] The visit was decisive. The partners' reasons for making up their mind in favour of buying an engine of the new model may be given in Parratt's words:[2] 'they [the Bloomfield and Willey engines] were worked with less Fuel and Steam was saved by a double Cylinder with a lever and many other improvements for which Messrs. Boulton and Watt had obtained an Act of Parliament. The apparent advantages which an Engine of this sort promised and the constant Disorder attending those on the old Construction led us to determine upon having one built under the direction of Mr. Watt and Mr. Boulton. The terms were that we should pay for all the Materials and allow them one-third of the savings in the consumption of Coal.'

The contract was soon executed and in March 1776 the new engine began its work at Hawkesbury. It was the fourth Watt engine to be put into commission and the largest steam-engine that had ever been seen. For a brief while its fame seems to have been equal to its enormous dimensions. The immediate performance may not have been up to expectations. According to the historian of the Boulton and Watt firm, the colliery-owners expressed a good deal of dissatisfaction in communications to the Birmingham firm.[3] Small trace of discontent appears among the memoranda. The old Newcomen and new Watt engine at Hawkesbury were given a regular trial, in January 1779. The old engine, it was found, needed ten tons sixteen cwts. of fuel a day, the new was content with four tons sixteen cwts. Elsewhere it is jotted down: 'the New Engine gets the Water down in 14 hours. The Old Engine gets the water down in 16 hours.'[4] The great Hawkesbury engine continued to enjoy some of its early fame for many years after. One of the last entries in the diary is a copy, in a different hand, of the deed of sale by which this engine was ultimately disposed of by the colliery, nearly twenty years after its setting up.

In the meantime the company had adopted steam for winding in the shaft, as well as pumping. This was a development of the last years of the century. No doubt in answer to queries, Matthew Boulton recommended in December 1790 a portable three h.p. engine, able to draw

[1] For these early engines, see Erich Roll, *op. cit.*, pp. 27-30.
[2] *ibid.*, pp. 13, 14.
[3] Erich Roll, p. 39; s.a. 1777.
[4] Memorandum, p. 22.

sixty tons of coal in twelve hours from a depth of 114 or 120 yards. The estimated cost was about two hundred pounds or guineas. Whether this new engine was that which was put in place in the spring of 1794 it would be hard to determine, but in May of that year a drawing engine was being operated by the colliery and 'performed very well'; so that steam winding in the shaft was thenceforward in being. This closes the experimental work of the Bedworth Colliery Company with that portent of change, James Watt's steam-engine.

Production problems naturally filled a large part of the mind which the partners applied to their business affairs. Negotiations and leasings for coal; borings, whose expenses are duly noted; questions of power and gas, absorbed much of their energies and attention. But it would be hard to say whether the actual getting of coal required more or perhaps even so much of their time and thought as its sale and the encountering the wiles of competitors!

Naturally, the Warwickshire pits competed among themselves. The Newdegate property at Griff seems to have been a thorn in the side of Bedworth. The colliery at Griff opened December 1774; it sent a wagonload of coal into Coventry on Thursday 29th December. Sometimes the advantage which it won over Bedworth was purely temporary; as in a combination of snow and frost with bad roads, when Griff and other collieries might enjoy a brisk sale, while the business of the partners practically stood still.[1] Griff, however, was supposed to possess advantages of more permanent nature; coal more easily worked, pits shallower and nearer together, fewer men needed.

The markets served to keep alive competing Griff, Bedworth and a number of other collieries on the field, notwithstanding bickerings. This was due in part to the spread of the canals and the extra business which they brought. But it was also due in part to the Warwickshire collieries being capable of acting together. The nature of their markets encouraged a certain amount of combination and their notion of profitable business included it, though no doubt as the exception to the rule.

The Warwickshire coalfield owed a considerable debt to the canals. Parratt evidently thought it important that in 1774 the Coventry canal was finished and the Oxford canal completed in its fourth stage to Braunston. He may have been an investor in the Oxford canal, for he watched its progress with a loving care. The autumn (November) of 1775 saw the boats coming up as far as Fenny Compton, where there

[1] Memorandum, p. 50.

was a tunnel over half a mile long. Two years afterwards, a junction between two canals was begun at Longford in the immediate neighbourhood of Hawkesbury and finished within a few months.[1] Now not only did the Coventry canal link directly Coventry with the Bedworth Company's pits, but the extension of the Oxford canal gave the company also new markets, south of Coventry. Owing to these developments, the Bedworth Company found it possible and well worth their while to maintain a considerable stock of coal at Banbury. The words used in discussing a change in the price of this Banbury coal, in 1779, suggest that some kind of agreement may have existed on the subject, among the different collieries. 'In August great complaint was made of the large stock of coal at Banbury and we were much urged to lower the Price that they might be sold off. Mr. Taylor and I saw that our Coals were in good condition but the rest in a State of Decay. We therefore were averse to having them lowered. However they were lowered to our very great loss.'[2] This distinctly suggests a price arrangement, which here worked against the interests of the Bedworth Colliery.

The Warwickshire mines felt themselves particularly united on the necessity of preventing, if possible, any descent of South Staffordshire coal upon their markets. Every colliery company was apt to wish a canal for itself, but none for its competitors; and the same sentiment, less definite and concrete, existed in the relations between the different fields. The spread of canals in other parts of the country was watched with a sort of unwilling acquiescence, as the disagreeable price of the privileges which came one's own way by 'canal navigation'.

The committee of the Oxford canal, meeting at Banbury in 1781, received with encouragement a proposal to take a canal from Birmingham to Napton, on the Oxford canal, not far from Daventry. Such a connection between the Oxford canal and Birmingham, which was already linked up with the Black Country collieries by canal on its western side, would have brought the South Staffordshire pits into communication, via Birmingham, with the territory on the east then dominated by the Warwickshire mines and the Oxford canal. This, says Parratt, whose reference to the minutes of the committee makes it pretty certain he was present, 'would have hurt the Interest of the other Part of the Canal and Collieries', and was a plan not likely to go unchallenged by the Warwickshire colliery-owners, especially if they had already, as they would regard it, conferred a favour on the Oxford

[1] Memorandum, p. 17.
[2] ibid., p. 25.

canal by taking up some of its shares. The committee were evidently persuaded to re-examine the scheme and, goes on the journal in some triumph, 'upon mature consideration they thought proper to drop it'.[1] The plan later went through and is the origin of the present Birmingham and Warwick and Warwick and Napton canals.

The following year, 1782, produced a more serious fright among the Warwickshire men. A move was being made to obtain a Bill to construct a canal from the Oakthorpe Colliery, near Ashby de la Zouch, to join the Coventry canal at Griff. This was the germ of the present Ashby de la Zouch canal, which runs past Oakthorpe and joins the Coventry canal, as was feared, at a spot immediately opposite Griff and Bedworth! The interest of Griff in the Coventry market felt itself affronted by so barefaced a proposal; so, too, did that of other colliery-masters. It was decided to put up a common front and 'by the Opposition by Us Mr. Curson (Charity Colliery) Sir R. N. [Sir R. Newdegate, of Griff Colliery] and Mr. Barber the Bill was thrown out'. Then two most interesting but tantalizing references follow: 'See page 75 An Account of the Expences attending this Affair See Page 78 An Agreement as to the Selling of Coals.'[2] Unfortunately the documents spoken of belong to some other manuscript book, which has been lost or in any case is unavailable. But the incident was another example of the fewness and comparative isolation of the Warwickshire pits and the existing imperfection of competition on their chief local market, Coventry, leading to combination.

The Warwickshire owners felt themselves compelled to intervene in another canal proposed a few years later, though here the issue was of a rather different kind; not the building of a canal, but the charges for canal use. An Act of Parliament passed to oblige the several Midland canal companies to complete their lines. The old Birmingham canal, which linked Birmingham with the Black Country mines around Wednesbury and Tipton, was to make a cut from Farmer's Bridge to Deritend, and to build a branch to Fazeley, where a big junction was to be created with the Coventry and Grand Trunk Canals. The Grand Trunk and the Coventry in their turn were to build up to Fazeley, while the Oxford canal was to finish its canal between Banbury and Oxford. Dubious as this far-reaching weaving together of the canals must have seemed to the Warwickshire owners, who thus had the South Staffordshire coal brought in against them from Birmingham and

[1] *ibid.*, p. 32.
[2] Memorandum, p. 37.

Fazeley, they were much more annoyed and alarmed by a clause in the Act which was understood to have arisen out of a meeting of delegates of the canals at Coleshill. According to this agreement, coals brought down the Birmingham canal from Farmer's Bridge to Fazeley, and thence to Oxford, were to pay less in tonnage than coals moving between Fazeley and Oxford. The first class of coal was to pay one penny a mile tonnage; the other class, three halfpence a mile. The object of this provision was to encourage the canal companies to carry out the new plans. But it is hardly surprising that the Warwickshire colliery proprietors became indignant. To them the clause seemed designed to subsidize the coal coming the greater distance, at the expense of the Warwickshire pits. A strong opposition was whipped up and victory inclined its way. In December 1785, 'the Warwickshire Coal Owners obtained a Repeal of that unjust Clause in the Canal Oxford Act respecting the partial tonnage'.

Despite internal bickerings and competition, the Warwickshire companies could always act together with energy and decision, when the occasion seemed to demand their combination. Their position in the Coventry and Oxford markets had always been somewhat oligopolic. Competition was largely limited to their own circle and their numbers were few. Combination was thus relatively easy and arose accordingly, whenever called forth by the threatened competition of other fields.

However sharp the occasional fears of the Bedworth partners, the evidence of these memoranda is of prosperity rather than adversity. There is only one trace of a real crisis in their twenty years. Financial pressure arose under the panic circumstances of 1793, a year of crisis 'remarkable for the distressed State of the Bankers particularly the Small ones', as one entry runs in reminiscent mood. At this moment, when creditors everywhere were putting the screw on their debtors, it is perhaps hardly surprising that the Coventry banking firm with whom the partners dealt expressed themselves, in the old phrase, 'dissatisfied with our Business'.[1] The company were paying five per cent for their accommodation and they remitted to the bankers in May fifteen hundred pounds. This was not sufficient; 'still they were desirous that we should balance all Accounts on a sudden. Their Proceedings we felt were illiberal.' The colliery owed big sums. In January of the following year, 1794, 'Woodcock visited Whieldon and Ferny at Newcastle'; they then accompanied him to Stafford, and he received

[1] The name of the Coventry bank is not referred to, except by initials; from other memoranda, it seems to have been Little & Co.

there £1,500, 'which procured a Suspension of Hostilities very seasonably'. The partners endeavoured to pacify their creditor by a further remittance of £1,500 in February; but still they could not satisfy. A meeting was consequently arranged at Coventry and here it was decided to pay the rest of what was owing 'in our proportionate Share Each Viz £2000 for mine £2000 for Why and Fy.' However, the candid entry follows: 'This was promised they should receive in a fortnight but it has not yet been done.'

The diary tells us just enough of the Warwickshire coal-owners to make us willing to hear more, not least of the colliery which these memoranda concern. But of one set of people living by the mines it says nothing. The colliers who kept Watt's engine busy in the shaft and whose hidden activities helped satisfy bankers and keep canal companies prosperous, scarcely appear. In July 1775 we hear the colliers are now allowed coal, instead of the coal money which has for some time past been allotted them. The charter system crops up and was probably general on the Warwickshire field. 'Two Yard Coal getting and 5 Winds', runs a rough memorandum of the methods at Griff, 'makes the charter 3s. 3d.', but the colliers 'pay the winding up, which makes the Charter 2s. 10d.' The Griff miners also paid towards the wood used in the mine and their share, unspecified, of coal for the engine. It would be interesting to know if such payments were peculiar to Griff among the Warwickshire mines for some reason or other; they may have been, as it was thought worth while to make a note of them.

This is meagre information of the life of the collier. But as the workings of Warwickshire coal capitalism in the eighteenth century come further to light, so, too, will the lives of the colliers. Perhaps in this connection a guess may be hazarded. An examination of Midland business, even within the confined space of the eighteenth century, shows us capitalists existing in a great number of different groups and carrying on their work under immensely varied conditions. Some are capitalists engaged in industry which requires fine technical knowledge, such as chemical manufacture or steam-engineering; they are men of marked scientific culture, even inventors and original thinkers. Others are far from being cultivated men, but make their living by a knowledge of the markets, combined with bargaining ability. The essential conditions of their business vary greatly. At one end of the scale lies the genuinely monopolistic concern, such as a Boulton and Watt firm exploiting its patent and, still more, the lack of substitutes for its product; but below it are all sorts of markets, more or less imperfect, encouraging every form of business policy from the freest competition to the combinations, hidden or avowed, temporary or of long standing, which existed among the Warwickshire colliery-owners when they fought a Canal Bill, or the Stourbridge glass manufacturers when they once cartellized the English market for window glass, or among the Black Country nail-ironmongers when they set wages at Dudley quarter-day in the later years of the century. So, too, it may be expected that if we ever see clearly the Midland working class of the eighteenth century they will tend to lose the simple but vague outlines of class, to take on instead the clear, sharp, conflicting lines of many groups of people, differing in social character and outlook according to their working conditions. Competition in the labour market was never more perfect than it was among the businessmen, nor men more interchangeable than the goods they made.

8 Industrial Organization and Economic Progress in the Eighteenth-century Midlands

British industry is so wide and varied that there will always be danger of narrowness in studying it in the form of regional history. Local patriotism and the antiquarian spirit judge many details interesting which no one unfamiliar with the district can by any stretch of the imagination find instructive or profitable. Besides, the causes of economic progress or decay, which are, or ought to be, the main object of investigations of this sort, cannot be pieced out wholly from the experience of any one part of the country or any particular industry or group of industries. The most that can reasonably be hoped is that the history of the district chosen will bring into relief some special angle of the general economic problem.

The most obvious feature of Midland industry is the enormous range of the industries which have become localized within a limited area. Of course, big changes have taken place from time to time both in the nature of the product and the processes employed. Some of the principal industries of the district today were not among its most notable manufactures or were altogether unknown in mid-Victorian times. There was a specially fast and heavy shift in the industrial interests of South Staffordshire and Birmingham, as Professor Allen has shown, in the slack times and depression of the years 1876–86, following the boom of the Franco-Prussian War and the early seventies.[1] In those years, the Black Country finally declined as an important coalfield and as a main centre of iron production. With the working out of the coal and iron-ore reserves of the district and the modernizing and redistribution

[1] G. C. Allen, *Industrial development of Birmingham and the Black Country* (1929), pt. III, ch. iii and iv.

of the national iron and steel industry which took place in the last quarter of the nineteenth century, a profound change came over the Midland trades. Heavy structural engineering followed the new steel industry to the north, while the Birmingham district, from being the centre of a multitude of hardware trades based upon iron, took on increasingly its present-day aspect of a light engineering centre based mainly upon steel, although larger and more active than its former self.

I want to direct attention at the moment not to these modern arrangements but to the Victorian structure which came to perfection round about the time of the war of 1870-1, when it flourished exceedingly until the collapse of trade in 1875—a structure which was beginning to be undermined even then and has now passed out of living memory. There was a sharp distinction in Victorian days between the industries of the Black Country and those of Birmingham. South Staffordshire concerned itself more with the heavy industries and the cruder iron manufactures. It turned out in the early seventies roughly a third of the country's wrought iron and a ninth of its pig iron; upon these, it had built up industries of heavy structural ironwork. The principal small metal trade was the hand-wrought nail, although the district also possessed several intensely localized and flourishing trades of other sorts—chains at Cradley, locks at Willenhall, saddlery and harness ironmongery at Walsall, nuts and bolts at Darlaston, hollow-ware at West Bromwich and Wolverhampton, flint glass at Stourbridge, and so forth. Birmingham competed with the Black Country in some of these products, for example, flint glass, edged tools, and saddlery and harness. But the four main industries of the city were not of the Black Country sort at all; they were the brass and copper trades, the manufacture known as jewellery, which included the output of an infinity of Victorian knicknacks, the making of small arms and the button industry. Other manufactures were metal pens, brass bedsteads and wire goods.[1] Birmingham had applied its capital and skill, it will be observed, not only to products of iron, but also to manufactures in other sorts of metal. Peculiar as this collection of industries may appear today, it was highly characteristic of the district and the time and natural enough, judged by the requirements and taste of the age and the local ability to supply what was wanted. It was also highly

[1] The best contemporary account is to be found in a series of reports collected by the Local Industries Committee for the meeting of the British Association at Birmingham in 1865, edited by Samuel Timmins and published under the title of *Birmingham and the Midland hardware district* (London, 1866).

profitable—the surest indication, as many thought, of what is both natural and desirable—and the foundation of a type of English provincial social life which it is a pity that no leisurely matter-of-fact Trollope has left us a picture of.

The size and the methods of the many firms carrying out this wide range of manufactures were almost as varied as the products themselves. Big capital and plenty of power were employed by the pig- and wrought-iron manufactures and by the owners of the numerous metal-rolling mills in the district. But most of the finished manufactures, with some conspicuous exceptions, still depended on a skilful pair of hands and simple tools rather than on power-driven machinery. They were carried on in small workshops. Here a capitalistic organization of a different kind was common, which turned upon the factor. The functions and authority of the factor varied from trade to trade, but his main responsibilities were to initiate and finance this or that branch of production and to market the goods. There was a combination, therefore, in Midland industry between the factory-capitalism which we know so well today and the domestic system of production of an older time. But there was also a tendency for the large centralized organization to gain ground, as against the older methods. In some industries, we read, the large unit had developed not because power-machines had been introduced, but because the processes of making this or that product had been divided among numbers of semi-skilled workers, who required supervision to co-ordinate their energies. In other industries, certain manufacturers with a reputation and market of their own had found it worth while to bring all their workpeople together, for the sake of maintaining the quality on which their sales depended and to increase their lead over competitors.[1]

Anyone who is acquainted, however distantly, with the industrial history of the Midlands at an earlier date than the Victorian town and district thus hastily described, must be struck by the age and continuity of the industrial processes which still persisted in such vigour down to the middle of last century and beyond. The assumption of some writers that the industries of the Midlands go back hardly further than the eighteenth century, is, of course, no more correct than that the Lancashire textiles date from the same age. Both districts have a long record of previous industrial history.[2] Seventeenth-century England took

[1] Allen, op. cit., p. 446.
[2] For early Lancashire, see A. P. Wadsworth and J. de L. Mann, *The cotton trade and industrial Lancashire, 1600–1780* (1931); for the Midlands, W. H. B. Court, *Rise of the Midland industries, 1600–1838*, book i (1938).

important steps towards an industrial future; steps so varied and interesting that they may tempt us into supposing them to have been more important than they actually were. So far as the Midlands are concerned, the slow but increasing exploitation of the native coal and iron of the district bind together the seventeenth with the eighteenth and the nineteenth centuries in an unbroken whole.

Often the continuity has been one of a personal character. The example might be quoted of a family who were continuously interested, as factors, perhaps in the early days as craftsmen also, in the old hand-wrought nail trade from a time well before the Civil Wars until the early years of Victoria. Then the family record finished in a typically nineteenth-century way, for the eldest son sold out and spent most of the capital accumulated over two centuries in setting up as a Warwickshire country gentleman and in railway and joint-stock speculation. I do not believe this sort of personal continuity to have been in the least rare or exceptional in the isolated and homekeeping Midlands of pre-railway times.

The continuity of the processes of industrialization in the Midlands can, of course, be easily paralleled from other parts of the country. It suggests of itself another consideration; which is, what a great deal of industrial progress was possible without the aid either of steam-power or the factory. For the well-known partnership formed in 1775 between James Watt and Matthew Boulton of Birmingham, which began the manufacture of the steam-engine, belonged distinctly to the later rather than the earlier phases of Midland industrialization. A large output over a wide range of industrial products had already been achieved before the steam-engine came to make it larger. It is enough to remember that the district was already one of the most important coal and iron centres in the country, both a large producer and consumer of bar iron. The making of the hand-wrought nail was already what it remained for part of the next century, the most widely spread of the local iron manufactures, while the South Staffordshire specialities, such as locks, saddler's ironmongery and harness, flint glass, and so forth, were well established. The broad outlines of the industrial geography of Birmingham and the Black Country in the mid-nineteenth century, as it presented itself to Carlyle when he visited it in 1824 and Clerk Maxwell[1] in the fifties—travellers with characteristically different views, for the one compared the place to Hell while the other evidently felt the happy

---

[1] J. A. Froude, *Carlyle's early life* (Silver Library Edition, 1896), I, 238–9; Campbell and Garnett, *Life of James Clerk Maxwell* (1882), pp. 168–85.

scientist's conviction that if this was Hell then it was a very interesting spot—these outlines had been laid down a hundred years before.

The wide range of products and the large output achieved before the nineteenth-century phase of industrial life was reached had comparatively simple roots. Industrial progress, in this as in other parts of the country, depended upon two indispensable conditions; first, the possibility of increasing the output of the products of the region without a proportionate increase of industrial costs, and second, the finding of a market, without which the larger output would have been not worth attaining; for the production methods of a Matthew Boulton would patently have been economic madness for an earlier age. There will be no time to consider here the fulfilment of the second condition, the finding of a market for Midland goods. It was an extremely interesting and complicated process, which could be well illustrated from the career of Matthew Boulton; for if Boulton is chiefly famous for the effect of his work upon the reduction of industrial costs through cheap power, he was also, at every stage of his career, both before and after the partnership with Watt, an indefatigable and adventurous, or as some contemporaries thought, crack-brained searcher for markets. In considering the problem of increasing returns in Midland industry, I shall assume it to be borne well in mind that the reduction of costs and the sale of the product stood in so intimate a relation to one another as to be little more than the two sides of a single process.

Small-scale enterprise was the main instrument for increasing the return to Midland labour through this early period of the seventeenth and the eighteenth centuries and for the bulk of the industrial output of the district in terms of final products. There were many traces of this still in Victorian Birmingham, with its factors and numerous backstairs workers. In the previous century it was still more marked, despite the frequency of concerns, especially in the iron industry, which were large for their day and even more of a medium size. The abundance at that date of industrial units of the smallest known type, the family shop, directs our attention to a very interesting phase in the growth of industrialism, which is, to be sure, well known from the side of the textile trades but was no less important for the metals.

One of the principal results of the experiments of the late eighteenth and nineteenth centuries in large-scale industrial organization, usually described as the Industrial Revolution, was to create the modern study of all those forms of economy which form the internal economies, in Marshall's phrase, of the individual firm; the problems of management as large industrial concerns know them today.[1] Here again Matthew Boulton and James Watt might serve as example, although their work was outstripped by their successors, the two sons, Matthew Robinson Boulton and James Watt, Jnr. Of the latter it was said in 1930 that there was nothing that Taylor, Ford or other modern experts in scientific management have devised which could not be discovered, at any rate by anticipation, in their work before 1805, while their system of costing was superior to that employed by many very successful firms today.[2] Problems of large-scale organization in industry began to receive, from such men, a degree of attention which in earlier times was more commonly bestowed upon similar questions in the sphere of war or government.

It would be absurd to say that tasks of industrial administration of this sort were new, but steam power certainly threw an altogether new emphasis upon them and gave them a universality which was new. And to that extent, they draw our attention away from and perhaps make us less able to appreciate the industrial problems of ages when large-scale organizations were large by the scale of their own time rather than by that of ours. In the eighteenth century an engineering firm like Boulton and Watt was unique in the Midlands, and large concerns of any kind were the exception rather than the rule. It is clear, therefore, that economies must have been secured in other ways, to account for the large output which Birmingham and the Black Country were disposing of upon national and world markets before the end of the century.

The sources of industrial progress in those days are to be found largely in the region of Marshall's external economies of the industry and in Adam Smith's even larger conception of division of labour,[3] than in that of the skilful management of large works. There were three ways specially in which an output could be secured which was truly extraordinary when compared with the state of industrial technique ruling. They were briefly:

[1] The *locus classicus* for this distinction between internal and external economies is, of course, Alfred Marshall, *Principles of economics* (8th edition, 1920), bk. IV, ch. ix, p. 7.

[2] Professor J. G. Smith, in the introduction to E. Roll, *An early experiment in industrial organisation being a history of the firm of Boulton and Watt, 1775–1805* (1930), p. 15.

[3] On the relations between the ideas of Marshall and Adam Smith on this point, see Allyn Young, 'Increasing return and economic progress', *Economic Journal*, vol. XXXVIII (1928), especially pp. 527–9. I must here acknowledge a considerable debt to Professor Young's handling of the subject.

(1) by geographical specialization or, as we say, localization of industry;
(2) by occupational specialization or division of processes;
(3) by a less well-defined process of industrial differentiation, by which whole new industries intervene between the first handlers of the product and the market, so that production becomes more roundabout in proportion as it becomes more efficient, judged by the test of ability to increase output without sending up costs in proportion.

All three processes had a single object, increased returns to human labour, which they approached by different routes. The simultaneous employment of all three methods provides the key to the astonishing diversity, even before the steam-engine came on the scene, of the industrial life of the Midlands.

I suppose that the whole concentration of the iron trades upon the coal and iron ore of South Staffordshire might be taken as an example of geographical specialization. But it may be more profitable to resort to a single industry. The hand-wrought nail trade might appear to be the most generally spread of all the local industries, the one least tied down to locality. There was certainly hardly a district in which nail-making was not at some time or other carried on. Yet this very common trade had a curious affinity for places, down to its last days.

Although there was no division of labour in the production of a single nail, except perhaps the spike-nail, the production of the different types of nail was localized. Dudley, in the heart of the Black Country, produced horse and mule shoe-nails. These require more skill than other nails, and the work was better paid. Rowley Regis turned out rivets, hob-nails and small nails, Bromsgrove all small work, hobs, brush-nails and Flemish tacks, Halesowen large spike-nails, and so forth, throughout the nailing country. The localization was always changing but was always marked.[1] Striking as the localization of the nail trade certainly was, it is in some ways a bad example to quote, for I am not satisfied that I know as well as I should like to know what economic advantages the various types of nail-makers drew from being where they were. One assumes that advantages there were, but it would take a considerable local knowledge to put a finger on them. I suspect that they had much to do with the factoring; that it was as convenient to have one district for which one went for one class of nail, as it is to have different

[1] E. I. Davies, 'The hand-made nail trade of Birmingham and district' (Thesis, Birmingham University Library), pp. 3–5.

shops or different parts of an open-air market for different products. On the other sides, no doubt, it paid the nailer to stick to the class of nail in which he had the most proficiency, and particular classes of work became specialized among particular families and consequently in particular districts.

The specialization of the nailing districts is only one more instance of the local specialization which is found over and over again in the Midland iron trades, within the general framework provided by the raw materials of the district and the cost of their transport—not only coal and iron but limestone and fire-clay as well—without which it would not be possible to explain the presence in the Midlands of industries such as flint-glass making which have nothing to do with iron-working at all. But the attachment to district went on long after the local raw materials had ceased to be of much importance; for if there is not one advantage or one set of advantages in being in a particular place, then there will be another advantage or another set of advantages. Hence industry, once it had come to the Midlands, remained, although there was constant change within the district. It does not, of course, follow that every motive behind an enterprise being where it was, was economic. In the days when business was run by partnerships, all sorts of personal incidents, such as quarrels with a former partner, influenced the calculations behind what we now call localization.

As for occupational specialization, the first wide growth of industrial occupations in the Midlands took place in the century between Queen Elizabeth and Queen Anne, during the first vigorous development of the iron-ore and coal of the district. It was, in fact, nothing more than another aspect of the localization of iron trades which I have just mentioned under the name of geographical specialization, except that it was a side to the process of industrialization which was tied down less to place and natural resources than to the actual processes of manufacture and the constant tendency to divide them among new crafts.

The division of processes had gone far among the established trades by the end of the seventeenth century. It could scarcely have been carried further than among the lorimers or makers of saddlery and saddler's ironmongery—who were important men in a horse-riding age—at Walsall. There, so Dr. Plot tells us, men of four crafts collaborated in the making of the spur. The same habit of specialization extended to the making of other parts of horseman's equipment, and it was rarely that a man turned from the making of one part to that of another.[1]

[1] Plot gives a detailed description: *Natural history of Staffordshire* (1686), pp. 376–7.

The division and simplification of processes had its logical conclusion, as it has often been pointed out, in the introduction of the machine to take over one process after another. Whether this was the inevitable result or not, the coming in of the machine for manufacture of the final product was only a late stage in the process—in the Midlands, mainly a nineteenth-century one—and was preceded by two centuries of growth effected mainly by the increasing skill of the human hand and of simple tools.

By industrial differentiation I mean the peeling off, if the phrase may be allowed, of whole new industries, and especially of those which did not introduce a new product but intervened in the making of an old one between the first handlers of the materials and the consumer. The general effect of these was to reduce manufacturing costs among an immense range of final products. The natural place for such industries to grow up among the Midland trades was in the preparation of metals in the early stages, and their successful establishment was one of the prime causes of the competitive success of the Midland industries.

A good example of this kind of development would be the introduction of the slitting-mill into the district in the seventeenth century. The poorly paid maker of hand-made nails has already been mentioned as the most universal figure among the metal-workers of the Midland counties down to the early nineteenth century. But the extension of the nailer's craft was to no small extent a result of the slitter's success in providing him with the strips of iron which formed his raw material, in the sizes which he required and at a price which enabled the nailer, through the factors, to supply the whole country and the colonies. But the iron slitting-mill was but one development among many in the smelting, hammering and rolling of metals. Other trades owed as much to the copper-roller, who by the eighteenth century rolled metal, as someone grandiloquently said, for all Europe.

The rise of these more roundabout processes of production, of whole industries devoted to producing materials for other producers, and the large plants which were necessary where the materials being used were the metals, has attracted the attention of many good observers and is consequently well known.[1] The growth of big capitalistic enterprise in the primary processes was often highly dramatic. Furthermore, since it progressed by way of the large-scale enterprise, which leaves more

[1] See especially the excellent standard descriptions of T. S. Ashton, *Iron and steel in the industrial revolution* (1924), and H. Hamilton, *English brass and copper industries to 1800* (1926).

abundant records behind it than the handicraftsman or the employer under the domestic system ever did, it is comparatively easy to trace. It is hardly surprising that enterprise of this prominent type has received more attention than the obscure organization of many of the trades dealing with final products.

Large-scale organizations seem for long to have been almost confined to the primary trades in the Midlands, although in such trades they already had a long history behind them when the eighteenth century began. The new thing which the men of that century undertook seems to have been the extension of the method of large-scale organization to the final products. This development found a well-known support in the increasing use of steam power at the end of the century, but the large works was destined to come, in some trades, even if steam had never been invented. It was a natural outcome of the methods by which industry had come to be carried on. The constant separation of processes and the complicated nature of some of the products which Midland, and especially Birmingham industry, was now turning out, made supervision more and more a necessary task of the entrepreneur. He could no longer content himself with putting the work out and collecting it again. The factory in the Japan trade run by John Taylor at a time a little before the American war shows this trend in business methods. Power of any sort seems to have been unimportant at his works, compared with the need to keep an eye on the details of the work and maintain the firm's reputation for quality, such as it was. But here again the extraordinary and never-satisfied energy of Matthew Boulton made him a pioneer whose labours have far outshadowed the shadowy Taylor. Boulton's factory at Soho became in later days the first home of scientific engineering and the prime cause of the growth of other factories in the Midlands and far beyond them, but the document in which Boulton himself sums up his reasons for building the factory in the first instance contains no word about power. The important matter in his eyes is to have the workpeople 'under our eyes and immediate management . . . every day and almost every hour'.[1] The history of the Soho factory shows that while the art of modern factory management, as has already been said, was largely a result of the introduction of steam, it also inherited much from pre-steam days.

The successful introduction of the new technique of power pro-

---

[1] From a statement by Matthew Boulton, preserved with other papers relating to his partnership with John Fothergill in the Assay Office, Birmingham.

duction rested upon a number of economic conditions or prerequisites. These were broadly three in number:
(1) an industrial wage-earning class, with an aptitude for the class of work required;
(2) an industrial managing class, prepared to tackle the problems of large-scale organization and already in some degree familiar with them;
(3) a class of industrial investors.

The success of the Watt-Boulton partnership came from the fact that owing to the industrial developments which have been glanced at above, all these conditions could be fulfilled. On the other hand, the partners' difficulties in the workshop and the counting-house and perhaps no less with their bankers showed how large and how novel the enterprise was which they had set themselves.

Very solid links have been shown to unite the old and the new forms of industrial enterprise during the eighteenth century in other parts of the country. They seem to have been at least as firm in the north as in the Midlands, to judge by the career of such a man as Samuel Oldknow in the cotton industry.[1] There is a resemblance between his movement from one form of industrial organization to another and that of Boulton, although they worked upon different products and in different generations. The same transition must have been made by many thousands of people. It represented the industrial revolution in a most evolutionary aspect.

One can of course exaggerate the continuity of industrial life. Nature may not make leaps, but men do. And the adoption of steam power was a leap into the dark for society at large, despite all the forward-lookingness of Boulton and the Scotch caution of James Watt. It was a jump away from centuries of human experience, and no words can be too strong to describe the truly revolutionary side of that great event.

But the continuity, rather than the breaks, of industrial life has been deliberately emphasized in this paper, for a particular purpose. For there was an underlying unity between the new forms of industry and the old, although it was the unity not of a product, or of a single enterprise or industry, but of a continuous economic process.

Thoughtful observers in the eighteenth century itself believed that

[1] George Unwin and others, *Samuel Oldknow and the Arkwrights* (1924), gives the facts of Oldknow's career. The suggested comparison with Boulton is mine, not Unwin's, and he would possibly not have agreed with its validity.

they had found the key in what they called the division of labour, by which they meant that separation of manual processes which goes to make new occupations. A contemporary of Adam Smith, Lord Shelburne, who visited the town in 1766, described its industries in language which, if it had been written a few years later, might have been thought to have slipped out of the draft of the *Wealth of Nations*. 'A button', he remarks, 'passes through fifty hands and each hand perhaps passes a thousand in a day, likewise by this means the work becomes so simple that, five times in six, children of six or eight years old do it as well as men, and earn from tenpence to eight shillings a week. There are besides an infinity of smaller improvements which each workman has and sedulously keeps secret from all the rest.'[1] One could truthfully add to his lordship's observations that they went for more than buttons, and applied to almost every industry in Birmingham and the Black Country.

The division of labour was an astonishingly fruitful economic conception and obviously throws floods of light on the evolution of the Midland trades, among others. But in the casual phrases of Shelburne, as he would have been the first to admit, it was far from being a complete explanation. He thought of it wholly in terms of manual skill, omitting to mention the specialization of men whose business it is to manage, although the rise of that class in the Midlands as elsewhere was one of the most important of all the aspects of the division of labour. And he forgot to specify, what he was certainly not ignorant of, the financing functions of capital.

Since the days of Shelburne and Adam Smith the functions of capital have received so much attention from thinkers that it would be easy to sketch a quite different explanation of the rise of the Midland industries from that given by Shelburne; one which would lay all the emphasis not on the specialization of the worker but on the leadership of the capitalist. This might be termed the Sombartian type of explanation, and indeed Sombart's *Moderne Kapitalismus* contains the best general account known to me of the organization of industry before the industrial revolution.[2] The organization in the Midlands does not appear to have differed essentially from that of metal trades in other parts of Europe at that time, for example in Germany, and it turned, here as there, upon the organizing and financing powers of the capitalist as much as upon the increase of manual skill.

[1] See the whole description, Fitzmaurice, *Life of Shelburne* (1875), I, 402–5.
[2] W. Sombart, *Der moderne Kapitalismus*, Zweiter Band (München und Leipzig, 1928). This volume was published in two separate half-volumes.

Economic Progress in Eighteenth-Century Midlands 247

The growing pull of the big capitalist was a feature of Midland history, as it has been of industrial development almost everywhere in modern times. But in the trades organized domestically, with the possible exception of the nail trade, the big factor does not appear to have dominated the scene so absolutely as he is said to have done in the contemporary woollen trade of the west of England,[1] and after 1785, when Watt's announcement of rotary motion led to heavy investment in the new form of power, the factory-owner multiplied himself with a most notable slowness in the Midland trades.

In other words, the operations of the capitalist in this region were comparatively modest and undramatic, at least until the nineteenth century. It is always possible in the earlier period to look over the big man's shoulder at the many lesser persons who were responsible, according to the best of our scanty evidence, for a very important part of the total industrial output. His activity was never so remarkable as to obscure the importance of the working man's growing skill or of the still unexhausted mineral resources of the district. This being the case, there is little temptation to overrate the importance of the capital owner in the Midlands, or to interpret his position in the industrial order of the seventeenth and eighteenth centuries in terms of an inevitable trend towards the high capitalism of the very different world of a later day. The quite different problem appears: how to account in terms of contemporary economic and technical conditions, for the persistence side by side of enterprises of many different sizes, organized in a curious variety of ways.

Our knowledge of the old forms of industry begins to appear at this point most defective and unsatisfactory. A simple description of the rich natural resources of the district, or of the many industrial occupations of its inhabitants, or even of the methods by which the capitalist employer organized his business—although that goes deeper—does not help us very much. The fundamental unity of Midland industrial development over two centuries appears in the vast expansion of output, to which many products, many industries and many types of organization contributed. This increasing mass of goods was its outward and visible sign. But its reality must have been the continuous movement of costs and prices and the relationship in which they stood to one another, as regards any one product or industry or business, at any given time.

We know far more of the external forms of organization in the

[1] This is the impression created by the account of the West Country trade in the eighteenth century in E. Lipson's *Economic history of England*, II, 13–69.

Midlands than we do of these determining economic relations. Yet upon these the outward forms depended, and without a knowledge of them we know little more than the face of the landscape, without being familiar with the invisible forces which over the long period created it. One is obliged to confess that there is a great deal that is hypothetical about our knowledge of industry at this early period. Presumably the major groups of Midland trades were subject to increasing returns over long periods. This must have been so especially towards the end of the eighteenth and the beginning of the nineteenth centuries, when war demand, combined with the rapid advance of technique in the iron industry, brought about a swift building up of the iron industry and of many of the subsidiary industries which it fed. There are signs of a fall of costs in the iron trade at that date which might fairly be called revolutionary. But we know little about it and less still of the return to Midland resources in the trade in final products.

What is wanted to give fullness and life to our conception of the older forms of industrial organization is, there can hardly be a doubt, knowledge both statistical and descriptive of the relations between the expansion of output, the efficiency of industry and the size of the concern, if concern it can be called, at different times. There can also be no doubt that the poverty of the material puts out of our reach for ever such studies of this kind as have been made for nineteenth-century industries. It would be impossible, unfortunately, for any one to construct a study of increasing return in the South Staffordshire iron industry for the eighteenth century, similar to the late G. T. Jones's interesting analysis of the Cleveland pig-iron industry between 1883 and 1925,[1] or to attempt to work out the elasticity of return (the ratio between the rate of expansion of the industry and the rate of fall of real costs) in the Black Country coalfield in the same age. The necessary public and private statistics could not be found, quite apart from the formidable technical and theoretical obstacles which stand in the way of such investigations, even when the information exists.

But it is to be hoped that the slow process of the examination of the records of firms, especially of firms of long standing, whose operations endured over substantial periods, and were fairly representative in their scale of the industries to which they belonged, may provide us as time goes on with clues worth having to the general movement of industrial costs and to the returns obtained upon them. The interpretation of such records appears to require, at any rate for important parts of the work,

[1] G. T. Jones, *Increasing return* (1933), pt. IV.

powers more often found among accountants and engineers than among historians. On the rare occasions when men of those trainings have turned their attention to historical problems, the results have sometimes proved most valuable and interesting. Economic historians already owe, for instance, a considerable debt to the Newcomen Society for the history of technology and engineering. The growing popularity of economic history studies may persuade others to undertake similar researches or some historians to find in themselves an unsuspected capacity to deal with figures and technical facts.

The work at any rate would be worth doing. Questions of quantity, such as most of these are, are the breath of life to ordinary industrial human nature; the size of the pay packet, the dimensions of the profit, the quantity of goods delivered. Reconstruction of the extinct calculations which once passed through Midland heads, often unlettered heads, cannot be more than unheroic work. But the calculations were men's common thoughts about the things of their common experience. There is Maitland's authority for saying that to rethink such thoughts is one of the duties and privileges of a historian.[1]

[1] F. W. Maitland, *Domesday Book and beyond* (1897), last page.

Index of Subjects

Africa, 193
  South African War, 70, 73, 131, 174, 185, 187–8
  J. A. Hobson, 185
America,
  coal industry, 162, 199, 202, 204, 208, 215
  international trade, 68–72, 79, 154, 174
  New England colonies, 19, 22–4
  war resources, 113–18
  World War I, 93, 98, 100
anthropology,
  B. Malinowski, 21
art,
  Bassani, 10
Australia, 157, 174
Austria,
  E. Dollfuss, 44–5
  economy, World War I, 62
  R. Hilferding, 186
  F. Josef, 48
  G. Princip, 65
  relations with Germany, 44, 47
  Vienna, 48–9
  Young Bosnians, 65

Bank of England, 107–8
  history of, 142–3, 150
Birmingham,
  in the thirties, 31–6
Birmingham, University of,
  J. Chamberlain, 29, 31
  and local politics, 32
  J. G. Smith, 29–30, 37

Calvinism,
  and capitalism, 18
  in New England Colonies, 19
Cambridge,
  Clapham, Sir John, 14, 55–6, 141–50
  Downing College, 16
  Heretics Society, 21
  History School, 14, 17

capitalism,
  Calvinism and capitalism, 18–19
  Lenin, 38
  R. H. Tawney, 17–18, 22, 46, 56, 127–43, 176
Cirencester, 2–3, 5–6, 10, 23
coal industry, 67, 225, 234
  Cardiff, 32–3, 162, 196
  Cheshire, 214
  Derbyshire, 211
  engine use, 225–9
  Glamorganshire, 33, 204
  interwar years, 195–224
  leasing arrangements, 227
  Sir Walter Monckton, 214
  Northumberland, 204–5
  Nottingham, 211
  F. Parratt, 226
  Samuel Commission, 206
  Sankey Commission, 203
coal mines legislation, 203, 205, 210–12, 214–15, 216–20
colonialism,
  English colonies, 38
  H. Merivale, 183–4
  New England colonies, 19
  G. Wakefield, 183
Communism, 27, 34, 43
  and imperialism, 180–94
Czechoslovakia, 48–9, 220

economic history, 33–6, 151–79
  Birmingham, University of, 25
  M. Bloch, 149
  Sir John Clapham, 14, 55–6, 141–50, 151–79
  E. Gay, 20, 22–4
  Hammond-Webb approach, 164
  Professor Pigou, 164
  E. Power, 134–5
  J. Saltmarsh, 56
  G. Schmoller, 144
economics,
  W. Ashley, 29

Index of Subjects

economics and history, 160
  R. Firth, 136
  P. S. Florence, 21, 30
  S. Harris, 21
  G. T. Jones, 21
  M. Keynes, 5, 34–5, 91, 136, 144, 160
  H. Marquand, 30
  A. Marshall, 55, 141, 145–6
  E. Mason, 21
  Mill, 182, 184–5
  C. Ruini, 49
  Richard Henry Tawney, 17–18, 22, 46, 56, 127–43
  O. Taylor, 21
  G. Walker, 30
  A. Young, 21
education, 8–13, 25
  Education Act, 1902, 13
  Education Act, 1944, 133
  educational reform, 12–13
  Hegel, Ranke, and Marx, 28
  E. Sharwood Smith, 12–13
  social science and history, 37

Fascism,
  in Europe, 27
  O. Mosley, 34
  universities and industry, 34
France, 19, 40, 92, 142
  M. Bloch, 149
  Franco-Prussian War, 235
  French Revolution, 87, 168
  occupation of Morocco, 187
  occupation of the Ruhr, 43, 204
  World War I, 47, 62, 65, 71, 85–7, 88–100
  World War II, 50–1

The General Strike, 1926, 16–17, 123
Germany, 5, 34, 40, 45, 58, 71, 78–9, 84, 94
  and Africa, 187–8
  Berlin, 92
  Bismarck, 49, 190–1
  coal industry, 208–9, 215, 220
  and Czechoslovakia, 47–8
  economic depression, 40–3
  economy in World War I, 62, 142
  and France, 50–1, 85
  Goebbels, 52
  Goethe, 26–8
  Hitler, 41–2, 45–6, 48–50, 52, 54
  invasion of Norway, 60
  and Italy, 50, 58
  Munich, 47, 49
  unemployment, 40, 43
  G. Schmoller, 144
  Weimar, 57
  Government, 9, 16, 167–71

Asquith-Bannerman-Campbell administration, 4, 66, 78, 131
Balfour administration, 66
Chamberlain Government, 49
Labour Government, 30, 32, 40, 132

History,
  Lord Acton, 141
  Professor Ashton, 162
  B. Croce, 49
  Sir George Clark, 36
  J. G. Droysen, 22
  German philosophy of history, 28
  G. P. Gooch, 28
  Guicciardini, 152
  K. Hancock, 37–40, 45, 54–5, 190
  J. Hawgood, 47, 49
  F. W. Maitland, 141
  B. Malinowski, 21–2
  S. E. Morison, 12, 20, 23–4
  L. Namier, 17
  and sociology, 18, 158
  R. H. Tawney, 17–18, 22, 46, 56, 127–43, 176
  H. Temperley, 14
  D. Ward, 16, 19, 22, 25, 28, 43

imperialism,
  and capitalism, 38
  and Communism, 180–94
India,
  Sir Theodore Gregory, 39–40
  Herman Merivale, 183
industrial relations, 15–16, 34–5, 163, 165–6
  G. D. H. Cole, 112
  the General Strike, 1926, 16–17, 123, 205
  H. Marquand, 30
  Sir F. Tillyard, 29–30
  Whitley Committee, 123
Ireland, 78, 162
  post-war disturbances, 38
  J. G. Smith, 29
Italy, 98–100, 162
  B. Croce, 49
  Germany, 50, 58
  Mussolini, 44, 47, 49
  Rome, 92
Japan, 52
  attack on Manchuria, 40

Labour Government, 40, 132
  H. Marquand, 30, 32
Lancashire,
  Chartist Movement, 7–8

Index of Subjects

coal industry, 195, 211, 214
cotton trade, 36
League of Nations, 119, 209
London, 6, 16–17
  Charles Booth, 16–17, 73, 133
  W. O. Hart, 52
  The Saturday Review, 187–8

Manchuria, 40
Midlands, 31, 34, 36, 68, 235–49
  coal industry, 195, 210, 214, 233–49
  W. H. B. Court, *Rise of the Midland Industries*, 36
Mineworkers Federation, 215
Ministry of Shipping, 52–3
monopoly,
  and imperialism, 186–9
Munich, 47, 49

natural history, 8, 11–12
  M. Catesby, 12
  C. Darwin, 8, 11–12
  J. D. Hooker, 11
  E. Isaacs, 32–3, 41, 43
  A. R. Wallace, 8, 11
New York, 20–3

poetry,
  Goethe, 26–8, 57
  E. de Selincourt, 30
  W. E. Dodds, 30
philosophy,
  R. B. Braithwaite, 21
  B. Croce, 49
  B. Malinowski, 21
  Marx, 18, 21, 28, 34, 38–9, 57, 76, 135, 160, 176–7, 184–5, 189–92
  Mill, 182, 184–5
  philosophy and the Bible, 58–9
  philosophy of war, 80, 138, 193
  Ranke, 28
  R. H. Tawney, 17–18, 22, 46, 56, 127–43, 176
Poland, 50, 208–9, 220
population, 67–8, 103, 148
  Malthus, 157
  Ricardo, 182
Portugal, 99
poverty, 3, 6, 7, 17, 55, 120–1, 124, 224
  Poor Law, 76, 148, 163
  unemployment, 17, 24, 32–6, 40–3, 70–1, 102, 111, 123, 136

religion, 7–8, 19, 26, 56–7, 155
  Calvinism and capitalism, 18, 135, 143

C. Darwin, 11–12
H. H. Milman, 8
The Old Testament, 58
socialism and religion, 17–18, 129–31
W. Temple, 56
Russia, 34, 38, 45, 58, 62, 65, 83, 86, 98–9

Sarajevo, 65, 78, 83
Scotland,
  coal mining, 195, 201, 210
Serbia, 98–9, 119
shipping, 52–6, 80–3, 85, 92–3, 99
silk industry, 10
socialism, 101
  Christian Social Union, 129
  German National Socialist Revolution, 43, 47
  C. Gore, 129
  Labour Party, 76
  H. S. Holland, 129
  F. D. Maurice, 129
  J. Saltmarsh, 56
  R. H. Tawney, 18, 56, 129
  W. Temple, 129
sociology, 158
  J. Clapham, 14, 55–6, 141–50
  Fabian Essays, 129
  P. S. Florence, 21, 30–1
  Goethe, 26–8
  B. Malinowski, 21
  W. Morris, 129
  R. H. Tawney, 18, 136–9
  G. Unwin, 123, 141–2, 148–9
  A. Young, 21
Spain,
  J. Bell 46
  Civil War, 45–6
  J. Cornford, 46
St. Petersburg, 92
Stock Exchange, 58
syndicalism,
  Tom Mann, 76

textile industry,
  in Stroud, 6–7
trade unions,
  Arthur Henderson, 112
  G. Barnes, 112

unemployment, 17, 24, 32–6, 40–3, 70–1, 102, 111, 123, 136
urbanization, 67–8

Versailles Treaty, 5
Vienna, 48–9, 92

Index of Subjects

Wales,
  coalfields, 202, 210
Warwickshire,
  mines, 230–8
working classes, 7–9, 32–3, 109
  people's Charter, 146
  Great Exhibition, 146
World War I, 4, 5, 14, 55, 61–71, 62–3, 87
  Allied Maritime Transport Council, 100
  American resources, 113–18
  Armistice of 1918, 5
  Clausewitz, 88
  Committee of Imperial Defence, 84
  financing and resources, 61–126
  Marshal Foch, 5
  Inter-Allied Food Council, 100
  Inter-Allied Munitions Council, 100
  League of Nations, 119
  Munitions of War Act, 111
  prewar industry, 197–202, 207
  recruitment, 89–90
  unrestricted submarine campaign, 99
World War II, 46–60, 63
  Hiroshima, 24

Yorkshire,
  coalfields, 211

Index of Persons

Acton, Lord, 141
Allen, G. C., 235
Arnold, Matthew, 133
Ashley, William James, 29, 166
Asquith, H. H., 78, 131

Barnes, George, 112
Bassano family, 9, 10
Bathurst, Lord, 3, 4
Batt, Walter, 11
Baykov, Alexander, 51
Beit, Alfred, 187
Bell, Julian, 46
Beveridge, William, 133
Bismarck, 79, 190–1
Bloch, Marc, 149
Booth, Charles, 16, 73, 133
Boulton, Matthew, 228, 238–40, 244–5
Boulton, Matthew Robinson, 240
Bowley, Arthur, 73
Boyle, Hugh, 53
Braddon, Rose, 8
Braithwaite, R. B., 21
Brooke, Anthony Charles, 11, 134
Bukharin, N., 186

Caird, Edward, 128
Carlyle, Thomas, 238
Catesby, Mark, 12
Chamberlain, Joseph, 29, 31
Chamberlain, Neville, 40
Churchill, Winston, 82, 131
Clark, Sir George, 36
Clapham, Sir John, 14, 55–6, 141–50
Clausewitz, 88
Cole, G. D. H., 112
Coolidge, Calvin, 12
Cornford, John, 46
Cosgrave, Richard, 38
Cousins, Donald, 30
Cranfield, Lionel, 138
Croce, Benedetto, 49, 193

Cunningham, William, 141–5

Darwin, Charles, 8, 11–12, 23
de Selincourt, Ernest, 31
Dodds, W. E., 31
Dollfuss, Engelbert, 44, 45
Droysen, J. G., 22

Eliot, George, 8

Ferneyhough, 225–6
Finzi, Gerald, 53
Florence, Lella Sargant, 30
Florence, Philip Sargant, 21, 30–1
Foch, Marshal, 5
Frazer, Sir J. G., 8
Freud, Sigmund, 13

Gay, Edwin, 20, 22–4
Goethe, J. W., 26–7, 57
Goitein, Hugh, 30
Gore, Charles, 129
Gooch, G. P., 28
Goodier, Norman, 16
Gregory, Sir Theodore, 39, 40

Hammond, J. L., and B., 148
Hancock, Keith, 37–40, 45, 54–5, 190
Hancock, Theaden, 37–8, 45
Harrington, James, 137
Harris, Frank, 187
Harris, Seymour, 21
Hart, W. O., 52
Hartnell, Norman, 53
Hawgood, John, 47, 49, 51
Haworth, Norman, 30
Hayes, Charles, 24
Heckscher, Eli, 145
Hegel, G. F., 28, 57, 177
Henderson, Arthur, 112

Index of Persons

Hilferding, Rudolf, 186
Hitchman, Alan, 25
Hitler, Adolf, 40–51, 54
Hobson, J. A., 185
Holland, Henry Scott, 129
Hooker, John Dalton, 11
Hoover, Herbert, 12
Huxley, T. H., 11

Isaacs, Edwyn, 32–3, 41

Jones, G. T., 21, 248

Keynes, Maynard, 5, 34–5, 91, 136, 144, 160

Lee, Frank, 25
Lee, Robert E., 15
Lenin, V. I., 38, 185–90
Lloyd George, David, 82, 97, 111, 131
Luxemburg, Rosa, 189–92

Macchiavelli, 170, 176
Maitland, F. W., 141, 249
Malinowski, Bronislaw, 21
Malthus, T. R., 182, 192
Mann, Julia, 36
Mann, Tom, 76
Marquand, Hilary, 30, 32
Marshall, Alfred, 55, 141, 143, 145, 147, 239–40
Martineau, Professor, 29–30
Marx, Karl, 13, 28, 34, 38–9, 57, 135, 176–7, 184–5, 189–92
Mason, Edward, 21
Maurice, F. D., 129
Maxwell, James Clerk, 238
Merivale, Herman, 183
Mill, John Stuart, 182, 184–5
Milman, Henry Hart, 8
Monckton, Sir Walter, 214
Montagu, Edwin, 102
Morgan, Lloyd, 12
Morison, Samuel Eliot, 12, 20, 23
Morrison, Herbert, 51
Mosley, Oswald, 34
Mussolini, 44, 46, 49
MacNeice, Louis, 31
McKenna, Reginald, 82

Nachtigal (Imperial German Commissioner), 190

Namier, Lewis, 17, 127
Napoleon, 87
Newdegate, Sir R., 231

Ochs, Alfred, 187
Oldknow, Samuel, 245
Oliphant, Marcus, 30
Orwell, Sonia, 53

Parratt, F., 226, 229–30
Parratt, Stanier, 226
Peel, Sir Robert, 147
Peierls, Rudolf, 30
Pigou, A. C., 144, 164
Plot, Robert, 242
Postan, Michael, 54
Power, Eileen, 134, 142
Pound, Dean, 21
Princip, Gavrilo, 65

Ranke, L. von, 28
Rhodes, Cecil, 187
Ricardo, David, 144, 160, 164, 182
Roosevelt, Franklin, 23
Rosebery, Frank, 25, 41
Rowntree, Seebohm, 73

Sankey, Mr. Justice, 203
Schmoller, Gustav, 144
Schumpeter, J., 39, 136
Sharwood Smith, Edward, 12, 14
Shelburne, Lord, 246
Showell, Arthur, 31
Smith, Adam, 11, 152, 160, 178, 181, 192, 240, 246
Smith, John George, 29–30, 37
Sombart, W., 144, 246
Stalin, J., 34, 38
Stamp, Josiah, 136
Styles, Dorothy, 48
Styles, Philip, 48
Sue, Eugene, 8

Tawney, Richard Henry, 17–18, 22, 46, 56, 127–42, 149, 176
Taylor, Overton, 21
Temperley, Harold, 14, 15
Temple, William, 56, 129
Tillyard, Sir Frank, 29–30
Thormahlen, Messrs., 190

Unwin, George, 123, 141–2, 149

Vinogradoff, P., 21

Wadsworth, Alfred, 36
Wakefield, Gibbon, 183
Walker, Gilbert, 30
Wallace, Alfred Russell, 8, 11
Ward, Dennis, 16–17, 19, 22, 25, 28, 43
Watt, James, 36, 227–9, 238–40, 245, 247
Watt, James, Jnr., 240
Webb, Sidney and Beatrice, 131, 166

Weber, Max, 18, 135, 176
Whieldon, 226, 232
Whieldon & Fernyhough, 232
White, Reginald, 43
Whitley, J. H., 123
Woermann & Jantzen, 190

Young, Allyn, 21

Zimmern, A. E., 9